La Grange Public Library

Book Club Corner
Sponsored by
The Friends of the Library

IN THE
COUNTRY
WE LOVE

IN THE COUNTRY WE LOVE

MY FAMILY DIVIDED

Diane Guerrero

with Michelle Burford

Henry Holt and Company
New York

Henry Holt and Company, LLC
Publishers since 1866
175 Fifth Avenue
New York, New York 10010
www.henryholt.com

Henry Holt® and ⬛® are registered trademarks of Henry Holt and Company, LLC.

Library of Congress Cataloging-in-Publication Data

Names: Guerrero, Diane, 1986– | Burford, Michelle, author.
Title: In the country we love : my family divided / Diane Guerrero with Michelle Burford.
Description: First edition. | New York : Henry Holt and Company, 2016.
Identifiers: LCCN 2015040990 (print) | LCCN 2015045324 (ebook) | ISBN
    9781627795272 (hardback) | ISBN 9781627798334 (Spanish language paperback) |
    ISBN 9781627795289 (electronic book)
Subjects: LCSH: Guerrero, Diane, 1986– | Guerrero, Diane, 1986– —Family. |
    Actors—United States—Biography. | Children of illegal aliens—United States—
    Biography. | Immigration enforcement—United States. | BISAC: BIOGRAPHY &
    AUTOBIOGRAPHY / Personal Memoirs. | BIOGRAPHY & AUTOBIOGRAPHY /
    Cultural Heritage. | SOCIAL SCIENCE / Emigration & Immigration.
Classification: LCC PN2287.G7455 A3 2016 (print) | LCC PN2287.G7455 (ebook) | DDC
    791.4302/8092–dc23
LC record available at http://lccn.loc.gov/2015040990

Our books may be purchased in bulk for promotional, educational, or business use.
Please contact your local bookseller or the Macmillan Corporate and Premium Sales
Department at (800) 221-7945, extension 5442, or by e-mail at MacmillanSpecial
Markets@macmillan.com.

Note: Some names and identifying details have been changed to protect the privacy of
individuals.

First Edition 2016

Designed by Meryl Sussman Levavi

Printed in the United States of America

10 9 8 7 6 5 4 3 2 1

To my Papi and Mami—

Whether we be near or far,
hand in hand or divided by continents,
may our love remain forever whole.

To Toni Ferrera—

Your memory lives on in the
hearts of all those you touched.
To me, your light shines the brightest.

Contents

IN THE
COUNTRY
WE LOVE

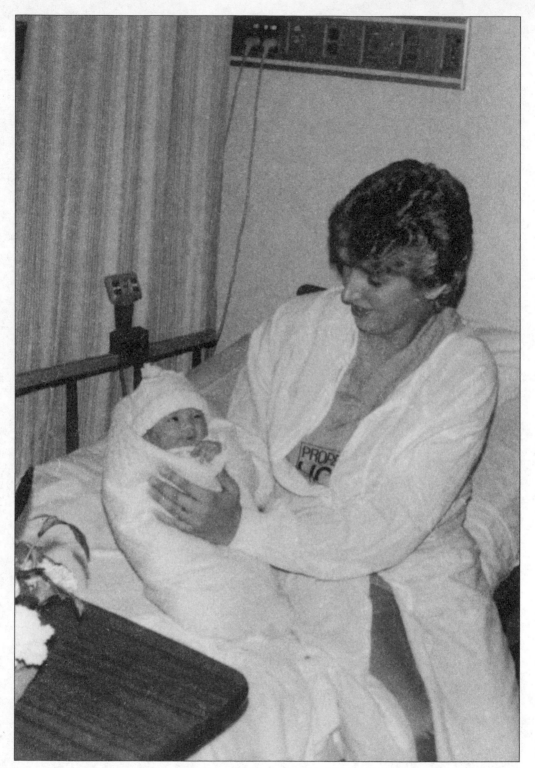

To the left is my father's little apple (*manzanita*). My parents said I looked like a little apple when I was born. To the right is the nurse, Diana, who helped deliver me.

Introduction

There are chapters in every life
which are seldom read and
certainly not aloud.

—Carol Shields,
Pulitzer Prize–winning novelist

One moment—that's all it takes for your entire world to split apart. For me, that moment came when I was fourteen. I returned home from school to discover that my hardworking immigrant parents had been taken away. In one irreversible instant—in the space of a single breath—life as I'd known it was forever altered. That's the part of my story I've shared. This book is the rest of it.

Deported. Long before I fully understood what that word meant, I'd learned to dread it. With every ring of my family's doorbell, with every police car passing on the street, a horrifying possibility hung in the air: My parents might one day be sent back to Colombia. That fear permeated every part of my childhood. Day after day, year after year, my mom and dad tried desperately to become American citizens and keep our family together. They pleaded. They planned. They prayed. They turned to others for help. And in the end, none of their efforts were enough to keep them here in the country we love.

My story is heartbreakingly common. There are more than eleven million undocumented immigrants in America, and every day an average of seventeen children are placed in state care after their parents are detained and deported, according to US Immigration and Customs Enforcement (ICE). Those numbers don't take into account the scores of others who, like me, simply fell through the bureaucratic cracks. After my parents were snatched away, no government official checked up on me. No one seemed to care or even notice that I was on my own.

It's not easy for me to be so open about what happened in my family, especially after spending so many years hiding in the shadows. I've really struggled with putting my business out there. So why am I choosing to reveal so much now? Because on that afternoon when I came home to an empty house, I felt like the only child who'd ever dealt with something so overwhelming. And in the agonizing years that followed, it would've meant everything for me to know that someone, somewhere had survived what I was going through. For the thousands of nameless children who feel as forgotten as I did—this memoir is my gift to you. It's as much for your healing as it is for my own.

Just as one moment can bring despair, it can also lead to a powerful new beginning. A different life. A dream for moving onward and upward rather than backward. What you'll read in these pages is ultimately about that hope—the same desire that once led my family to this nation. That hope is the only thing that has sustained me through this frightening ordeal.

These days, we're surrounded by a lot of talk about immigration reform. Border security. A path to citizenship for the millions of undocumented workers who live among us. Behind every one of the headlines, there is a family. A mother and father. An innocent child. A real-life story that's both deeply painful and rarely told. At last, I've found the courage to tell you mine.

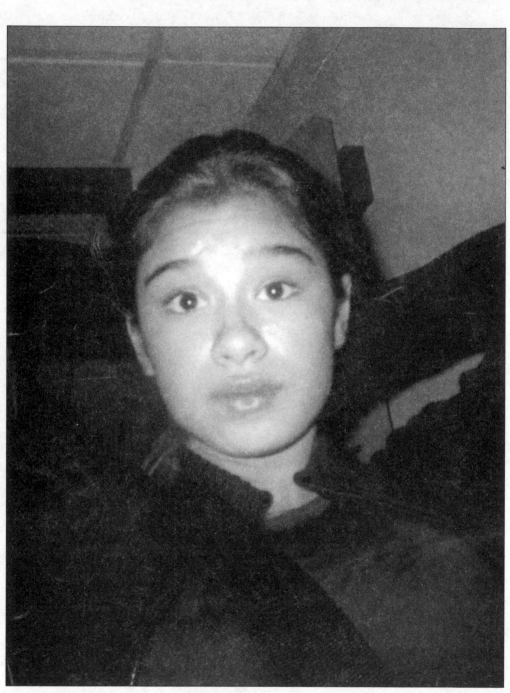

Real fresh as a freshman in high school.

CHAPTER 1

The Silver Key

Every doorway,
every intersection has a story.

—KATHERINE DUNN, novelist

Spring 2001—in the Roxbury section of Boston

My mom was making me late—and I hated to be late. Especially for a school I loved. And most especially when I was preparing for my first solo. It was a big deal for a freshman to land a solo. Huge, actually. In fact, even getting into Boston Arts Academy had been a miracle. It was my ticket out of the hood.

"Diane, come eat your breakfast," my mother called from the kitchen.

"I gotta go!" I yelled, because—let's face it—like many fourteen-year-olds, I had 'tude.

"You've got another second," my mother said, following me down the hall. "You need to eat something."

"No, I *don't* have another second," I snapped. "Why do you always do this to me?" Then, before she could say another word or even hug me good-bye—*slam!*—I stormed out the door and off to the train.

It was nice out, around seventy degrees. After a freezing winter, the weather was finally improving—and so, it seemed, was my family's luck. The day before, my dad had won the lotto. Not a crazy amount of money, mind you—a few thousand bucks—but for us, it was the jackpot. And on top of that, the love was flowing again in our house. My four-year-old niece, who'd been away from our family since my older brother, Eric, and his wife had separated, was back to spending time at our place. I saw it as a sign that things were looking up. That better times were coming.

As I dashed onto campus, I looked at my watch. *Three minutes until the bell.* Even before eight a.m., the place was buzzing. Do you remember *Fame*, that eighties TV series about a performing arts high school in New York City? Well, going to BAA felt like stepping onto the set of that show. In one room, there'd be all these kids dancing around and going berserk. Next door, another group would be belting out songs or creating art on the walls. The energy was insane, particularly right before Springfest—the one night our parents got to see us perform. It was one of the most special nights of the year. And my number—a love song duet called "The Last Night of the World" from *Miss Saigon*—was part of the finale.

Right on time but a bit out of breath, I rounded the corner into humanities class. That's how our day was set up: First, we had our academic subjects like math and science, and then came the afternoon courses I lived for—theater, art, music. And because Springfest was only three weeks away, I'd also started staying late to squeeze in some extra practice time. I didn't want my solo just to be good. I wanted it to be absolutely perfect.

The morning dragged by. Nine. Ten. Eleven. Noon. And with each hour that passed, I felt more and more weird. Not *Twilight Zone* weird, but more like that pit in the stomach you get when something is unsettled. I figured it was because of how I'd treated my mom; I knew I needed to apologize. Then again, I wouldn't actually *say* I was sorry. To avoid that awkwardness, I'd cry a little to show her how much I loved her and hadn't meant to be such a dick.

At last, the school day was over—which meant rehearsal time. When I got to the music room, a big studio, my teacher, Mr. Stewart, was already there. So was Damien—the sweet black kid with a 'fro and glasses who was the other half of my duet.

"You need to warm up?" Mr. Stewart asked me. As usual, he was wearing a tie, a dress shirt, and that big grin we all knew him for. He was seated at the piano.

"I'm cool," I said. I stashed my backpack in a chair and quickly took my place near Damien. Mr. Stewart spread out his music sheets, rested his fingers on the keys, and played the ballad's opening notes. Damien's part was first.

"'In a place that won't let us feel,'" he sang softly, "'in a life where nothing seems real, I have found you . . . I have found you.'"

Next was my verse. "'In a world that's moving too fast,'" I chimed in a little off-key, "'in a world where nothing can last, I will hold you . . .'"

Mr. Stewart stopped playing. "You sure you're okay, Diane?" he asked.

I shrugged. "I'm fine, I guess," I told him. "Just rusty."

Crap. I'd been practicing this song in my bedroom mirror for days; I knew it up and down. But for some reason, it wasn't coming out right. Probably nerves.

"Let's try it again," Mr. Stewart said.

I stood up tall and cleared my throat. The music began. As my part approached, I closed my eyes so I could concentrate.

"'In a world that's moving too fast,'" I sang, "'in a world where nothing can last, I will hold you . . . I will hold you.'"

I opened my eyelids long enough to see the teacher nod. *Exhale.* All year, I'd been trying to figure out whether this music thing was for me. Whether I could really make it as a singer. And thanks to Mr. Stewart, I was starting to believe I had a shot. He'd taken me under his wing and was helping me find my sound. My voice. My place. I couldn't wait for my family to come and hear me.

On the way home, I stopped at Foot Locker. After my papi's Powerball win, he'd proudly given me a crisp fifty-dollar bill. "Buy yourself something nice, sweetheart," he told me. "Anything you want." I'd decided to splurge on sneakers, this cute pair of classic Adidas shell-toes. I'd had my eye on them for weeks; I thought I was Run–D.M.C.

They were fresh as hell (yeah, I was living in a '90s dream). "Aren't these hot?" I said to my friend Martha, this shy girl from my neighborhood who happened to be in the store that day. She smiled, showing off a mouthful of braces. "You can wear them out of the store if you want," the clerk said. "I'll wrap up your other pair." Moments later, I handed over my cash, stuffed my old tennis shoes in my bag, and headed off to the T—the Orange Line. That was at five thirty.

At six fifteen, the train pulled into the Stony Brook station. I strolled across the platform, the whole time staring down at my Adidas. *So dope.* Outside, the sun was setting a bit. I knew my parents would be wondering what time I'd get home. I decided to stop and call.

I spotted a pay phone—yes, pay phones were still a thing—and walked toward it. I removed a quarter from the back pocket of my jeans, pushed in the coin, and dialed. *Ring. Ring. Ring. Ring.* "You've reached Maria, Hector, and Diane," said my mother's voice on the machine. "We're not here right now. Please leave us a message." *Beep.*

One of my parents was always home by this time. Always. And neither of them had mentioned having plans. *Where could they be?* With my hands trembling, I searched my pockets for a second quarter. Empty. I threw off my pack, unzipped the back compartment, and swept my forefinger along the bottom edge. Bingo. I forced the coin into the slot and pressed hard on each digit. *Ring. Ring. Ring. Ring.* Again—no answer.

All at once, I swung on my pack and jetted. I'd run these three blocks to our house dozens of times; I knew the route in my sleep. *Let them be home*, I prayed with every step. *God, please—let them be there.* The faster I sprinted, the slower I seemed to be moving. *One block. One and a half. Two blocks.* A girl on her scooter called out, "Hey, Diane!" but I was way too out of breath to even answer her. My right shoelace came undone. I didn't stop to retie it.

When I made it onto our street, I saw my dad's Toyota station wagon in the driveway. Relief. *They didn't hear the phone,* I reassured myself. *They've gotta be here.* I rushed up to our porch and pulled out my set of keys, riffling through them until I got to the silver one. I slid it into the dead bolt, held my breath, and tried to brace myself for what I'd find beyond that door. I still can't believe what I found.

Mami and Papi looking real '70s. Two-year-old me in Boston Commons. The British are coming! The British are coming!

CHAPTER 2

Mi Familia

*The family is one of
nature's masterpieces.*

—GEORGE SANTAYANA, philosopher

As a kid, I watched a lot of television. One of my favorite things to do was to find a spot on our sofa, curl up with the remote, and flip through all my beloved shows on PBS, WB, Fox, and Nickelodeon. I also had this huge collection of Disney movies on VHS. I knew every Disney character by heart, from Princess Jasmine, Belle, Cinderella, Mowgli,

Simba, Pete and his dragon, the whole bedknobs and broomsticks crew, Cruella, and Pocahontas—yeah, they were the homies. By kindergarten, I'd become convinced I was Ariel from *The Little Mermaid*. I dressed like her. I sang like her. I let my hair cascade down my back like hers. And of course, I knew all the details of her dream to escape from her life to another. Ariel was my kind of girl. I got her.

My brother went along with my fantasy. "How does your song go?" Eric teased me one Friday. "Is it 'Under the ocean'?"

"Shut up," I said, rolling my eyes. He'd apparently overheard my rendition of the mermaid's musical plea. I'd hollered into the mic, otherwise known as my mother's hairbrush, singing "Under the Sea." As frequently as I'd watched the movie, each time might as well have been the first. And— spoiler alert—when Ariel fell into Prince Eric's arms, I cried. Yes, I feel things.

Eric, who is ten years my senior, kept an eye on me when our parents were out. Can you imagine growing up with a sibling who's a full decade older? It's like being an only child. Think about it: When I was six, Eric was sixteen. Which means that, for the most part, he did his thing and I did mine.

Not that he didn't try to include me; he was actually pretty cool. "Come on, baby girl," he'd say on afternoons when we'd scrounged up loose change from beneath our couch cushions. "Let's go down to Chuck E. Cheese." Once there, he'd play video games while I jumped myself silly in the inflatable bouncer. After we'd used up our short stack of coins, we'd head back and park ourselves in front of the tube again. When it came to TV hang time, Sundays were the best. Eric would mix up one of his chocolate shakes or fruit smoothies and settle in next to me so we could watch *The Simpsons* and *Married with Children*. It was our weekly tradition. Our other fave was *The Wonder Years* on Wednesday nights.

My mother and father—or Mami and Papi, as I affectionately call them—worked. And I mean super-hard. That's what it takes to make it in America as you're struggling for citizenship. From the time they arrived from Colombia, they accepted the sort of low-wage, under-the-table jobs that make some people turn up their noses. Scrubbing toilets. Painting houses. Mowing lawns. Mopping floors. My dad, Hector, left for his shift as a restaurant dishwasher well before sunrise; at noon, he traded his kitchen apron for a factory uniform. Monday through Friday and sometimes on weekends, my father clocked in. It's how he made ends meet.

My mother, Maria, was home more with Eric and me, but she also did everything from babysitting to cleaning hotels and office buildings. When I was small, she took me along for her shifts. As she wheeled her supply cart through the aisles, stopping to vacuum and wipe, she let me roam. "Put that back, Diane," she'd scold if she caught me swiping candy from an executive's desk. Almost immediately, I was on to other mischief— swiveling in a chair and pretending I was a secretary. I could entertain myself that way for the longest time. She'd look at me and smile. "That's why you have to do well in school and work hard, so you don't end up like me." I'd look up at her slyly like, "Moms, I got this."

My parents usually finished work by dinnertime. At five, the smell of Mami's rice and beans, fried plantains, and *sancocho*, a Colombian soup, wafted through our halls, rising to mix with the sound of our beloved salsa music faves from El Gran Combo, Grupo Niche, Frankie Ruiz. My mother and father are both fantastic cooks; in fact, neighbors would flock to our house to eat their specialties. Mami had her signature dishes and Papi was always conjuring up something interesting, sometimes adding an American, Chinese, Italian, or Dominican twist.

One thing is for sure—our fridge was never empty. Papi would always say we didn't have much but at least we had food. I didn't ask for a lot, as long as he'd make me my favorite weekend snack of *pulpos* and *papitas* (octopus and fries). Papi would cut a hot dog in half and slice it in the middle two ways so the hotdog looked like it had tentacles, and when fried, the tentacles would come out looking like an octopus. My dad was always doing fun little things like that for me. When he made yucca, he'd peel the yucca skin and make vampire teeth for me and him, and we would chase each other all over the house. Papi was so cute and silly.

I was easy to please: I'd eat pretty much anything, as long as it had ketchup on it . . . and the foods didn't touch each other. "Ooh, that's delicious!" my mother would declare upon sampling her creation. Then as she prepared my plate, she'd pour the beans directly over the rice. "Mami!"

I'd protest. "Can you please keep them separate?" I hated it when my food touched. I still do.

Dinner was my chance to take center stage. Once the family had gathered around the table, I'd belt out whatever Selena or Whitney Houston hit I'd just learned, lifting an arm to add drama. My parents applauded as if I'd brought down the house at Carnegie. "That's wonderful, honey!" Mami exclaimed. At her insistence, I did a second number. Followed by a third. Until finally, Papi cut my concert short. "Okay," he'd say through laughs. "That's enough, *chibola*!" He'd given me that endearing nickname after he'd heard it on a Peruvian TV show; it's slang for "my little girl." Whenever he said it, I cracked up.

Between my nightly performances and Los Hermanos Lebron blaring from our radio, rarely was there a quiet moment. Did the ruckus annoy the people on our street? Not in the least. In immigrant communities all over the globe, celebrating is part of the culture. It's a survival mechanism. When your relatives are thousands of miles away, you make up for it by connecting with others who speak your language. Eat your food. Love your music. Understand your traditions. Our neighbors weren't only our neighbors; they were our extended family. We showed up for one another's barbecues, baptisms, anniversaries, *quinceañeras*. And the holidays? Off the chain. We partied our way from one residence to the next. In fact, I don't remember a single quiet Thanksgiving or Christmas. Ever.

We moved a lot, but all within the small radius of Boston's neighborhoods, some more blighted than others. If the rent was due to increase at the end of a lease term, my parents had to search for a more affordable option. Until I was three, we lived in Hyde Park. From there, we relocated to Jamaica Plain, and then to neighboring Roslindale when I was around seven. And finally, when I was twelve, to Egleston in Roxbury. I liked Roslindale. It was mostly a residential area filled with working-class families who stayed away from trouble. Egleston, on the other hand, was frickin' scary. Gunshots rang out at midnight. Reports of stabbings made the headlines. Graffiti covered the buildings. Dudes in lowriders blasted rap or reggaeton or Puerto Rican freestyle jams as they rolled down Washington Street. Not exactly the Hamptons, but it's what we could afford.

Our homes were small and often crappy; some were funkier than others. Tiny bedrooms. Eric usually had his own space, and until I was five, I slept with my parents. As I got older, Mami carved out a makeshift bedroom for me, mattress and all. We typically had a yard. Sometimes, we lived in an apartment; other times, we were in a two-family house. I didn't care as long as we were together.

Compared to some neighborhoods around Boston, ours felt like a different planet. On a Sunday when Papi wasn't working, he'd drive us to Wellesley, as well as to nearby Newton, Weston, and Dover. As we weaved our way through the beautiful neighborhoods, passing the stone clock tower and the ivy-covered colonial homes, I'd stare from my window and imagine what it must be like to live there. Luxury cars, pools, ladies lunching—you know, typical white people stuff.

"God," I'd pray as I gazed dreamily from the backseat, "it would be so nice to live here one day." I wasn't asking for the biggest or most charming house; just a little house that was our own, just ours. A child in Wellesley surely couldn't have the same problems as a brown girl from the hood. If you were white and wealthy and impeccably manicured, your life had to be perfect. In my head, that's how the fairy tale unfolded.

My mother did all she could to make our surroundings nice. She hung lacy sheer curtains that she'd purchased on sale from Marshalls or Macy's. She spruced up our bathroom with a blue, fluffy toilet seat cover and matching floor mat. On her days off, she dusted and organized our entertainment center, which held dozens of old CDs, albums, and cassettes from all the best Latin artists. She also had a thing for scented candles. During the Catholic holidays, she'd line up a row, lighting each to fill our living room with a sweet aroma.

Mami's desire for good aesthetics extended to her own appearance. She took pride in how she looked, valuing cleanliness as much as she did an honest day's work. Now that I look back on it, she was somewhat of a glam girl: She saved her pennies so she could occasionally splurge on Victoria's Secret lotion and Lancôme lipstick; she kept her nails polished. And before bed, she brushed her shoulder-length, black mane until it was silky.

Papi was well groomed, too. His short hair was swept neatly back, his mustache perfectly trimmed. He wore cologne daily. And no matter how close he and Mami came to the financial cliff-edge, they made sure Eric and I were presentable and always rocked at least one cool outfit. They couldn't buy us many extras, but they taught us to make the most of what we had and to look our best. They also passed on an important lesson—that our bond with each other and with the people in our community was the one luxury that should be most treasured.

Halloween is my favorite holiday. It was at a neighborhood get-together that I met two of my closest friends. I was five. Mami had gotten to know this nice Colombian lady, Amelia, who lived several blocks over from us in Jamaica Plain. "Why don't you come by on Saturday?" she asked. She was having a gathering, just because; Colombians don't need a reason to party. Mami agreed, and that weekend, I made my debut as Tinker Bell. Amelia's daughter, Gabriela, also five, was dressed as Snow White; her cousin, Dana, was Minnie Mouse. When a flying fairy, a stunning princess, and a polka-dot-clad mouse come face-to-face, there's zero need for small talk. That's why I cut to the chase: "Wanna dance?" I asked. Both girls nodded and grinned. After we'd shown each other our best steps, there was no looking back; I had two best friends for life. A couple of hours later, Mami had to drag me out of there.

The next Halloween at a church costume contest, I expanded my BFF circle by one. "Nice tutu," I said to this girl named Sabrina, who'd shown up wearing the same white ballerina outfit I had on; I had a total "bitch stole my look" moment . . . like hell, this little girl is not going to out ballerina me! I am not the one. We both bolted onto that stage, full throttle. She clearly wasn't going to bow down—thirty pliés, sautés, and whatever shit we were trying to pass off as ballerina moves. Later we both lost the contest; her cousin Dee, who wore a rad Little Mermaid costume made by the one and only Venesolana, the best costume maker and seamstress in the neighborhood, won it. Sabrina and I realized there was no other way to come out of this ordeal but to become besties.

"Mami," I'd beg after school, "can my friends come over?"

"They can if you've finished your homework," she'd say, cutting up a pepino cucumber ahead of supper.

My mother's answer was all it took to send me scurrying to round up the girls. Some days, I'd hang with Dana and Gabriela; other times, it was just me and Sabrina. But whenever all four of us got together, we were like the barrio rat pack; and we did not sit still. We Rollerbladed. We rode our bikes. We splashed in the public pool. But mostly, we lingered in the yard with our dolls so my parents could watch us. Every thirty minutes or so, I'd shuffle in to sweet-talk Papi into giving me Popsicles. "You're not going to be hungry for dinner!" Mami would cut in. Before she could interfere, I was back outside, handing out the frozen treats to my playmates.

On days now when I'm feeling out of balance, when the world is spinning too fast, I close my eyes and recall those afternoons. Papi, sticking his head out of the screen door simply to check on me and my friends. Mami, stirring her stew while humming and swiveling her hips to the rhythm of *cumbia* or the sounds of her *novelas*. Us girls, lost in our laughter, disappearing into our world of dolls, books, board games, and imagination. There, in the most ordinary of days, the greatest joys of my childhood resided. Supper on the stove. Music in the air. Love all around. My wonder years.

* * *

My mother and father loved Colombia and hadn't planned to come to the United States. Mami, the fifth eldest of seven, was raised in Palmira—a rural town in the Cauca River Valley, the southwestern part of the country. That region is naturally gorgeous, its residents twice as warm as the tropical sun overhead. Farmers, with carts of mangoes, plantains, avocados, and papayas, line the dirt road leading into the main square. In the silence before daybreak, mothers rise to collect their children's colorful garments from the clotheslines strung between tenement windows. Most locals get around by bike, pedaling to and from their jobs as fieldworkers. Plant workers. Civil servants. Fishermen. Maids. Cooks. In the evenings, as dusk gives way to nightfall, families share their meals. Their stories. Their hardships and aspirations. As impoverished as many Colombians are—nearly a third of residents live below the poverty line—they've maintained a spirit of resilience. There's an optimism that things can and will improve.

My mother's parents clung to that belief. They had none of the basics many of us take for granted, such as indoor toilets and often electricity, yet they held on to their desire to give their sons and daughters a leg up. For three decades, they worked their fingers to the bone, harvesting sugarcane in the fields. They used part of their income on schooling, and, in one sense, their investment paid off: Three of my mother's siblings are college-educated. My uncle Pablo is a schoolteacher licensed in mathematics. My aunt Mare was becoming a lawyer. And my uncle Carlos became an industrial engineer. Yet in Colombia, getting a degree doesn't bring the same opportunity as it can in America. Jobs are scarce. The economy is dysfunctional. Government corruption abounds. Those with a master's or doctorate often can't make a living. It doesn't matter how admirable your work ethic or education if you can't put either to use. And, of course, there's a major economic and social divide. For those who don't come from money, it's almost impossible to become successful.

Nonetheless, Mami set out to become a teacher. Life, however, had different plans. While completing her program at a local university, my mother fell in love. She left school, married, and became pregnant, all in the year leading up to her eighteenth birthday. She was in her first trimester when she made a crushing discovery: The man who had married her and who'd pledged to love her forever was already married and had another family, one he'd hidden from her. Under the weight of that enormous betrayal, their vows crumbled. Mami wasn't just upset; she was completely shattered. Alone in her misery, she wept her way through the remainder of the pregnancy until, in August 1976, doctors delivered my brother as a preemie. It was just Eric and my mom now.

My dad, who grew up a few streets over from my mother in Palmira, survived his own series of heartaches. He was fourteen on the day his father died suddenly of an aneurism. Amid the anguish of that misfortune, he was forced to help with his family's expenses; he, the seventh of eight children, became one of his family's breadwinners and began picking beans in the fields even as he continued his studies. More tragedy followed. Four years later, Papi's widowed mother and sister were on a bus when the bus's brakes failed. The bus careened off the road and burst into flames. Every passenger made it off alive except for one—my father's mother, my grandma Carlota. She breathed her final breath while saving her daughter. After he lost his mother, my father set aside school altogether to work full-time in the fields. Like my mother's family, Papi and his siblings grew up with so little, yet made the most of what they had. My aunt Luisa and aunt Nancy eventually became teachers; my uncle went on to work as a clerk. Maite, the eldest of the siblings, had always taken care of the family using her earnings as a seamstress. My uncle Johan had already left Colombia in search of work abroad. And some of the other brothers and sisters pursued college.

My parents didn't know each other as children. They met when he was twenty-five and she was twenty. A mutual friend introduced them. In those days, my mother's family was known in the neighborhood for throwing dance parties; my father went to one, and while there, he spotted this goddess ballerina. My mother was the best dancer in the room, and to this day, she is a very poised and elegant dancer. Papi was attracted by Mami's moves, as well as by her brilliant smile and spirit. By then, my father already had a reputation as an amazing salsa dancer. He was also fly. His sister Maite, who'd been a seamstress, was always making him these John Travolta–looking outfits. Around town, people called him Chino Pinta, which is slang for "well dressed." My mother already knew of him and had a crush from afar.

Practically from the moment she laid eyes on him up close, Mami knew she wanted to be with my dad. He was as handsome, fit, and olive-toned as he was charming and reserved—a perfect balance for my mother's outgoing personality. Papi wasn't the one to settle down, but my mom put in the work to bag it up. He thought long and hard before committing until he could no longer resist her bewitchment. Even now he's the kind of man who doesn't easily commit to anything. They didn't marry, but they did struggle along together on the little money Papi could earn in his job in a sugarcane plant. Papi made so little that both he and Mami had to continue living with their families because they couldn't afford a place of their own. Mami also worked for a bus company called Palmira Express. In a nation where employment is so difficult to find, romantic love sometimes comes second to survival.

My parents had been with each other for only six months when Mami experienced another misfortune: Her younger sister was killed in the crosshairs of random gunfire. Exactly one year later, on the anniversary of my aunt's passing, my mother's mom was sitting in her living room, nursing the agony of her daughter's death. As she wept, she suffered a massive heart attack. "Your grandmother died of a broken heart," my mother has often told me.

Those tragedies shook Mami to the core of her being. On many mornings, she was almost too distraught to crawl out of bed; her love for Eric and my father is what kept her going. Even as she carried on, she yearned to escape the despair all around her, to start over someplace else. She wanted my brother to have a better life, one that wasn't possible on a plant worker's pay. Years earlier, my mother's older sister, Milly, had moved with her husband from Colombia to Passaic, New Jersey. They'd been granted permanent residence. Mami, who'd visited my aunt numerous times with my brother in tow, saw an abundance of opportunities there, a place far from her crippling losses.

"We should go stay with my sister and get on our feet," Mami told my father. Papi, known for his caution, wasn't persuaded. But even with working from dawn to nightfall, he made less than $200 a month. Not only were he and my mother emotionally traumatized by the sorrows of their early lives; they were also financially desperate. So in 1981, with all their belongings stuffed into two suitcases, they arrived in Passaic, on a four-year visitor visa—the type of visa that was easiest for them to attain because they were invited and hosted by family members who were here legally. My dad had his doubts about making the trip. My mother planned never to look back.

America wasn't initially the dreamland my parents thought it would be; as fervently as they tried, they couldn't land even the lowliest of jobs. With the help of my aunt and uncle and their friends, they eventually hustled up a few part-time positions. Yet with the work unsteady and the funds low, they argued about whether to remain. Mami wanted to stay; Papi, who was particularly bothered by the fact that they were in the country undocumented, considered going back. He hated living with the fear that, without warning, they could be deported. But my mother talked him into sticking it out. "Let's see if we can make it work," she told him. My father—aware that, as little as they were bringing in, it was far more than he could make in Colombia—reluctantly agreed. And even amid their bickering, my parents saw eye-to-eye on one thing: Somehow, some way, they needed to work toward legal permanent residence. That's why, from the minute their visas expired, they began strategizing about how they could become citizens.

One year stretched into five. They still had just enough cash to keep themselves fed and clothed, and yet my mother wanted to have another baby—to put down roots here with my father. For a long time, he held her off. But by 1985, the two were in sync. Papi loved my mother and wanted to raise a child with her. So they moved forward with what they've told me is their proudest accomplishment: having me. It's so Third World of them, not to mention hilarious. The point is that I wasn't an accident; they *chose* to get pregnant. Who says immigrants aren't planners? Not much else had gone right for my parents, but I was right—110 percent.

On July 21, 1986, I entered the world with a privilege that has shaped my entire existence. Because I was born on US soil, I received a right guaranteed by the Fourteenth Amendment of our Constitution—citizenship. The two people who made that blessing possible for me would've traded just about anything to have it for themselves. They'd grown to love this country and longed to call it their homeland.

Mami was still breast-feeding me when our family moved from New Jersey to Boston. "You'll be able to find more work there," a friend had told her. "It's a great place to raise kids." In January 1987, on the eve of a big snowstorm, Papi loaded up all eight of our possessions and drove us four hours north. Ahead of the trip, my parents had managed to set aside a bit of savings. On the morning we moved into our apartment in Hyde Park, my father handed the landlord a neatly stacked set of bills, the lion's share of everything he had. At least our rent was covered—for the first month, anyway.

* * *

My family had its share of drama. For starters, my brother and father did not get along, particularly once Eric reached adolescence. When he was fifteen, my brother fell into an emotional slump. He couldn't see a future for himself in this country; it's nearly impossible to dream big when you don't even have your legal papers. As smart as Eric is—he's excellent at math and English—he lost interest in school. His grades slipped. Instead of hitting the books, he spent long hours with his girlfriend, Gloria. He stayed out past his curfew, and when he did come home, he refused to say where he'd been. It takes a lot to rile up my father. My brother's behavior did the trick.

"Where were you last night?" he said to Eric one Sunday morning when my brother dragged into the kitchen. I, then seven, was eating a bowl of Lucky Charms. Mami and Papi were seated with me at our table.

Eric didn't look at my father. "None of your damn business," he mumbled. My mother and I traded glances.

Papi stood and walked toward my brother until he was about three inches from his face. Eric stepped back. My dad moved closer. "You listen to me," he warned. "You don't curse in front of our daughter, you hear me?"

Eric glared at him. "You're not my father," he muttered. "I don't have to do what you say."

All at once, Papi grabbed the neckband of Eric's T-shirt and pulled my brother toward him. "You watch your mouth!" he shouted as the two stumbled from the stove to the fridge. "In this house, you're going to show some respect!"

Right then, Mami leaped from her chair, charged toward the two, and tried to wedge herself between them.

"That's enough!" she yelled. "Calm down!"

My father let go of Eric's shirt. The instant he did, Eric stomped from the kitchen and into his bedroom, slamming his door so hard that the milk in my bowl swayed. I was too afraid to speak or make a sound.

As young as I was, I knew what was happening between my dad and brother. I didn't have the maturity or words to explain it back then, but I could sense it. Eric was furious about the way his life was turning out. Because of the circumstances surrounding his birth, he'd been cheated out of a father. While my parents showered me, their princess, with affection, my brother felt misunderstood. Criticized. Like a misfit in his own family. My dad, as honorable as his intentions were, made his viewpoint clear: I was his baby girl, Eric was his stepchild. And the closer my brother got to a manhood I'm sure he was frightened to navigate, the more intense his power struggle with my father became.

Papi had his own sore spots. I could see how much he wanted to cre-ate a stable situation for us—to make his risk of coming to America turn out to be worth it. He was also still reeling from the blows he'd sustained when he was Eric's age; I don't think you ever quite get over such devasta-tion. Following his father's death, my dad became a grown-up overnight. The responsible one. Above all, he wanted to pass on a similar sense of responsibility to my brother. He was just doing so in the shadow of a pain-ful past.

As for me, all I wanted was peace. The fight that began that morning ended the way they all did: with my parents blaming each other. "You're babying Eric!" my father yelled at my mother that night. "*Alcahueta!* Let him grow up!" There I sat, in my small rocking chair in our living room, witnessing the hostility and feeling helpless to end it. The screaming escalated until Mami, her face covered in tears, grabbed a box of buttons on a credenza. She lifted her arm to hurl it in Dad's direction, and in an attempt to block her, I darted from my seat and pulled the bottom edge of her hair. But it was too late. The buttons—big ones, little ones, dozens of them in different colors and shapes—scattered across the floor.

"Stop it!" I screamed through sobs. "Stop it or I'll call the police!"

Silence fell over the room. My father, who'd been standing near the entertainment center, slid down onto the couch near me. From her chair on the other side of the room, Mami gave me a blank look. For as long as I live, I will never forget what she said next.

"Go ahead and call the cops," she whispered, her voice raspy from the yelling. She paused. "Then they can come and send us all back to Colombia."

I gazed at her but couldn't bring myself to respond. My thoughts raced as I tried to make sense of what I'd just heard. "What are you talking about, Mami?" I asked, my eyes filling with tears. "What do you mean, they'll send you back?"

She shifted forward in her chair and dropped her head. "I mean they'll deport us, Diane," she said. "They'll take us all away from you."

I stared at my mother, then over at my father, and then at Mami again. By this point, I already knew my parents' legal status. In fact, I don't recall a time when I *didn't* know they were undocumented. In our house, that was just understood. A fact of life. The way things were. But at seven, I hadn't fully comprehended what their status could mean for me. I hadn't realized that, with a single phone call, I could lose them. For the first time, Mami had spilled the truth.

After midnight, my parents continued their argument behind their closed bedroom door. I hated it when they fought; it made me so anxious. In the dim light of my corner in the living room, I rose from my little mattress and turned on a lamp. At the foot of my bed lay a large nylon bag; my costumes were inside. I hoisted the bag onto the bed and dumped out its contents. Among the jumble of tiaras and bright metallic fabrics, I spotted my white tights, a pair that went with a princess getup. I picked them up and slowly pulled them onto my hair like a stocking cap, letting the legs dangle down past the shoulders of my pink gown. Mami's heels, the ones she wore to Mass, sat near the couch. I slid in one bare foot at a time, wobbled a bit, but then stood up straight. On this night, I would be Molly. Or Tina. Or Elizabeth. Or Carrie. Or any little white girl whose parents didn't bicker. Whose brother didn't hurt. Whose family would never, in a million years, be pulled apart. There, in my land of make-believe, I could always find a happy ending.

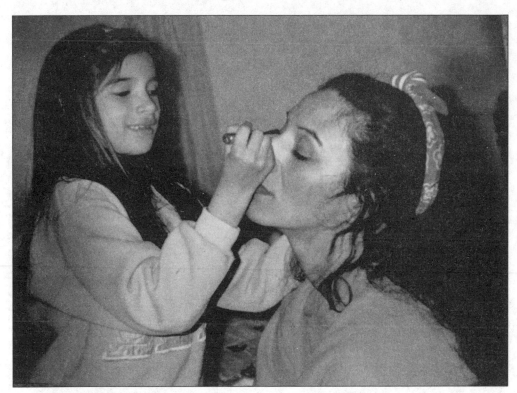

I had no teeth but I was a great makeup artist. Me and Mama.

Papi and me at our favorite place in the whole world,
Nantasket Beach, Massachusetts.

CHAPTER 3

Underground

*When we came to America . . . we
became invisible, the people who swam
in between other people's lives, bussing
dishes, delivering groceries . . .*

*The most important thing,
Abba said, was not to stick out.
Don't let them see you.*

*But I think it hurt him,
to hide so much.*

—From *Ask Me No Questions*
by MARINA BUDHOS, novelist

When you're the child of undocumented immigrants, you learn to keep your mouth shut. Someone wants to know where your parents are from? It's none of their friggin' business. Like everyone else in our secret network, we followed the First Commandment of life under the radar: Do nothing that might bring the cops to your doorstep.

"*Nuestra situación no esta resuelta*," my father frequently told me. "Our situation isn't settled." Which is why the simple ring of our bell was all it took to make us panic. "Did you invite anyone over today?" Mami would ask Papi. "No," he'd say—and within seconds, he'd be lowering the blinds.

My papi was also incredibly careful whenever he was out. He stayed more quiet in public than he did at home, never wanting to say or do anything that might draw attention. And when he drove, he followed the traffic laws carefully. No running yellow lights. No switching lanes without signaling. No unnecessary honking. And definitely no speeding. He didn't want to take the chance that we'd be pulled over by the police. That would immediately blow our cover.

Our house was like a stop on the Underground Railroad. When my parents' friends or the relatives of our neighbors fled here from Colombia, they often slept on our floor. "We need to help them get settled," Mami would explain as she scooted over my mattress to make room for the visitors. "They'll only be here for a few weeks." During that time, the community would do for them what they'd once done for my parents: Hook them up with menial labor. Connect them with a landlord willing to accept rent in cash. Show them where to get groceries and household goods on the cheap. And above all, encourage them to pursue what my mom, dad, and brother longed to receive: legal residence, which most of them did. I'm not bitter, but what the fuck? What about us? Why were we the unfortunate family?

Our lives revolved around my parents' quest for citizenship. Nearly every week, Mami and Papi strategized about how to get their papers. Lamented that they didn't yet have them. Or argued about whether they ever would. A few years after we settled in Boston, Mami scraped together money to pay a local lady who promised to secure a work visa for us; a neighbor had hooked my mother up with her. As it turned out, the woman was a notary public, not the lawyer she'd claimed to be. By the time my mother heard that from several others who'd been hoodwinked, the con artist had left town.

In 1986, the year I was born, President Reagan extended a temporary lifeline to families like mine. His Immigration Reform and Control Act gave foreigners who'd illegally entered the country before 1982 an opportunity to apply for amnesty. "Let's file our papers," Mami pleaded with my father. "This is our opening." Papi, ever the reluctant one, tried to talk her out of it, but Mami filed for amnesty anyway. She was denied because she'd been in Colombia during six months (between 1980 and 1982) when she needed to be in America. Dad later applied himself, but was too scared to follow up with the process.

Comprehending my father's reluctance takes understanding what is a reality for millions of foreigners. As much as my dad respected this country, he also had a deep mistrust of its system. He honestly believed that if he presented himself to authorities, he'd be handcuffed and immediately deported for having overstayed his visa. Given the rumors and misinformation constantly circulating among those around us, it makes sense that he thought that way. From time to time, we'd get the news that someone had indeed been granted a pardon. But then a month later, we'd hear that another person, during the application process, had been torn away from his or her family and carted off to prison. Like so many others around us, my dad wanted to do the right thing. He was just paralyzed by enormous fear.

That changed in the spring of 1997, when I was eleven. Amid relentless pushing and coaxing from my mother, Papi at last mustered the courage to step out of the shadows. A friend had also given him a strong nudge and a resource. "I know a lawyer who can do all the paperwork for you," the woman told him. She handed him a business card bearing the attorney's information. "You should go see him. I've heard he's good. He's a Harvard law school graduate." In our neighborhood, most business was done by word of mouth.

That evening over supper, my father pulled the card from his wallet and slid it across the table toward Mami. He smiled. "I'm going to check out this guy tomorrow," he told her.

My mother picked up the card, turned it over a couple of times, and brought it right up to her face. She then lowered it and ran her fingertip across the gold-embossed lettering. "This looks good," she said. "How do you know this guy?"

"You know Betty, the Guatemalan woman at the end of the block?" he said. Mami nodded. "Well," Papi continued, "she heard that this lawyer is helping people get their green cards."

My mother's lips spread into a grin. "Good," Mami said, setting aside the card to begin clearing the breakfast dishes. "Maybe Diane can go with you."

Damn right I'd go—neither of my parents speaks English fluently. Not that they didn't try. In fact, my dad wanted to learn English so badly that, over the years, he signed himself up for several classes and practiced into the wee hours. But as a teenager, he'd lost hearing in his left ear while working in a sugarcane plant. A pipe burst, water shot out and knocked him to the floor, and his eardrum was permanently damaged. So he had difficulty picking up the language and was very shy about speaking it. Mami's skills were stronger, yet she didn't understand dozens of words. So when Eric wasn't around to interpret, I became my parents' official translator. I read everything from our electric bills ("What does this mean?" my dad would ask me, pointing to a word on the statement) to the ingredients on our food packages. I accompanied my parents to doctors' appointments so I could explain to them what their physicians were saying. So for Papi's visit with the attorney, I'd definitely need to tag along, no question about it. And besides, I was Papi's little friend. He took me almost everywhere.

On the Saturday of the appointment, we pulled into the lot of a towering office building in downtown Boston. My father was clean-shaven and had on his nicest clothes—gray slacks, a jacket and tie, and newly shined shoes; I wore a floral cotton dress and white sandals. "Stay close to me," Papi whispered as we made our way through the sliding-glass doors and into the lobby. "It's on the twelfth floor."

We emerged from the elevator onto a long carpeted hall. Beneath fluorescent lights, we meandered down the corridor, scanning each door in search of the suite number. We passed a temp agency. An accounting firm. A dental practice. At the end of the hallway we reached the law office. The attorney's name was engraved in all-capital gold letters across the door's placard. I don't remember the name, but I do recall that it sounded all-American—something like Bradley Scott or Dylan Michaels, JD. He definitely wasn't Latino.

Papi turned the handle and cracked open the door. My father stepped inside and I followed. There, in a room the size of a small studio, a man who appeared to be in his forties sat behind a large oak desk covered in papers. He wore a three-piece suit and had a warm smile. The top of his head was bald and shiny. He was fit with an athletic build. He stood and extended his hand.

"It's Mr. Guerrero, right?" he said. My dad gripped the man's palm.

"Have a seat, sir," he said, motioning toward two cushiony chairs near his desk. "*Bienvenido*."

Exhale—this man spoke some Spanish. Not *great* Spanish, I'd soon learn, but good enough to lighten my translation duties. "*Cuéntame tu historia*," the lawyer butchered like a gringo. "I need to hear your story."

Papi leaned forward in the chair. He peered over at a painting on the wall, this cheesy poster of Lady Justice holding up an ancient scale; below it was the framed Harvard diploma. My dad then looked back at the man and cleared his throat. "Well," he said softly, "I left Colombia so I could earn more money for my family."

"How long have you been in the United States?" the man asked.

"Since 1981," Papi said.

"Have you ever applied for citizenship?"

My father shook his head.

"Do you have a family member who's a citizen?"

"Well, my daughter," Papi said, looking over at me. "And my daughter's mother has a sister here, but she's a resident, not a citizen."

The lawyer inhaled deeply. "Well then, we've got a lot of work to do," he said. He reached for a maroon binder on the top corner of his desk, opened it, and removed a thick packet. "In order for me to help you," he continued, "I'll need you to fill out this questionnaire." He gave my father the twenty or so stapled pages.

Papi flipped through it. "So how many months does it take to get a green card?" he asked.

The lawyer chuckled. "Mr. Guerrero," he said, "I'm afraid it's years, not months. For some of my clients, it takes ten years or longer—especially if there's no family member who has citizenship."

My dad stared at him and tried not to let his jaw drop down to his knees. "Ten years?" he said.

"That's right," the man said. "It can even be longer than that. But you never know. You might be one of the lucky ones."

My father scowled. "*Cuanto cuesta?*" he asked. "How much does it cost?"

The man shrugged. "That depends on how long your case takes," he told him. "My rate is three hundred an hour."

Papi gasped. "We don't have that kind of money," he said, rising from his chair. "I think we'd better go."

The man rose from his chair. "But wait a minute," the man cut in. "I can set up a monthly payment plan. I've assisted many people in your predicament."

My father didn't look convinced, but he did return to his seat. "So what would I need to pay you up front?" he asked.

"We can start with seven hundred dollars," he said. "But why don't you go through these papers, return them to me next week, and we'll talk about it then. I'm sure I can come up with a plan that fits your budget." My father thanked the man and we left.

Back at home, Mami rushed out to meet us when we turned into the driveway. "So," she said before we could get out of the car, "how did it go?"

Papi sighed. "Okay, I guess," he said. "I'll have to find myself a third job."

"Why?" Mami pressed. "What's the price?"

"Seven hundred bucks *minimum*," he told her.

She frowned. "Well," she said, "I could take on some extra baby-sitting. And we do have some savings."

"True," said Papi. "I'll have to see what I can work out with him."

Every day that week, I got the plum assignment of—surprise, surprise—tackling that packet for my parents. The following Sunday, when my dad and I returned to the lawyer's office, he seemed impressed that we'd pulled it together so quickly. "Very good, Mr. Guerrero," he said, flipping through the pages to be sure all were complete. "Now we can talk about the payment terms."

"I've been thinking about that," my father said. He paused. "And the best we can do is five hundred up front. That's the highest I can go."

The man paused. "You've got yourself a deal, Mr. Guerrero," he finally agreed. My dad's face lit up. "I'll start your case tomorrow and give you a call soon to talk about the next steps."

The two rose, clasped hands, and shook vigorously. On the way out, my father reached into his wallet, pulled out three bills he'd folded together, and gave the attorney his fee. "*Gracias*," he said, holding back tears. "I appreciate this very much."

The whole way home, Papi kept glancing over at me but didn't speak. He didn't have to. We both knew what the meeting could mean for us. At last, we had a plan. We had a payment in place. We knew the route to citizenship might come with setbacks, but at least we'd taken a step forward. A big one. Someone wise once said that hope is the best medicine. In our family, in our community, in that attorney's office, hope wasn't just the finest remedy. It was the only one we knew.

* * *

I loved school—from elementary on up. And yet thanks to having the attention span of a gnat, I wasn't the best student. I did get As in music and gym, and I could sometimes swing a B in English. But math and science? Let's just say I had to do a few summer sessions. My parents pushed me to do better; after all, they'd come here, in part, to give me a solid education. And yet Mami and Papi had their hands so full with keeping Eric on track and earning a living that they couldn't give much attention to improving my performance; it's not like they had the funds for tutoring. They recognized I was striving to be a good girl, that I took my courses seriously. So given everything going on in our house, my average grades had to be sufficient.

Papi was strict about homework. "No cartoons until you're done with math," he'd tell me. I'd sit there, fumbling with my eraser and fidgeting at our kitchen table, my mind wandering off to anything but multiplication tables. I envied those kids who could zip through their assignments. *Why can't I be like that?* I'd think. *Why can't I concentrate?* Years later as a young adult, I made two discoveries. First, I am dyslexic with numbers and words. And second, I have attention deficit disorder. This is terrible for anyone, but even more so for a person on my career path. My brain is like a busy bee—continuously on the move, rarely ever quiet. That explains many of the challenges I had. As hard as I tried, I could. Not. Seem. To. Focus. My family's in-limbo status didn't make that any easier. And my parents couldn't afford to get me help or the proper tutoring.

My first school was great. Mami got me into Ohrenberger Elementary in West Roxbury; Eva, Sabrina's mother, recommended it to my mother. Sabrina, who's a year older than I am, was already enrolled there. The campus was clean, the curriculum solid. Starting in kindergarten, Mami thought it was a good idea to put me in bilingual classes. She wanted me to learn to read and write in both English and Spanish. To this day, I don't think that was right for me. Yes, I got a little of both languages, but I never really mastered either of them. Thanks, Mom. I did, however, discover my first musical love: jazz. Around third grade, my chorus teacher introduced my classmates and me to legends such as Louis Armstrong, Billie Holiday, Dizzy Gillespie, and Ella Fitzgerald. I was hooked from the opening note. I'd found my thing, which is good, because fractions certainly weren't it.

Ohrenberger was one thing; the public schools around Roxbury were another. Standardized test scores were often below the national average. The classrooms were understaffed and overcrowded. The facilities were old and falling apart. There were seldom enough books or pencils to go around. Using her own money, my sixth-grade English teacher once purchased a batch of spiral notebooks. "Here," she said, handing one to each of those who needed them. "Write out your vocabulary words in these tonight."

I lived within blocks of Washington Irving, my middle school; so did Sabrina, Gabriela, and Dana, who attended with me. Following the final bell, the four of us would meet up and walk home. "Stick together," our mothers often reminded us. "And steer clear of trouble." We knew the drill: We were supposed to have each other's backs if anything wild went down. And on a Wednesday toward the end of my sixth-grade year, something did.

"Wanna come over to my place?" Sabrina asked as we strolled along the sidewalk, loaded down with our backpacks.

"My father's not gonna let me," I said. "I've got a ton of history."

"Yeah, me too," Gabriela added. "I need to get home."

Just as we turned onto my street, these two Puerto Rican girls rolled up on their bikes. One had on Timberland boots and thick black eyeliner circling her eyes; the other wore Daisy Dukes and a tank; she had a tattoo of a cross on her right boob. I recognized them from campus. The one in the booty shorts glared at me.

"What's up, wetback?" she sneered.

I took a step back. So did Sabrina and Dana. Gabriela didn't budge. Of the three of us, she'd always been the tough cookie. The strong one. The girl who tolerated zero bull. I peeked over at Gabriela in hopes she'd take the lead. She did.

"Dude, why don't you leave her alone?" she snapped. "You don't even know us."

"Shut your mouth!" spat the girl. "All three of you need to take your flat, ugly faces back to Colombia!"

My hands shook as I clutched onto the padded straps of my backpack. (Disclaimer: I've always been a bit of a pussy.) I didn't know what they wanted with us, but I wasn't about to stick around and find out. All at once, I hauled off down the street, the blood coursing through my veins as I sprinted. "Let's get outta here!" I shouted. Sabrina and Gabriela were right on my heels. We didn't stop to look back until we'd reached my front door. Thankfully, the girls had vanished.

That wasn't the first time we'd been bullied. In our area, which was mostly filled with Puerto Ricans and Dominicans, anybody who wasn't in one of those two groups was usually considered a dirty immigrant. We were spat on. Cursed at. Looked down upon. And perceived as unattractive because of our indigenous Indian features. I know, I know: Other Latino groups look similar. That goes to show how stupid discrimination is.

"We can't let them scare us," said Gabriela, out of breath. Too late for that: I was already shaken up. Once inside, I didn't tell my father what happened. Instead, I buried my head in my history book and did my best to forget the incident. With everything in me, I wished that we lived someplace else. I wanted to be a "normal" child. I wanted to be like the teenagers on *Saved by the Bell*. Their biggest "problems" were whether they'd get asked to the prom, not whether they'd be jumped by some 'round-the-way girls or have their parents deported. For the remainder of that year, whenever I spotted the two badasses in the cafeteria, I ducked out and avoided eye contact. I couldn't risk a beat-down, especially during my dad's work with the lawyer. Rule numero uno: The best way to win a fight was to sidestep it in the first place.

As tough as my middle school was, it did have one major thing going for it—a slew of extracurricular activities. You name it, I was involved. In fifth grade, I joined the basketball team and chorus. In sixth, I became a cheerleader. I was fit—probably the only time I ever had a six-pack. As if my schedule wasn't already crazy-busy enough, I also signed up for Peer Leadership Program during seventh grade. I, along with a group of others chosen by the faculty, attended training sessions on topics such as drug prevention and safe sex. Once a week, we then went around and talked to our classmates about how they could protect themselves. I loved it. For the first time, I felt useful, like I had a voice. A purpose. A contribution to make. Something that set me apart from all these bullies and simple-minded hoes.

Deep down, I somehow knew I was better than my environment, that I was capable of rising above the riffraff. In the hours before sunup, as Papi prepared for his first shift, I lay awake on my bed, imagining a magical future that was a universe away from my own. I could picture it: Me at center stage, a golden spotlight shining down on my beaming face. A crowd roaring with applause. The lush-velvet curtains rising, then lowering, then rising again for another encore.

The older I got, the dimmer those fantasies became. Could a brown girl from an immigrant family ever find a place on the Great White Way? It didn't seem likely. Only one in a million girls reaches a dream like that, but in some small corner of my soul, I secretly believed I could be that girl. Yet before the desire could completely take root, my family's circumstances would jolt me awake. In the space of a few seconds, the dream would move from feeling impossible, then possible, then back to improbable, and even nuts.

My mother clearly thought I had what it took to go far. "You're a shining star!" she'd proclaim each time I regaled her and my dad with a new song. When I was little, Mami's encouragement made me blush and giggle. But starting at around twelve, her words began to sting. "You don't know anything!" I screamed at her one night after she'd announced I was destined for Hollywood. "Stop saying that!" My mother, stunned by my reaction, just stared at me.

Mami hadn't changed; it was me who was shifting. I yearned to become a singer, to find my way into the limelight, as much as my parents wanted that on my behalf. And yet the sheer improbability of that desire—the reality of "*nuestra situación*"—made it painful to linger on such a long shot. So I placed a tight lid over the top of my dreams. I kept them concealed, only to be acknowledged in the dim light ahead of daybreak. I pretended not to want what I wanted, mostly because I feared I'd end up disappointed.

* * *

My brother became more and more disillusioned. For most of my childhood, I looked on helplessly as my parents did all they knew how to do to get Eric on track. They pressed him to focus on his courses. They grounded him when he came in past his curfew. And at one point, when things got really heated between Papi and him, my mother asked my aunt and uncle in New Jersey to intervene by talking with my brother. None of it helped. He continued to feel down—he'd lock himself in his room and sleep for hours at a time—and my parents didn't have the cash to send him to a counselor. Truth is, among low-wage earners busting their tails to make the rent, one's feelings are seldom discussed or acknowledged. Emotional wellness is a First World luxury.

A year after leaving school, Eric discovered that he and his longtime girlfriend were expecting. That didn't go over so well with either of their families. Gloria's parents thought the two weren't ready for a baby; Mami and Papi agreed. But Eric and Gloria had made their choice. Not only did they intend to stay together, they also wanted a child.

A few months into her pregnancy, Gloria moved in with us. Did I mention our quarters were cramped? Well, with five people in a teensy two-bedroom, our place became particularly crowded. And tense. Which led to arguments between Eric and my parents. Which led to bickering, usually about money, between Eric and Gloria. Which led me into deeper fantasies about a home in Wellesley and a life far away from the friction.

In June 1996, the newest member of our family arrived. Eric drove home in his Toyota with Gloria and their sweet newborn. The whole way, my brother could hardly keep his eyes on the road as he glanced over his shoulder to check on his princess in the backseat. When the car pulled into the driveway, Mami and I hurried out front; for the previous hour, I'd been hounding my mother about when we could expect them. Gloria unhooked the carrier from the car-seat base and carefully balanced it over my brother's arm. The baby, swaddled in a soft pink blanket, had her lids tightly shut.

"What's her name?" I asked, peeking over the carrier's edge.

"It's Erica," Eric told me. He leaned down and pecked her on the forehead, which made her stir a bit and open her eyes. "Isn't she cute?"

I nodded. She looked like a living doll. Rosy cheeks. Delicate lips. A bald head. She was the most beautiful baby I'd ever seen.

In the months following Erica's birth, Eric stepped up like never before; his new role as a father gave him motivation. He landed work painting houses and mowing lawns. Rather than hanging out late with his buddies, he spent time with Gloria and the baby. In fact, their relationship began going well enough that they tied the knot. Soon after, Gloria began filing the papers to sponsor Eric for citizenship. With a green card, my brother could look for an above-the-table job and bring in a minimum-wage income. They knew it would take months and perhaps even years to complete the process. But they'd be on their way to financial stability.

Or at least that was the plan until my brother stumbled off course. Maybe he started feeling blue again. Maybe he was discouraged about how little cash he could piece together to provide for his family. Whatever the trigger, his old behaviors returned: Staying out until the wee hours of the morning. Disappearing with no explanation. Challenging my parents' authority. On the evenings when he was home, he and Gloria quarreled constantly. "I need you to help out more with the baby!" I once overheard her telling him. "And where were you last night?" Their marriage became so rocky that Gloria and the baby went to live with her parents in Hyde Park.

At that point, my brother went from despondent to broken. He stopped working. He barricaded himself in his room. When he did drag himself out to go to the fridge, he and Papi got into it; as usual, Mami tried to referee. That was enough to keep a lid on the tension for a few days—until the next brawl rolled around.

* * *

I am a daddy's girl. Through and through. Mami and I are tight as well, but Papi and I have always had this special connection. For starters, we're both ultrasensitive. When my aunt came from Colombia for a visit, she brought some pictures of my dad as a kid. "You were kinda ugly," I said jokingly to my father—and I truly was pulling his leg. He was so offended that he snatched the photos from me.

"I'm sorry, Papi!" I shouted, shocked that he was reacting so strongly. "I promise I won't say it anymore!" I knew I'd hurt his feelings; they always were so easily hurt. Papi was also a softie in other ways: I'd catch him tearing up during one of those World Vision commercials with the starving children in it. He'd try to keep his emotions under cover by claiming he had a cold, but his "sniffles" were tears. He's almost as easily moved as I am—which is saying a lot, since I cry over anything and everything.

In the evenings when my dad came through the front door, we had our own ritual: "Come here, *mi amorcito*," he'd say, sweeping me into his strong embrace. "How was your day?" I remember how he smelled after work—like a factory—and for some reason, I liked the scent. On the occasional weekend when my father was off, he'd take me down the street to get ice cream. With my vanilla cone sloping to one side and dripping under the sun's heat, we'd walk together to the park or library. Even when I reached that age when most children can't be bothered with their parents (eleven and up), I hung out with my papi. In his presence, I felt understood. Seen. Validated. Safe.

Days at the coast with Papi were amazing. We'd get up early, pack some snacks, load up our station wagon, and set out on the hour-long drive to Nantasket Beach, southeast of the city. Some weekends, Mami went with us or I'd invite my friends along; other times, it was Papi and me. Once there, we'd hit the promenade and wander toward the Paragon Carousel.

By fifth grade I'd grown a few inches, but he'd nonetheless hoist me onto the back of a horse and stand at my side as I spun around in delight.

Down by the shore, we'd build sand castles and watch the waves wash them away. "Papi, come in the water!" I'd plead. "Not today," he'd say; because of the issue with his ear, he couldn't get water in it. "Please!" I'd beg; if I persisted, he'd pull some cotton balls from his pocket, stuff them into his ear canals, and tiptoe into the water. "I'll stay in for a sec," he'd tell me—but twenty minutes later, we'd still be splashing and laughing our butts off.

Even once he got out and left me to play on my own, he'd yell directions from his beach chair. "Don't go too deep," he'd caution. "*El mar es traicionero*—the ocean is deceiving! A wave can come and knock you over without warning!" I'd test the boundaries by wading in up to my thighs, the entire time glancing over my shoulder at my dad. But I'd stop short of diving in all the way. If Papi had to save me, I worried about him getting water in that bad ear.

Upon returning home, my mother would wash a bucket's worth of sand from my hair and set out fresh clothes for me. Papi, worn out from our adventure, would doze off on the couch as Mami brushed my hair a million times to get out the tangles. "Wake up, *mijo*," she'd whisper to my dad when the sun had gone down. "Time for bed." Before moving into their bedroom, Papi would lean down and put his forehead against mine. I'd raise my chin so he could tickle my neck with his stubble. "Good night, little girl," he'd whisper. "Now it's time to sleep. *Es la hora de dormir.*" It was the kind of day I wished could go on forever. No tension between my parents. No drama or fighting about Eric. Just perfect.

Papi and Mami made every celebration special—and Lord knows we had a lot of those. Birthdays were particularly big in our house, and for my tenth, I had a luau. The party was filled with flamingos, grass skirts, and pineapple—lots and lots of pineapple. All my besties were there— Sabrina, Dana, and Gabriela. It was everything! My father came in with my birthday cake. My face lit up as brightly as the row of tall, flickering candles my father had placed on top. "Make a wish!" he urged, standing over me with his Kodak. I drew in a breath, prayed that my family would never be separated (and, of course, that I really would one day become a shining star), and blew out the flames.

As summer gave way to autumn and stretched into the holiday season, Papi decked our halls with twinkling white lights and a pine tree. "Have you been naughty or nice this year, *chibola*?" he'd ask teasingly as he balanced the glistening star on the tree's top branch.

"Nice!" I'd yell, laughing. In the days leading up to Christmas, we gathered with other families to observe *La Novena*, a Colombian holiday and Catholic tradition. As we made our way from one house to the next through a winter wonderland, I stuck close to Papi's side. "You okay, hon?" he'd whisper, his breath so cold I could see it. "I'm good," I'd reassure him. Indoors, in the warmth, my dad and I stood hand in hand as neighbors recited scriptures and sang along to the sweet *villancicos* of "Mi Burrito Sabanero" and "Tutaina." There, swaying in our friends' living room and clenching my father's palm, I knew for sure I was cherished. I still know it.

My papi. My haven. My anchor. The daddy whose arms I rested in, whose shoulder I leaned on. The father who worked so tirelessly to provide me with not a perfect childhood, but one far happier than his own.

On a cold winter day seemingly a lifetime later, the man I love so much returned to visit the lawyer. Among the binders, legal forms, and citizenship applications plastering the attorney's desk, he'd perhaps find a path forward. A safe passage out of hiding. A passport from the underworld. The next chapter of our story.

My first communion, laughing at Gaby's imitation of one of the church ladies urging us to blow out our communion candles. (*Apaguen la luz, apaguen la luz.*)

CHAPTER 4

The Good Girl

I always know it's Sunday because I wake up feeling apologetic. That's one cool thing about being Catholic . . . it's a multifaceted experience. If you lose the faith, chances are you'll keep the guilt, so it isn't as if you've been skunked altogether.

—JANET EVANOVICH, novelist

My parents raised me Catholic. Like most Colombians, Mami and Papi had been brought up in that faith and were intent on passing the traditions to me: Sunday school and Mass every week. The Rosary. The holy water. The Ten Commandments. Confession. They weren't super-devout themselves, but they did want to give me a solid spiritual grounding, to teach me how to be honest and generous and good. I was an eager student. I didn't just learn the Catholic Way. I completely embraced it. By middle school, I'd taken the whole Good Catholic Girl thing to its highest level.

To be Catholic was to live by the rules—a slew of Thou Shalt Nots and Hail Marys. In our house, which had become increasingly tense, the guidelines gave me something to hold on to. Something to focus on. Something steady and unchanging. No matter how heated the arguments got, no matter how precarious my family's situation seemed, I could always light a candle or review the catechism. I was convinced Catholicism was the answer to every problem, the one sure way to bring good things into your life. Gabriela, Sabrina, and Dana all went to my parish, Sacred Heart, which made showing up to parish all the sweeter. Not only did I feel close to God, but Catholicism also gave me a sense of community—of being part of something bigger and more significant than me alone.

Papi frequently reminded me how I should behave. "Be careful how you talk to your mother," he'd tell me if I snapped at her. "God is always watching you." I came to know the Heavenly Father as, yes, the Great Protector, but also as the Ultimate Judge—one I feared deeply. I envisioned Him sitting up in heaven on His throne, scanning the Earth below with an all-powerful eye. Like Santa Claus, He knew who'd been naughty and who'd been nice, and He kept a record of it. Anyone who consistently disobeyed His commands and refused to repent would end up in hell. Starting when I was in second grade, I became keenly aware of this. If I, say, rolled my eyes at my teacher, I'd rush home, lock the bathroom door, cry, and then slap myself or pull my hair. It was my way of doling out punishment on myself before God could step in and do it.

At age ten, I began preparing for my First Holy Communion—a huge deal among Latino Catholics. There were classes to complete. Verses to memorize. Prayers to recite. And I took it all on with the kind of enthusiasm that must have surprised and secretly delighted my parents. On the Sunday when I officially committed to the faith and accepted God into my life, I stood there beaming and dressed from head to toe in white before the congregation. I'd been baptized and confirmed. I'd received the Body of Christ (the bread) and the Blood of Christ (the grape juice). At the time, I actually thought it was wine. "I'm so drunk," I'd tell my friends as I stumbled back to the pew. Afterward, at home, friends and neighbors gathered for a special dinner hosted by my mother and father. People gave me gifts and flowers. From then on, it was me, God, the Virgin Mary, and Saint Anthony—and as far as I could tell, I had everything to do with whether the four of us stayed tight.

I prayed constantly. On my bed in the evenings, I'd pull out a small flashlight and look through my little New Testament that Mami had bought for me. After reading a few passages, I'd then squeeze my eyes real tight and ask God to keep my family safe; for some reason, probably because I'd watched one too many scary movie, I had this unreasonable fear that my parents would die. My favorite Hail Mary prayer was one I'd memorized in Sunday school: "*Santa María, Madre de Dios, ruega por nosotros pecadores, ahora y en la hora de nuestra muerte. Amén.*" After that, I'd go on to make all my other usual requests. A little house, any house, one we could at last call our own. Citizenship for my family. That I could one day become a star. And, of course, that we'd forever stay together. If I sought God fervently enough, if I lived according to His principles and never strayed, He would reward my faithfulness by protecting my family. I believed that with all my heart. Every Good Catholic Girl does.

* * *

Papi continued paying the attorney each month, and whenever he checked in, he received a fresh assurance. "Things are looking good," the man told my father. "We're getting closer." That was enough to keep my father's heart rate steady, but my mother was starting to get antsy. "What's taking so long?" she'd press. "We've been handing over money for months." "Just be patient," Papi told her. "It'll happen." For a while, Mami would chill, but then a couple of weeks later, she'd be stressing again. She wanted to do something more. She thought we should put as many irons as possible in the fire. So in spite of Papi's pleas for her to slow down, she took a giant leap forward.

Back when my parents were still living in New Jersey, Mami had reached out to a lawyer who promised to help her get a green card. She submitted papers for the agency to file on her behalf with the federal government, but before that was complete, she halted the process upon our move to Boston. "I should reopen the case," she told Papi whenever he tried to convince her to await the outcome of the attorney's efforts. "By the time you get your green card," she told him, "I'll also be close to having mine."

In the fall of 1997, Mami connected with a lawyer in Boston who reached back out to the lawyer in New Jersey, who pulled her file. "We still have your paperwork," the New Jersey lawyer told Mami, "but it was never actually submitted to Immigration. You'll just have to give us some updates, and then we can get started on your case again." When Mami told Papi what she'd heard, he didn't like the sound of it. "That was years ago that you filed those papers," he told her. "There's a whole new staff there now. How do they even know what was or wasn't already submitted? And why don't you just sit tight until I'm done with my papers, and then we can look into it?" But understandably, Mami was tired of biding time. She was beyond ready for our circumstance to shift—so she forged ahead.

* * *

I started sixth grade—and extracurriculars aside, the school was a bit of a hot ghetto mess, I'm not gonna lie. Dedicated administrators worked around the clock to pull students up to academic snuff, but they were battling what must've felt like an unwinnable war, because the issues that plagued our neighborhood showed up on campus. Fights broke out often. Students disrupted class by throwing paper planes and pencils at teachers. Some girls turned up pregnant. And tensions erupted between rival gang members who'd show up to school with knives. It all freaked me out. Of course, plenty of kids, like me, wanted to excel. But how can a teacher bring out the best in students when she's simply trying to keep the peace?

It's not that my classmates were bad children. Looking back on it, I can see that many were discouraged. They'd given up on themselves. They were caught in a cycle of poverty and low expectations. When parents have little education, and struggle to keep food on the table, the American Dream feels pretty unreachable. And let's keep it real: When you grow up in the hood, you're not exactly on the fast track to Yale. But I kept my head down and got through it.

On an afternoon during my spring semester, I came home ready to hit the books. Lily, one of Mami's closest friends in the area, had stopped in to see her. The two were talking in the kitchen as Mami prepared dinner for the evening.

"The strangest thing happened yesterday," Mami told her.

"What?" said Lily.

"I heard someone knocking on our back window," she said.

"Who was it?"

"I peeked through the blinds," Mami said, "but I didn't get a good look at him. Then he came around and knocked on the door."

"Did you open it?"

"Of course not," she said. "I just yelled out, 'Who is it?'"

"What'd he say?"

"He goes, 'Ma'am, I'm here from your utilities company. We're just checking things out.' When I didn't respond, he went away."

"Did you call for someone?" asked Lily.

"That's the thing," Mami said. "I didn't. And no one called to tell me someone would be stopping by."

Lily was quiet for a moment. "I'm sure it was nothing," she finally said. "He was probably just checking your meters in the back of the house." Mami nodded, and they went back to talking about how much they'd enjoyed the previous Sunday's Mass.

One morning about three weeks later, I arose super-early for school. I'd been working on a science project for our school fair, and because I needed to get it to class in one piece, Mami had agreed to drive me to campus. She dropped me off at around eight thirty a.m., and as she did, she tried to kiss me. "Mami, not here!" I snapped while pulling myself away. I'd reached that age when I didn't want to be seen smooching my mother in public. "I hope it goes well today," she said. "I'll be thinking of you."

The project was a hit with my teachers. I'd tested the hypothesis that aspirin makes plants healthy and strong by growing two potted evergreens—one with aspirin water added, the other without it. The first was the clear winner. Its plentiful leaves were a deep green compared to the yellowish leaves of the other. "Good job, Diane," said my science teacher. I grinned. Since science wasn't exactly my thing, any "atta girl" felt like a high five straight from heaven. *Wait until Mom hears*, I thought. She'd helped me with the project.

When I arrived at the front of the house, I immediately knew something was off. The door was cracked. Eric was peeking out of it. When I reached the entrance, he opened it and pulled me inside.

"What's going on?" I said. Lily was sitting on the sofa. Her eyes were red. She and Eric glanced at each other before he answered me.

"It's Mami," he said. He paused.

"What happened?" I asked, my pulse quickening. "Where's Mami?"

"She's gone," he said crisply. He looked down at the floor.

I gazed at him. "*Gone*?" I repeated. "What do you mean *gone*?" I dropped my book bag at my feet. My palms trembled. So did my lips. "Is she dead?" I asked.

"No, no, no," Eric said, shaking his head from side to side. "She's not dead. Immigration came and took her."

The room became blurry. I felt light-headed. My brother kept talking, but I couldn't comprehend all that he was saying. I was in the Twilight Zone, or more like that Disneyworld ride, the Tower of Terror.

"Are you even listening to me?" snapped Eric when he noticed how I was off in never-never land. His words jolted me back to the present. "Our mother is about to be deported," he repeated. "She's been locked up."

After Mami had dropped me off at school, she'd returned to the house to get her own morning under way. She went to her cleaning job. Afterward, she picked up some groceries. Eric's car was in the shop for repairs, so Mami agreed to drive him to an appointment that afternoon. She stopped at the house again and picked up my brother. An hour later, just as Mami turned back onto our block, the police pulled her over. The man who emerged was no ordinary cop; he was an immigration officer—and he was the same man Mami had noticed creeping around our house. He opened her door and asked her to step out—and when she did, he asked her to put her hands up. "We have a warrant for your arrest, ma'am," he told her as he slapped a set of handcuffs on her wrists. "You have a right to remain silent. Anything you say can and will be used against you in a court of law." Eric sat stunned and shivering in the front passenger seat. The officials didn't even question him. They just took Mami away, and a moment later Eric got into the driver's seat and pulled the car into our driveway. He first called Papi and told him to rush home from work. His second call was to Lily.

Moments after I came in, Papi stormed through the door. He flung down his lunch box on the floor, looked directly at Eric, and shouted, "What happened?" Eric gave him the blow by blow, and as he did, I watched every bit of life drain from Papi's cheeks. He was white by the time Eric got done speaking. If death itself had a face, it would've been my father's in that moment. He had no words.

The following hours were a blur. Papi went into his bedroom, yanked the door closed, and thought about what we were gonna do. Lily got down on the floor next to me and rubbed my back, trying to console me, but I cried even louder. "It's okay," she told me. "Everything will be fine." When Papi emerged from his room a short time later, he told me something similar. "We'll get through this," he kept saying. But his eyes and demeanor betrayed him. With every fiber in me, I knew he was as terrified as I was—maybe even more.

His conversation with Lily was proof of that. Later, in hushed tones in the kitchen, the two talked through the next best move. They thought they were whispering low enough to keep me from hearing. They were wrong.

"What do you think we should do?" Papi asked. "Should we go to Jersey—and what if they come back for me tonight?" That question alone was enough to overtake my heart with a new wave of panic. What would happen to me if *both* my parents were taken?

Lily sighed. "They might return," she told him. "They know where you are now, and—"

Papi interrupted. "But they knew where I was even before today," he told her. "If they'd intended to arrest me, they would've done that this time. They know exactly where we live. It's no secret."

Lily shook her head. "I don't know," she told him. "You probably shouldn't stay here. It may not be safe." I felt like I was Anne Frank, hiding from the Nazis. Next up: a nice cold attic and my very own diary to document the horror.

But we did stay. My father's theory was that Mami had put herself on the ICE's radar when she'd restarted her paperwork. Although the agency claimed her paperwork had never been submitted to the feds, perhaps it had been. Maybe that "utilities guy" had really been someone from ICE sent to stake out the place. If Papi was correct, then Mami had been walking around with a target on her back for weeks. And as long as we laid low, he figured they would leave the three of us alone.

None of us slept a wink that night. Nor the next. Nor the one after that. *"Padre Nuestro,"* I'd whisper to God as I lay awake on my bed, "please help us." I recited every single prayer and Scripture I'd ever memorized. I racked my brain about whether I might've done something, anything, to bring the Lord's wrath on us. I'd had a bit of an attitude with Mami that morning. Could that have been it? Or had I committed some other sin I hadn't repented for? All through the evening and into daybreak, I heard every single sound in the neighborhood. A barking dog. A passing car. An alarm going off in the neighbor's house upstairs. With every shadow across the walls, with every slip of a key into a dead bolt, I feared the police had returned for the rest of us.

* * *

"Everything okay, Diane?" my teacher asked, leaning in to whisper to me. A few moments before, he'd asked the class to rise for the Pledge of Allegiance. I was usually the first on my feet; I loved the pledge, and given the fact that I've always been the only American in my family, it had always had a special meaning for me. But on this morning, I stood, zombie-like, and mouthed the words as if my head was on another planet. The teacher had noticed.

"Oh, I'm fine," I said. "Just a little tired."

I told none of my teachers that my mother had been taken. In fact, I didn't reveal it to anyone at school. Only my closest friends knew what had happened, and frankly, if I could've kept it from them, I might've. That's how mortified I was. With Mami gone, there was no one to watch me after school. This meant I went straight from campus to either Gabriela's or Sabrina's house until my father could pick me up from there. Before, I would sometimes go over to my friends' houses after school to do homework together, but this felt different—and awkward. I just wanted to be home. I felt out of place. Girl in hiding. WTF.

A day after Mami had been taken, she called. From Papi's side of the conversation, I pieced together the details. She'd already been taken to a women's facility in New Hampshire, and within weeks she'd be deported from there. "Yes, we thought about moving," Papi told her. I was surprised to hear them talking so candidly since Mami was on a prison phone. "But I don't think they'll return. And besides that, I don't really have the money to move right now." Right before Mami's arrest, Papi had just made a double payment to the attorney. Toward the end of the call, Papi handed me the phone. "Your mother wants to talk to you," he said. I took the receiver.

Before Mami could say a word, I began to sob. "It's okay, Diane," Mami said. *Why the hell does everyone keep telling me it's okay?* I understood that she, my dad, and Lily were all just trying to make me feel better about the situation. But the more they tried to assure me that the world was right side up when it had clearly gone to hell, the more agitated I became.

"You're going to be fine," she went on. "Your father is taking care of everything. I just have to go away to Colombia for a while. This is all going to work out."

She paused and drew in a breath. "Diane?" she said.

"Yes?" I said, sniffling.

"Why don't you come to Colombia with me?"

I froze. I'd never even fathomed the idea of a life away from Boston. Away from America. Away from the only country I'd ever lived in. Although I'd grown up hearing plenty about my parents' homeland, it felt more like a concept than a real place; it was a world far, far away, one we couldn't even visit because of my parents' in-limbo status. I was also really scared to leave my father and brother alone without me there to referee.

"No, Mami," I said, my voice shaking. "I can't go with you. I have to stay here with Papi."

The line went dead silent. "Take care of yourself, honey," Mami finally said. "I love you. I'll see you again when I can."

In the following days as I watched my father slide from devastation into despondence, one thing became clear to me: Papi blamed Mami for her arrest. And if I'm being honest about it, so did I. Behind his closed bedroom door, Papi argued with my mother nightly. Why hadn't she left well enough alone? Why did she need to go sniffing around for those papers? Why hadn't she listened to him? And why did she have to go around being the neighborhood socialite, letting anyone and everyone know our business? "You're too open," he told her. "Just too damn friendly. Maybe it was that stupid paperwork that got you caught—but it also could've been someone around here who secretly wanted to take us down." Those were harsh words, especially for a woman sitting in prison, but our family was falling apart. The stakes were high and the pain was raw. The mix of panic and fury came spewing out like untreated sewage. This wasn't the time for politeness or niceties. We were in crisis mode.

No way was I going with Mami, and as one week stretched into three and she kept pressing me about that during our phone calls, I resented her for even proposing that I leave the States. Aside from loving my homeland, there was another reason I didn't want to go: I was so scared that my dad and brother might kill each other. I thought I needed to play mediator, the way I'd seen Mami do for so long. I couldn't relocate. I needed to keep my remaining family in America intact.

In the days following Mami's deportation, my greatest fear began coming true. Eric and my father fought nonstop; the arguments nearly turned violent a couple of times. "No!" I'd scream, wedging myself between them. "Stop it!" My father, who was usually the cooler head, was in no state to tolerate Eric's BS. And there was plenty of it: He'd mouth off to my father. He'd come and go as he pleased, with no regard for the rules. And when Papi confronted him, things would get so tense, I would try to distract them by making myself look crazy by screaming and pulling my hair, just like I did when I punished myself for being a "bad" girl. I didn't want for them to fight, or for my brother to leave the house in danger.

A couple of weeks after Mami had gone, someone broke into the house during daylight and stole our TV and stereo. "I bet it was one of those punk friends of yours," my father spat at Eric. My brother denied it and slammed the door in my father's face. Papi was so livid that, on a couple of occasions, he came close to socking Eric in the face. I'd never seen him like this, so close to the edge. In between his wars with Eric and his many hours at work, he sat hunched over the couch and stared blankly at the television. He was physically there but emotionally wrecked.

I turned inward. I just wanted to finish up the school year and keep the truth hidden from my classmates. I tried to talk to Eric a few times, but he was just as overcome with grief as I was; his way of showing it was to cause more trouble around the house; my way of showing it was to pretend it hadn't happened. For hours, I'd disappear into my fantasy worlds, into my television shows, into my music, into my little New Testament Bible. Into anything that would temporarily make me forget the sorrow that hung over my family. For that first month following my mother's departure, I bet Papi and I didn't exchange more than ten words. Other than the same old "You cannot tell anyone what's going on"—and my answer of "I get it, Dad"—we hardly spoke.

Mami called frequently from Colombia. "I miss you so much, Diane," she'd tell me over and over. "You should come here."

I noticed a strange optimism in her voice—one that had been absent when she'd been in prison. "If you came here," she told me, "we could start over. Things are a little better here now than they were before. We could get you into school."

In hindsight, I now understand where Mami's hopefulness stemmed from. In her first weeks at home, she experienced a Colombia she hadn't known previously. Danger and poverty and violence were still rampant there, but she was buffered from it when she initially returned. She'd been away since the 1980s, and upon her return she saw her homeland through a honeymoon lens. Her family, many of whom she'd been sending money to for years, gave her the royal treatment. People were throwing parties for her. She was reconnecting with old acquaintances. The love was flowing. And she was feeling nostalgic. Don't get me wrong: No one was riding around in limousines. But her family was offering her whatever extras they had, like the finest meals they could prepare to thank her for all those years of financial assistance. The cruelties and hardships of daily life hadn't quite set in. So it makes sense to me now why she wanted me to come there so badly. For the first time, Colombia seemed like a place where she could build a life. But the only way that it would be a happy existence is if I, her only daughter, were there to share it with her.

That's crystal clear from where I sit now. But back then, every time she brought it up, my neck became extremely hot. "Instead of asking me to move there," I told her one evening, "you need to come *here*."

"I wish I could," she told me. "I would do anything to go back. But it's impossible right now."

I knew that was true. But while she was setting up her new life there, I couldn't help but be pissed that I was in charge of keeping World War III from breaking out in our house. I was like, *Are you kidding me right now? My life sucks without you, and if I have to deal with these assholes one more day, I am going to explode.* That didn't stop her from bringing up the idea of me going there. It got to the point that, whenever she called, I told my father to pretend I was asleep.

No one had prepared me for this. I'd always known there was a possibility that one or both of my parents would be taken, but what was the contingency plan? "You have to be strong," Papi would always tell me. I got that part. But what would happen after I put on a stiff upper lip? Would child services pick me up? Would I go back to Colombia with one or both of them? There were no answers, only possible eventualities Papi and I still weren't talking about.

I went mute. I also stopped eating much. Dad would offer me rice and beans in the evenings, and I'd push aside the plate. I got this weird tic in my neck that was probably from stress. And ever present was the thought that haunted me as I tried to get to sleep every evening: *Did I do something to cause this? Did I displease You, Heavenly Father?* I'd tried to be so obedient. I'd followed the rules. And yet God had allowed the very thing I dreaded to happen. And I didn't understand why.

* * *

Mami had been away for a little over two months when Papi came home with some news. "Your mother's coming back," he told me.

I glared at him. "What?" I asked.

"She found a way to get back into the country," he said blankly.

"But *how?*"

"I don't know all the details," he said in a matter-of-fact way that told me there was more to the story but that he wasn't going to share it with me. "She'll be here tomorrow," he told me.

I was stunned. A flood of questions filled my head. *How could she have found a way to get back into the States? Had the charges been dropped? Was that paperwork somehow sorted out? What's going on— and what isn't Papi telling me?*

Papi didn't seem thrilled. Nor did I. It's not that I wasn't happy to hear Mami was returning. But I feared that her return could put us all in danger of being arrested. I didn't question Papi any further about it. By this point, we both recognized the Don't Ask, Don't Tell policy we'd put in place.

The next evening around seven, Mami pulled up in front of our house in a taxicab. Papi, who'd been nervously eyeing the clock as if he was expecting her at a certain time, rushed out into the driveway to meet her; I followed. "My princess!" she said, dropping her suitcase to run up and hug me. "Oh my goodness, it's so good to see you both!"

She and Papi embraced a bit halfheartedly, as if all the previous two months' dramas stood between them. Mami didn't look like she'd just been through a horrifying ordeal. Her clothes were cute. Her smile was broad. Her energy seemed open. I hadn't quite known what to expect upon see-ing her again. I'd imagined she'd be undercover, maybe in a hat and glasses or army fatigues. Incognito. Neither Mami nor Papi told me the specifics of how she managed to get back across the border. To this day, I still don't know for sure. But I did know that only a mother who refused to live separately from her family would take the big risk of returning.

My parents immediately began making plans for a move. With Mami back, staying put was out of the question. We'd move to New Jersey. We wouldn't stay with my aunt and uncle—the authorities might find us there—but we'd find an apartment a few towns over and off the grid. That was the plan, and for a hot minute things seemed like they were about to come together for us. Until the day that, one week after Mami's return, she was arrested. Again.

That morning, my mother had been walking a couple of our neighbors' children to school—a side job she'd done for years prior. Single mothers who needed to get to work early would bring their little ones to our place before school. Mami would then feed them breakfast and walk them to class; in this case, it was summer school, which I'd also been attending. When I came home that afternoon, Lily was in our living room. Same spot. Same red eyes. Same look of exasperation. It happened again. We couldn't believe it. My dad had no words.

One of the children Mami was walking with was Lily's son; when the ICE officer pulled up alongside her on the street and got out of the car, Mami began to cry; she knew what was coming. "Ma'am, we're going to need you to come with us," the officer told her. He placed her in hand-cuffs as another officer gathered the children. I'm not sure how or when Lily and the other mothers received word that their children were being held at a local ICE facility, but when they did, Lily rushed to pick up her son. She then came directly back to our house, called my school, and requested that they send me home immediately. When I walked through the front door, filled with dread that the worst had indeed happened, Lily was there waiting. I could tell by her stone face that the news was exactly as I'd feared. "She's gone," Lily said, pulling me into her arms. "Your mother has been arrested again." This time, I was too stunned even to cry. Honestly, it felt like the biggest mindfuck ever. Was this really happening to us? What could we have possibly done to bring this on ourselves? How could my mother be taken not once, but *twice*?

Following this arrest, Papi wasn't taking any chances. "We're moving," he told me. "We've gotta get out of here." We didn't go far because we couldn't risk going and getting a lease somewhere. So we rented the little dingy basement apartment of Olivia, a friend we'd known for years. She lived upstairs on the top floor with her family and rented out the lower floors. The one-bedroom was so tiny that we had to get rid of most of our stuff and bag up the rest. The only piece of furniture we brought was a small loveseat. Everything we didn't sell, we boxed up—including all my dolls and costumes, and a lot of my clothes. Eric had chosen to move to New Jersey and try to start over there.

I wasn't expecting the Four Seasons, but this basement was scary. The ceilings were low. Dozens of boxes and storage bins lined the entrance. It smelled like mothballs. And the place was crawling with rats. Dad put my little mattress on the floor in his room, next to his bed. At nights, I could hear the rats scurrying and climbing inside the walls. I slept with one eye open and sometimes saw the biggest friggin' rats in the world gnawing at a crack in the ceiling light above my bed. I was so scared the light would break and the rat would fall on my face. Believe it or not, that wasn't the worst. The worst was when a rat would die in the walls, and the smell would permeate the entire apartment.

I didn't think my dad could get any more depressed than he'd been after Mami was taken the first time, but he sank even lower. For the first eight weeks, I think both of us were secretly hoping she'd magically reappear, as she had before. But two months came and went, and summer stretched into fall. No Mami.

In school, I did my best to stay focused. Not easy, given all that was happening at home. My grades slid. My math teacher called Papi.

"What's happening with Diane?" he asked. "She doesn't seem as interested in her work anymore."

"I'll talk to her," Papi promised. "I'm sure she'll get back on track soon." Of course, he didn't dare tell the guy the reality—that our family was trapped in the very definition of a living nightmare.

Papi worked even longer hours than before; he was sending my mother money in Colombia, plus supporting us. Suddenly, there was no distinction between a Monday or a Tuesday or a Friday. They all went like this: Papi got up. Left for work. Dropped me off with the neighbors upstairs, who gave me breakfast and sent me off to school. I'd sleepwalk my way through the day, and then return home at two thirty and fall asleep on the neighbors' couch. "Do you want to watch TV?" Olivia would ask. I'd nod, and she'd turn on *Peanuts*. For whatever reason, Charlie Brown was a source of comfort. I'd sit there eating a massive number of Cheez-Its, one cracker after another, while peering at the screen. I was just passing time until Papi came home around six. In fact, I was just passing time until God found it in His heart to lift us out of this mess.

Seventh grade is when things began changing for me physically. I was developing boobs; not gigantic ones, mind you—more like little apricots than grapefruits. But they were big enough for me to start pestering my father to buy me a bra. Normally, I'd never have such a conversation with

Papi. Mami had always been the one to be sure I had the clothes and undergarments I needed. She'd buy me these cute cotton undies and girly dresses, which explains why, once she was gone, I started dressing like a preadolescent boy—sneakers, T-shirts, fuzzy hair. These weren't ordinary times, so I had to get my father on the bandwagon.

"Papi?" I said. I think he was startled that I was even speaking, given how quiet I'd been.

"What is it?" he asked.

"Um, I need a bra."

"What?" he said.

"I think it's time for me to get a bra," I repeated.

Without looking at me, he shook his head. "Honey," he told me, "I don't think so. You're good."

But I insisted. It was the most awkward thing in the world to be talking to my dad about a bra, but a girl has to do what a girl has to do. For a whole week, I begged him. It was the most conversing we'd done in months. Finally, just to get me off his back, Papi relented.

He drove me to Bradlees, which was like a cheap version of Target. We headed straight to the preteen undie section. I wanted to get this over with as quickly as possible—so I grabbed the first bra I saw.

"That's too big for you," my father told me. "It's not going to fit."

Embarrassed, I slid it back on the rack and picked up another. It was pink and cotton and lace-trimmed. "That might work," he said. Before he could say another word (that someone might overhear!), I grabbed three of them in various colors and marched straight to the checkout. Talk about awkward.

Later on, Papi called Mami and told her about our adventure; both thought it was rather funny and, in a way, so did I. "I'm so sorry I'm not there to help with this," she said to me, half laughing—and half incredibly sad that she was missing my life.

"It's no big deal," I told her. "Whatever. It's just a bra." That was my attitude about anything that actually did bother me. I wished my mami was there.

I finally had my bra. Now I just needed a period to go with it. Mami had actually talked to me about my period even before she was taken the first time. "Has it come yet?" she kept asking me from Colombia. The answer was always the same: No. "Well, if it comes," she told me, "tell your dad right away. And call me. You can also talk to Olivia." It seemed every girl at school except for me had gotten her period. All I could do was wait. Every morning, I'd examine my underwear for any sign of red. Nothing. After a couple of months of paying close attention, I was so over it. I was like, *This is never going to happen.*

And then one evening, it did. Papi was in the living room, glued to a soccer match, when I emerged from the bathroom with a weird look on my face.

"What's wrong?" he asked.

"Um, I'm bleeding," I told him. I began to cry.

He turned off the TV and stood. "It's okay, Diane," he said, pulling me into his arms. "It's natural. Don't cry there, *chibola*. I'm here for you." Never had I missed my mother more than I did in that moment.

There's only one thing more awkward than buying a bra with your father—and that is buying maxi pads with him. Dad was cool about it and tried to make me feel as comfortable as possible by keeping his mouth closed. Olivia had told him what brand to get. I think my dad was as nervous as I was, and he dealt with that by stocking up. Big time. We left there with every kind of maxi pad known to womankind: Panty liners. Regular absorbency maxi pads. A pack for heavy days. He might have even picked up some Huggies, my poor father. But all good.

Until, of course, I started flushing my pads down the toilet. No one had told me that I should wrap them in tissue and bag them up to dispose of them in the garbage. Furthermore, I didn't realize I should let one get full before I changed it. If I saw even the tiniest trace of blood, I'd throw it away. Papi, who came into the bathroom after I'd just used it, noticed two things. First, the stockpiles of pads under the bathroom sink were already quite low. And second, he saw no sign of a pad in the trash can.

"Diane, can I talk to you for a sec, dear?" he said. *Crap.* I nodded and stared at him.

"You need to wrap your pads and put them in the wastebasket," he informed me. "Oh, and one more thing: You should wait at least a couple of hours before you grab a new one." Both of us blushed.

By Christmas of my eighth-grade year, I'd fully accepted that Mami wasn't going to return. I'd apparently done something so egregious, so unforgiveable, that no round of Hail Marys had been sufficient to block her recapture. This must be God's will. Papi seemed to have accepted that as well, and he was going through the motions of just soldiering through each workday. He talked to Mami once or twice a week; I talked with her even less than that. We'd both relaxed into the reality that life would have to move on without Mami in it.

And then she came back. For the second time. In January 1999. Not to Boston this time, but to New Jersey. I have no idea whether she told Papi she was coming; if she did, he certainly didn't pass along the good tidings. She moved in with her sister's son, my cousin whom I loved very much.

The first time we went to visit her, it wasn't exactly a sweet reunion. She was obviously thrilled to be back—"I can't believe I'm here with you again!" she kept saying as she hugged me—but honestly, I had mixed feelings. Of course, I'd missed her. I'd yearned to have her close again. But now that I had my wish, I wasn't so sure I wanted it anymore. Papi and I had established our rhythm, and Mami's reentry felt like an interruption. Really, I was just scared. Scared that I would be disappointed again, and I didn't think my heart could take it. Our weekends consisted of Papi and I driving all the way to Jersey. Very unsettling.

The visits were tense at first. Papi and Mami tried not to argue in front of me, but that didn't last long. I heard all the dirt: Papi was still furious about how careless Mami had been in requesting that paperwork and walking the kiddies to school. And while he knew how deeply she missed us, he didn't approve of her methods for getting back into the country. She wanted to come back to Boston briefly, but Papi flat-out refused. "If you're going to return," he told her, "then we need to move again and stay out of view." I didn't want to get in the middle of that argument. I just wanted our family to be normal. For once.

Mami eventually convinced Papi that we should all reunite in Boston. Truth is, even amid their bickering and the chaos, their love for each other was still strong. He missed having her around as much as I did. So after Mami had been back in the country for a few weeks, Papi and I moved from that basement into a two-family house in Roxbury. It wasn't very far away, but at least we wouldn't be at the same address if ICE turned up again. Mami moved in with us shortly after that, and from there, things started to look up. The new place was large enough for me to have my own room. At last, I got my stuff out of all those boxes. And within days of Mami's return, Papi's funk began gradually lifting. There were reentry speed bumps, of course. Mami didn't like some of the new friends I'd made in the area and let me know it. I was like, "Excuse me, but you can't tell me what to do." She got that message loud and clear and backed off.

It didn't take long for things to get back to normal—whatever normal is in a story like mine. By February of my eighth-grade year, she and Papi seemed more connected than ever. They argued, but with Eric gone, there was a lot less to fight about. Papi was still feeling quite hopeful about the lawyer; he'd assured us that, even with Mami's troubles, he could continue moving forward on Papi's case. And I was loving my room. Because we were in a different house—and, I hoped, out of reach of the ICE—I felt safe enough to actually sleep at night. Maybe I'd done something right. Something good. Something pleasurable to the Father above. Or maybe He'd simply chosen to look past my faults and reunite my family despite them.

Right to left: Gabriela, me, and Dana at our eighth-grade graduation.

CHAPTER 5

The Plan

I love to see a young girl go out and grab the world by the lapels.

Life's a bitch. You've got to go out and kick ass.

—MAYA ANGELOU, poet and novelist

"You all right, sweetie?" I sat, doubled over with my face in my palms, in the office of my guidance counselor. Near the close of the school day, I'd come by for our scheduled appointment. What was supposed to be a quick check-in had turned into a cry fest.

"I don't know what to do," I stammered, using my shirtsleeve to wipe my cheek. The counselor, an older woman with teased brown hair, reached for a box of tissues on her desk. She pulled one out and handed it to me.

"It's okay, Diane," she said. "Let's go over your choices again."

In May 1999, two short months from that day in the counselor's office, I'd be done with eighth grade—which meant it was time for me to choose a high school. And if you think my middle school sounded like a scene out of *American Gangster*, multiply that times three for some of the area's public secondary schools. By seventh or eighth grade, many of my peers had already fallen through the cracks. Teachers spent too much class time dealing with smart-mouthed punks. Students dropped out by the month. Those who wanted to do well were picked on. All of it made me more determined not to be the next statistic. So on the first day of that year, I'd gotten a spot on my counselor's calendar, plopped myself down in a seat across from her, and begun strategizing my way out.

"What about a charter or private school?" she had suggested. If accepted to the latter, she explained, I'd likely qualify for a strong financial aid package. Good idea. That fall, I had applied to not one. Not two. Not three. But six schools. Meanwhile, I lifted my grades from so-so to admirable. Those efforts, however, weren't enough to significantly improve my overall GPA; it was too little too late. On the Friday that February when I stopped in to see the counselor, I'd come carrying my sixth rejection letter. I was fresh out of options—and no amount of cooing, comforting, and tissues could change that.

"You know what, Diane?" she said, her face brightening.

"What?" I muttered without looking at her.

"I don't know why I didn't think of this earlier," she said, "but I know something else we could try."

I stopped sniveling, sat all the way up, and stared at her. "What?" I asked.

"There's this performing arts school that opened a couple years back," she said. She sifted through a stack of brochures on her desk and pulled out a leaflet. "Here it is," she said. "It's the Boston Arts Academy."

The pamphlet's front cover pictured a young man playing the violin and another one painting; in a third photo, a girl was in a dance pose. The counselor handed me the brochure, and I leafed through it a page at a time. "Has the application deadline passed?" I asked. This looked too good to be true; there had to be a catch.

"I don't think so," she said, turning to her computer screen. She brought up Google and typed in the school's name. A few clicks later, she had an answer. "You're in luck," she told me. "It says here that the audition deadline is still three weeks away."

I raised my eyebrows and sat forward. "You mean I have to *audition?*" I asked.

"That's right," she said, chuckling. "You'll have to try out. But you love to sing. You'd be a great candidate for this."

With the pamphlet in my backpack, I left the counselor's office and headed to the library. There, on a public computer, I read up on Boston Arts Academy (which, I learned, was the city's only public high school for the visual and performing arts). I stayed just a few minutes because I knew Mami would be expecting me home before dinner. "How was your day?" she asked when I shuffled through the door. "Fine," I responded. I kept the new possibility to myself because I didn't want to jinx it.

That evening, long after Mami and Papi said good night, I pulled out a blue journal I kept hidden under my pillow. I turned to a center page and wrote two large words across the top: "My Audition." Beneath the heading, I scribbled every song I'd imagined performing. *I could do some Mariah Carey*, I thought. *Or maybe a Broadway show tune.* The list stretched on for pages until, my eyelids heavy with exhaustion, I drifted off into my dream world.

* * *

Eric was doing well in New Jersey—at least at first. With the encouragement of my uncle, he'd nailed down a few handyman gigs and begun studying for the GED. But then as he was regaining his balance, trouble erupted. One morning when he was on his way to work, metal toolbox in hand, he stopped at a convenience store. As he was leaving, three dudes pulled up, jumped from their car, and attacked him. The guys surrounded him, pummeling his head with their fists. Eric, who thought he was being robbed, desperately tried to defend himself by flinging his toolbox at them. A passerby called 911. When the police arrived, they arrested all four. Although the three other guys had been the perpetrators, they pressed assault charges against Eric. A court date was set.

On the scheduled day, none of the attackers appeared before the judge. Eric's court-appointed attorney suggested what he thought was the best legal strategy. "Just sign this paper and say you were stalking them," he told Eric. "Stalking is a misdemeanor—and you'll be able to walk free." My brother took that advice. What he didn't know is that Gloria, who was considering divorce, had put a hold on his citizenship application. Without the protection of her sponsorship, Eric's "misdemeanor" was grounds for his automatic deportation; in immigration law, stalking is considered a felony.

Days after he scrawled his signature on that plea, Eric was shackled, put into a detention center, and shipped back to Colombia. It all happened so quickly that Mami, Papi, and I didn't get to visit him before his departure. I last saw my brother in this country in 1999—the spring of my eighth-grade year.

Mami was crushed. Her only son, her firstborn—the child she'd brought to America with a hope shared by millions of parents—had lost his footing.

"I wish we could've done more," she said to Papi through tears on the day of Eric's deportation. "I hate the way things turned out."

"We did what we could," Papi told her. "It was out of our hands."

I had mixed feelings. I was heartbroken that my big brother had become so disenchanted with his life here. That he'd grown up not knowing his own father. That he always felt like the odd child out in our family. That even once he turned himself around in New Jersey, hard luck knocked him to his knees. I was also sad about some of his choices, like getting caught up with a rowdy crowd. When you're undocumented in the United States, you don't get a pass under the heading of "youthful indiscretion." Eric knew that as well as anyone did. But like all of us, he's human. He faltered. And, instead of his mistakes bringing him a slap on the wrist, they cost him his opportunity for citizenship.

In the months after Eric was gone, I missed him terribly. I had finally gotten my own room, but that didn't feel very satisfying without Eric around. I longed for our afternoons down at the pizza joint. Our Sunday Fox marathons. Those times when he'd pick me up, hug me real tight, and then swing me around until I pleaded, through giggles, for him to put me down. And yet, as much as I wished that he'd remained here, a truth, one unspoken but understood among us all, hung in the space left by my brother. With Eric back in Colombia, Mami and Papi, with one less child to provide for, would have a stronger chance at their most fervent prayer. Mine, hidden away in the pages of a blue notebook, would remain my secret for a while longer.

* * *

Papi never missed a payment. Not one. For months, he dutifully gave the lawyer his fee, using the money he'd scrambled together with weekend janitorial and factory work. Before and after her deportations, Mami took on extra babysitting and housecleaning. In anticipation of a fresh start, my parents also ramped up their skills. Papi tried yet another English course at the community college; my mother enrolled in a computer course. When they could, they'd double up on the installments so they could speed up the application. And every couple of weeks, my father, increasingly eager to get things settled, called to check on his case.

"How's it looking?" he'd ask the attorney. "Are we getting close?"

"I can't say for sure," the guy often told him, "but it shouldn't be much longer, probably a few more months. We're making good progress." That exchange was typically followed by a request for us to complete more forms. We filled out enough of them to wipe out a forest.

On the heels of Eric's deportation, Papi became laser-focused on moving ahead. He called the law office frequently. One week, he left two messages for the guy. His calls went unreturned, which was strange since the guy usually rang back within a day. "He's probably out of town," Mami told my dad. "I'm sure everything's fine." The next week, Papi called again. When he still didn't get a response, he had me call. More silence. That's when my father chose a different approach. "Come on, Diane," he said to me one afternoon. "Let's go see him."

Through the sliding doors and up the elevator, Papi didn't say much; by the way he kept wringing his hands, I could tell he was nervous. The walk down that corridor, which had always been long, now seemed to stretch into eternity. When we got close to the legal office, I immediately noticed something odd. The lawyer's nameplate was missing. Papi and I glanced at each other, not sure what to make of it. My dad placed his palm on the door's handle and turned it to the left. It was unlocked. We entered.

The room was dark. When Papi flipped on the switch, fluorescent light flooded the space. Dad lumbered to the center of the empty office and looked around. The lawyer's desk was gone. In a corner sat a stack of cardboard boxes and some rolls of packing tape. Old newspapers lay scattered across the floor. Except for the nail upon which the Lady Justice picture had hung, the walls were totally bare. I turned to Papi, whose brown eyes widened. He put his hand on his head. "*No le puedo creer*," he murmured almost inaudibly. "I can't believe it."

A moment later, Papi rushed back to the door, pulled it open, and darted into the hall; I trailed. Several paces down, he stopped in front of a dental practice and rang a bell to the right of the entrance. Once we heard a buzz, we opened the door and stumbled inside. In the lobby, a secretary, this elderly Irish woman in reading glasses and with a poodle-curl perm, looked up from her clipboard.

"May I help you, sir?" she said in a heavy New England accent.

Papi stared over at me—which was my cue to become his spokeswoman. "Um," I said, "do you know that lawyer at the end of the hall?"

"Yes," she answered. "What about him?"

"Well," I said, "his office is cleared out. We're wondering where he is."

She squinted at me over the top edge of her reading glasses. "Oh, I don't know," she said. "I think I saw some moving guys here last week." With that, she returned her attention to her clipboard.

We walked back to the legal office as if, supernaturally, the attorney might've appeared. My father paced across the floor and slowly looked from one corner to the next. "How could this happen?" he repeated, his voice quivering more each time he said the words. "I don't understand.

Ayúdame Dios." His eyes filled with water. He then looked over at me and said, "Let's go."

Later, at home, in a moment I'd wish upon no child, I saw my papi, my rock, crumble before my eyes. "Why?" he said over and over. He kept rubbing his head in disbelief. He simply could not believe he'd been taken advantage of in this way—and especially in front of his little girl. So emasculating. What kind of hope could he offer his family? His daughter? Seeing my father in that state broke my heart. My sweet dad had been hoodwinked by this monster. In a feeble attempt to console him, I whispered, "It's okay, Papi. I'm sure we can figure this out."

Even as those words passed from my lips, I knew they weren't true. There was no way out of this mess. My parents had forked over thousands of dollars, close to everything they had. For nearly two years, Papi had worked like a dog to improve our family's position, believing that, at the end of that push, he'd find himself on the verge of a better existence. Instead, what he found was an abandoned office. A crooked lawyer who'd strung him along with broken promises. And little money left to his name.

I lowered myself onto the carpet and scooted right next to Papi. I put my arms around his neck, and, with tears streaming down my cheeks, I embraced him for the longest time. I cried not just because my daddy's last-ditch effort at citizenship had fallen apart. Mostly I cried because someone I cared for so much, someone I'd watched fight with everything in him, was hurting beyond words. In some ways, the heartache we feel for our loved ones is deeper, rawer, than any we could feel for ourselves. Witnessing my father in such despair still haunts me to this day.

Papi tried an old number he had for the lady who'd put us in touch with the attorney. She didn't answer. Later, in talking with others around the neighborhood, Papi found out that this woman was actually working for this fake lawyer; for each unsuspecting and vulnerable undocumented worker she'd bring him, he gave her five hundred dollars. And the Harvard degree? That was all made up. Thanks, bitch.

Dinner that evening was the most quiet in the history of our house. Mami sat stone-faced and sullen, as if there'd been a death, and in a way, there had been. "Are you sure he wasn't there?" she asked my father several times. She couldn't accept that we'd been scammed again. "Maybe he's coming back," she said. "You should go over there again tomorrow." Dad didn't respond. He got up from the table and left his meal half-eaten. I stared down at my food and said nothing. When you're back at the starting line of a race you have no reason to think you'll complete, there isn't much to talk about.

Later that night, I could feel his pain through the walls that separated our rooms. He wept not just for himself, but for me. How could he protect me if he couldn't protect himself? My father felt helpless—and on that evening as I struggled to get to sleep, so did I.

Sabrina and me on July 21, 2000, in Dedham, Massachusetts. My first grown-up birthday dinner at Uno's with the girls. Picture credit: Gabriela V.

CHAPTER 6

Ground Shift

*If you're never scared or embarrassed
or hurt, it means you never
take any chances.*

—JULIA SOREL, novelist

A week after my family's devastation, my audition for Boston Arts Academy came around. I finally told Mami about my plans to apply. "Wow, that's wonderful!" she said. As always, she was excited for me. She'd often call me her *hormiguita de bulevar*, which means "little ant of the boulevard." I was always on the move, searching for fulfillment and ready and open to opportunity. But then, when I was about to give her details of the audition, the phone rang—it was about my brother—and my excitement took a back burner.

As hopeful as I felt about the audition, her heart was still heavy from the recent blow. So was mine. In a way, the sting of the setback made me more certain about what I needed to do. I had to build a life for myself, one not dependent on my parents' circumstance. For me, this was more than a tryout. It was potentially my big break. I felt if I attended any other public school, I'd fall through the cracks, or I'd crack out.

On the morning of the audition, I rose early, showered, and put on my favorite sundress. At Mami's urging, I had oatmeal, made my way to the T, and at last reached the campus. *Wow, it's right across from Fenway Park*, I thought. *How cool is that?* The building wasn't much to look at, but many Boston public schools weren't. The school actually shared the building with Fenway High School, a media technology charter school. Whatever. Just by being there, I felt like I was taking control of my future.

I made my way across campus while eyeing some of the other kids who seemed to be there for the audition. *Shit—there's more?* I've always had a tendency to think I'm the only one doing things. Ha! Must be all the years pretending I was Kelly Kapowski from *Saved By the Bell*. Anyway, minutes later, I wandered through the doors of the music department. A perky blond woman greeted me. It was like I'd seen a ghost: "I see white people!" All *The Sixth Sense* and shit. I mean, of course I'd seen white folk, but at my old school they hadn't seemed all that perky and excited to be there. Most of the teachers were old and smoked too many cigs. It was like (insert thick Boston accent), "Jack sid-down for the last toime, or youar goin to the principal's office." Or "Do noat throaw projectiles across the rum." They were pissed and couldn't handle street kids like us. We ran amok.

"You must be Diane!" said the blond lady.

"That's right," I answered timidly.

"Come on in," she said. "I'm an assistant here in the music depart-ment."

She led me up a flight of stairs and into a back room. There, a group of about ten other kids had assembled. A Dominican-looking girl was warming up with some scales. A dude with short dreads and Dwayne Wayne glasses had his eyes glued to sheet music. Neither of them looked over at me.

"Do you have your music ready?" asked the assistant. I didn't.

"Oh, I thought I was supposed to sing a cappella," I said.

"That's totally fine," she said. "Wait here until we call for you. And good luck."

My turn came up first. Upon hearing my name, I ran my palm across the bottom half of my dress to be sure it wasn't wrinkled, and then I strode into a nearby music room and took a place in the center of the room. A girl by the name of Alyssa was there. I knew her from camp. Phew. She was always the cooler older kid and would often take me under her wing.

"What are you singing for us today?" asked Mr. Stewart, the head of the music department.

"I'll be singing *Si Tu Eres Mi Hombre*, by La India." I'd also do "L-O-V-E," an American standard made popular by Frankie Sinatra.

"Very well," said Mr. Stewart. "Let's hear it." My heart was racing but it was now or never. I could see Alyssa rooting for me.

I felt like I was outside of my body, watching my own audition from the audience and saying "Relax, damn it! Breathe! Use your diaphragm!"

"Thank you, Diane," said Mr. Stewart, staying poker-faced. "We'll be in touch."

"That's it?!" I blurted out.

He laughed. "Yes, that's it." My heart fell into my butt. *What just happened? Did I do well? Will I get killed at a ghetto ass school? How many licks does it take to get to the center of a Tootsie Pop?* Aaah . . . teenage anxiety.

Two weeks later, I scurried out to our yard when I spotted the postal worker pulling up to our mailbox. "Anything for me today?" I asked. She rummaged through several envelopes and lifted out a large manila one. My name, in all capital letters, was on the front. "I bet this is what you've been waiting on, young lady," she said. "Here you go." She gave me the package as well as the rest of the day's mail and sped away.

I pried open the envelope's flap, at first gently, and then with full force.

I slid out a stack of materials; on top lay a typed letter on fancy ivory-colored paper. I turned it over, and then back to the front, and scanned the first paragraph. My eyes fell on two sentences: "We are pleased to offer you enrollment for the fall of 2000," it read. "Congratulations, and welcome to Boston Arts Academy!" I stared down at the words, rereading them to be sure my eyes hadn't deceived me. My dyslexia gets the better of me sometimes, but damn, chill, dog! My hands trembled along the edges of the letter as I dropped the other mail onto the lawn. And during a moment that will forever live in my memory, the world, for once, was perfect. I was in.

* * *

Attending Boston Arts Academy felt like coming home. For the first time, I fit in. I could be myself—well, as much as I could without looking stupid of course. My inner nerd was free at last. No one called me a coconut (white on the inside, brown on the outside) because I attempted to speak well, participate, and study hard. I still had to be chill around the neighborhood—I'm cool, dog—but in school I could let down my guard. I'd found my people—artists who, like me, wanted to explore. Learn. Grow. The only downside was that my crew—Dana, Gabriela, and Sabrina—weren't in class with me; Dana had moved to Florida, Sabrina was at West Roxbury and liked it, and Gabriela was at a high school in Jamaica Plain. She later auditioned at BAA and got into the theater department, which made school extra sweet.

Showing up for school was actually fun. I seldom had a day when, once my alarm went off, I groaned, rolled over, and wished I could stay home. Every day brought something exciting. In the cafeteria during lunch, students gave theater or musical presentations. Artists like Spike Lee and Yo-Yo Ma visited campus and offered talks. We took field trips to the Boston Symphony, the Museum of Fine Arts, and the ballet. I was blown away by the opportunity, the access, the exposure. Simply being in that environment lifted my expectations for what was possible in my life, even with the uncertainty at home.

The fall I enrolled, BAA was only in its fourth year of existence. In the classrooms and hallways, you could sense a spirit of innovation, of pioneering. The whole place was like a giant laboratory; staff members experimented with new academic approaches and pushed us to think outside the box. We discussed race, ethnicity, and social-class systems in and outside the US. It was a well-rounded program designed to emulate college courses and discussion. This was perfect for the inner-city kid who often felt left out of the political conversation. It created an understanding of our socioeconomic status and the discrepancy in opportunity with our white privileged counterparts in Newton and Wellesley. In music class, I'd take that a step further by researching the music that complemented what I was learning in my other classes. From day one, I was motivated to give 100 percent and keep my grades on point. Teachers mentioned college as if they assumed we'd one day enroll. Even now, 94 percent of BAA graduates do.

My first semester, I was a bit on the shy side. I had a couple of good friends and enjoyed hanging with them, but I mostly sat on the sidelines and observed. Spring was a different story. That's when I began my journey. I still had a long way to go and still do, but by then, I was invested.

Our music classes were basically chorus rehearsals. About forty of us divided up into our sections: soprano (me), alto, tenor, and bass. Mr. Stewart chose our songs, which included just about every genre—from classical and jazz to pop, Broadway show tunes, and call-and-response spirituals.

The music was powerful. Sometimes you could feel the music spirits all around us. There is something special when a group of people work toward a common goal. And we worked hard. The entire music score from *Carmina Burana*, gospels like "Joyful, Joyful," "Edelweiss" from *The Sound of Music*, hits from *Jesus Christ Superstar* and *Rent*—in my head, I can still hear them. We would prepare for different events during the year. The two big ones were Winterfest and Springfest. Only upperclassmen had been invited to perform for winter and spring fests during BAA's initial years. But in 2001, the administrators chose to include freshmen for the first time.

At the end of chorus one day that March, Mr. Stewart pulled my classmate Damien and me aside. "May I see you two for a sec?" he asked.

"Um, okay," I stammered. I had no idea why he'd be calling us out.

"As you know," he said, "Springfest is coming." We both nodded. "Well, I'd like to offer you both a special part. It'd be amazing if you'd sing a duet."

Damien and I looked at each other. I said nothing, since it's tough to speak when your tongue is glued to your throat. I knew Mr. Stewart realized I was completely dedicated, but I was floored that he'd consider me for such an honor. "Okay," I said, letting out a nervous giggle. "Are you sure? Me? Really?"

"Look, Diane," he said, chuckling. "Do you want it or do you not?"

"Yeah, sure," I said before he could change his mind. Damien also agreed, and the next week we began staying after school to learn our number, "The Last Night of the World," a love-song duet from *Miss Saigon*. I was delighted—this is what I wanted. I was scared shitless, but God did I want it. I wanted it bad.

At home, things remained unstable. The dust had settled on the realization that Mami and Papi were nowhere close to citizenship. They continued their daily work grind so they could gradually rebuild their savings. Although they finished the courses they'd been taking, they couldn't afford to sign up for others, nor did they have much desire. At night behind closed doors, I'd hear them talking through their options; those discussions ended with arguments. I stopped even asking about their plans. I'd basically given up hope that they'd reach their goal and hoped that they could remain under the radar until I reached an age when I could help.

The one bright spot in our lives was my niece. Back when Gloria moved in with her folks, Mami was sent back to Colombia, and Eric relocated to New Jersey, I saw a lot less of Erica. That changed in early 2001. Not only did Gloria begin bringing her daughter around more; she made it clear that, even with Eric gone, she wanted us to be part of Erica's life. In the evenings, I'd spread toys across my bed so I could play with her. "Hi, sweetie," I'd say, luring her into my room by flashing a Disney coloring book. With a smile, she'd pick up a crayon, only to wander off a second later and bang on her mini-xylophone. With that cutie-pie in the house, there was never a dull moment.

One afternoon that May, I was entertaining my niece in the living room. Mami was in the kitchen, visiting with Amelia, Gaby's mom. I overheard their conversation.

"I had the strangest dream last night," Mami said. She lifted the lid on a pot, poked her spoon inside, and scooped out some soup to taste.

"What was it about?" her friend asked.

"I can't remember the whole thing," she said, "but at the end of it, I fell into a pond of dead fish."

"A pond of dead fish?" she repeated. "Hmm, *bueeeno.*" Amelia was known to be clairvoyant and often could feel things . . . supernatural things. She read "La Taza" (the cup), which could tell you some of your future simply by looking at the swirly remains after the reedy was finished. If a utensil fell on the floor, depending on what it was, she could tell you if a man or a woman was coming to your house. I would be spooked half the time because our family track record was so shitty. Bad juju. *Sacudela! "La Mala Suerte!"* I was scared by the unknown.

"I know," my mom said. "I woke up in a cold sweat. I don't know what it means." By the way she spoke, I could tell she was freaking out. "I have a bad feeling about it," she continued. "Maybe some bad luck is coming." Dead fish or any dreams about fish were not a good sign.

Right then, Papi, who'd been listening from his room, walked in. "Are you telling *that* story again, Maria?" he said, chuckling. Apparently, he'd already heard it that morning. "You're going to scare Diane," he said. "You're being superstitious. I'm sure it's no big deal." Mami smirked, began slicing some onions, and no one mentioned the dream again—until two evenings later.

On Papi's way home from the factory later that week, he stopped at a bodega to pick up a couple of items; as the cashier rang him up, he asked, "How about a Powerball ticket, sir?" At first Papi declined, but then he said, "Okay, why not. Might as well give it a shot." He paid the man, tucked the ticket in his pocket, and forgot about it. Following dinner, he retired to his room and turned on the news. When an announcer mentioned the live lotto drawing, Papi remembered his ticket and took it out. Five minutes later, he came charging into the living room. "Maria! *Chibola!*" he shouted. "Guess what?" Mami and I had been watching the novela *Betty La Fea*, the Colombian version—the first and best version. Back up, all you fake-ass versions of *Ugly Betty*! We bolted to our feet.

"What is it?" Mami said. "What's wrong?"

"My numbers match!" screamed my father, waving the ticket. "We won ten thousand dollars!"

"Let me see!" Mami said, taking the ticket from my father. "Are you sure, honey?"

Papi raced back into the room and returned with a piece of paper; on it, he'd scribbled the row of digits. "Look," he exclaimed, handing my mother the evidence. "The numbers match!"

Mami's eyed darted back and forth between the paper and the ticket. We all got quiet while she examined everything. "Oh my God, you're right!" she finally said, giving my father a huge kiss. "I guess my dream didn't mean anything!" she hollered. "We're lucky after all!"

For some families, ten thousand dollars wouldn't even cover the cost of a summer vacation. But for us, it was like a million bucks. And literally overnight, my parents went from feeling hopeless to optimistic. "We can use this money to pay a legitimate lawyer," Papi told Mami the next morning. "This is a miracle."

That afternoon, Papi left work early so he could go and claim his prize at the state lottery headquarters. He came home wearing the biggest grin. After so many months of turmoil, it was nice to see him smiling again.

On his way out the door that Thursday, Papi poked his head into my room. I'd just awakened.

"Good morning, honey," he said.

"Hi, Papi," I answered with a yawn. "Everything okay?"

He nodded. "I want you to have this," he told me—and that's when he handed me that brand-new fifty-dollar bill. I slid from my bed and hugged him. "Thanks, Papi," I said. "I love you." Every morning I'd wake up to three dollars on the nightstand, but this was way generous.

It was still pretty early when my father left, so I decided to squeeze in one more hour of rest. Ninety minutes later, when my eyelids flew open, I glanced at my clock and realized I'd overslept. *Shoot*—I'd be running behind for school.

For more than a decade, I've relived every detail of what happened during the next twelve hours. My argument with Mami. My rush to get to campus. The eerie feeling in my gut. The rehearsal with Damien, the pit stop at Foot Locker, and the voice on our machine saying no one was home, playing over and over again in my head. On the evening of May 17, 2001, out of breath and full of dread, I unlocked our front door, cracked it open, and crept inside. Nothing has been the same since.

Me and Papi, Mama and Vanilla Ice—(cough) I mean my big bro Eric.

CHAPTER 7

Taken

Something very beautiful happens
to people when their world has
fallen apart: A humility,
a nobility, a higher intelligence
emerges at just the
point when our knees hit the floor.

—MARIANNE WILLIAMSON,
spiritual teacher

The entryway was dark. Papi's boots, the pair he wore whenever he did yard work, sat muddy and unlaced near the door. I heard none of the sounds I'd usually hear after school. No noise from the television. No voices chattering in Spanish. No salsa blasting from the radio. I lowered my book bag to the floor next to my father's boots and noticed the light on in the kitchen. I darted toward it, my heart pounding with each pace.

"Mami!" I called out. "Papi! Are you here?"

I stood at the kitchen entrance and looked around. A plate of sliced plantains rested on the countertop; a pot of uncooked rice was on the stove's back burner. The faucet, which Papi had been trying to fix that week, leaked into the sink. *Drip. Drip. Drip.* On the table, that morning's newspaper lay next to a half-filled cup of coffee. Mami's apron, which she always folded and put away after preparing a meal, was dangling from a chair back. I pivoted to the hall and dashed to my parents' room. *Could they be sleeping?*

"Where is everyone!" I screamed at the top of my lungs. "Mami, Papi—I'm home!" I pushed on their bedroom door. It was stuck. "Are you guys here?" I yelled, banging on the wood with my fists. "Open up!" When I didn't get a response, I wedged the toe of my Adidas into the door's lower right corner, leaned into it with my full weight to force it open, and stumbled in. The room was bare. Mami's address book was open atop her nightstand; Papi's reading glasses lay near the foot of their bed. With my entire body shaking, I rushed to the bathroom. Then into my room. Then back to the kitchen. And finally, with a prayer that they might be outdoors, into the backyard.

All empty.

Right then, the doorbell rang. I stopped. *Could it be them?* In the shadows of the hall, I tiptoed to the front of the house. At the door, I stretched up to look into the peephole. There stood the neighbor who lived on the other side of our two-family house, a squat middle-aged woman who hadn't ever been very friendly to us. Leaving the safety chain hooked, I opened the door only wide enough to see out.

"It's me, Diane," she said. "Unlock the door."

My hands quivered as I slid the chain left and unlatched it. With my face flushed and my stomach churning, I stepped into the vestibule. The woman stared at me like I had three eyes.

"Your parents have been taken," she said glibly, as if she was reporting the weather forecast.

"Um, what?" I blustered. My head felt like it was about to fall off my

shoulders, tumble to the ground, and burst open right there in front of her. "What do you mean?"

"I mean the immigration officers came here and arrested them," she shot back. "They're gone."

I glared at her, all of a sudden feeling dizzy. The foyer began to spin, faster and faster, as if I was stuck in a washing machine. "No!" I wailed with my palms over my temples. I swayed forward, then back, and caught myself before falling onto the linoleum. "They're not gone!" I squealed. The woman didn't blink.

"Anyone you want me to call?" she asked. I was too distraught to answer. My moans turned to howls.

"Well," she said, realizing I wasn't going to respond, "let me know if you need anything, okay?" I didn't answer. I staggered into the house and slammed the door.

What am I going to do? My thoughts raced faster than my heartbeat. *I need to call someone.* I hurried to the living room and grabbed our cordless from its base. I dialed the number of my niece's mother, Gloria. *Ring. Ring. Ring.* She picked up.

"Hello, Gloria?" I whimpered.

She paused. "What's wrong, Diane?"

"My parents have been taken!" I shouted into the receiver. Hot tears escaped from my lids and splashed onto my T-shirt.

"What are you talking about?" she asked.

"The police came here and arrested them!" I hollered.

Dead silence.

Even in my hysteria, I was already trying to find a way to fix things— to line up a new life for myself. "Can I stay with you?" I asked between gasps. "Maybe you can move in here. I can watch Erica for you. I'll go to school and get a job."

She sighed. "Diane, that's not a good idea," she said. "I don't think it would work."

I heard what she said, but I couldn't quite comprehend what it meant for me. "So what am I supposed to do?" I sniveled.

"For now," she said, "don't open your door for anyone. We don't really

know what's happening yet. The police might return there. Stay out of sight until we can figure something out."

Beyond terrified, I scurried back to the front door to be positive it was chained and bolted. I turned off every light, closed all the blinds, went into my room, and locked the door. With the cordless in hand, I got on the floor and scooted all the way under my bed. Our house had never felt more quiet or scary.

I cried as softly as I could, my dad's words reverberating in my head. "If anything ever happens to us," he'd often told me, "you've gotta be strong." But I didn't feel strong; I felt weak and abandoned. I put the phone's dial pad right up to my eyes so I could see the digits in the dark. I called another lifeline—Amelia, the mother of my friend Gabriela.

"Amelia?" I whispered.

She picked up on my distress. "What's going on, sweetie?" she asked.

In hushed tones, I told Amelia all that had happened, from my discovery that Mami and Papi were gone. "Where are you?" she asked. "Under my bed." "Stay where you are," she told me. "Don't move. I'll be there as soon as I can."

Minutes later, the phone rang; I saw Amelia's name on the caller ID and picked up on the first ring. "It's me, Diane," she said on her cell. "I'm here. You can let me in." At the door, I looked through the peep-hole to confirm it was Amelia and not the police. After opening the door, I fell right into her arms. Gaby was there too. "It's okay, Diane," she repeated as she stroked my hair. "Everything's going to be fine now. Gaby, go make some tea."

The phone rang again. It was my father.

"Hector?" she said. "Yes, I'm here with Diane." I listened intently to Amelia's side of the conversation and pieced together how the day had unfolded. My parents had been taken separately. Mami, who'd been making dinner, was arrested in the late afternoon while Papi was on his way home from work. My father pulled into the driveway to discover that the immigration officers had surrounded the house; they were waiting to put him in handcuffs. Papi was driven to a facility for men, Mami to one for women. My father was allowed to make one short call. This was it.

Amelia, shaking her head in sorrow at what she'd heard, handed the

phone to me. "Your father wants to speak to you," she said. I pressed the receiver to my ear.

"Papi," I said with a scratchy voice, "where are you?"

"Listen to me, Diane," he said sternly. "Don't be afraid. You're a smart girl." My eyes filled with a fresh round of tears. "Don't cry, Diane. Do not cry. Now I need you to pay attention," he continued, "because I don't have much longer on the phone. Go in our room and pack our suitcases, one for me and one for your mother. We'll need some of our things in Colombia."

"What?" I shrieked. Mami and Papi had been in prison for less than twenty-four hours, yet my father was convinced they'd be deported. "But can't we do something to stop this?" I pushed.

"There's nothing we can do," he said matter-of-factly. The only way he and Mami might have a chance at staying, he explained, was if a top-level attorney took their case; even with Papi's stroke of fortune, he didn't have the money for a pricey lawyer. "I've asked Amelia if you can stay with her," he told me. I heard a guard ordering Papi to finish his call. "So you'll be with her, okay? I love you. I've gotta go now." *Click.* I put down the phone and sat there helpless.

A while later, I pulled myself together so I could complete the task Papi had given me; Amelia made some calls to her family while I slipped into my parents' room to pack. I scooted a ladder to their closet, climbed atop, and steadied myself. I carefully slid their bags from a shelf above; I threw the bags onto the nearby bed and stepped down. I had no clue where to begin. What the heck do you pack for two people who'll never return? I searched through their drawers and closet, pulling out random items. A lot of shirts and pants. Several pairs of shoes. And a couple of coats and sweaters. *Done.*

As I zipped the bags, I heard something. I peeked out the door and into the hall. The commotion was coming from the kitchen. I made my way there. When I reached the doorway, two men and three women, all neighbors from our street, peered at me. Word about my parents' capture had apparently gotten out. Amelia had let the neighbors in, thinking they'd come by to offer me their sympathies. What happened instead still pains me.

"What are you doing?" I asked one of the women. She was standing in front of our open fridge with a large plastic bag in her hand. It appeared she was packing up our fruits and vegetables.

"Your parents won't need this food anymore," she snapped. "We might as well take it." Before I could respond, Amelia walked in.

"Excuse me," she said to the woman. "Can you please put that back and leave?" The lady glared at her and slammed the fridge closed without returning the food she'd stolen. I was dumbfounded. I was already feeling so vulnerable, and the people my parents had called friends were looting their home. It was the ultimate insult. And ironically, it was in that moment, one with others surrounding me, that I felt most alone. In an effort to guard our remaining possessions, I marched from the kitchen and locked every door in the house.

With my parents' suitcases stuffed, I needed to prepare a bag for myself. I didn't know when I'd return to the house, or if I would; when everything you've known has just crumbled, nothing seems certain. I packed plenty of school clothes, my books, and a Norma Jean mini Cabbage Patch doll that Papi had given me for Christmas. When I went into the bathroom to gather my toiletries, more tears flowed. It was like I had crying Tourette's. All around me were signs of what my parents thought would be an ordinary evening. Mami's rosary hanging on the towel rack. Papi's cotton balls that he'd stuff into his ears before he showered. I opened the medicine cabinet, took out my toothbrush, and shut the glass again. There, in the mirror, I gazed at a face I didn't know. Puffy eyes. Numb lips. Raw.

Amelia tapped on the bathroom door. "You all right, hon?" she asked.

"I'll be out in a sec," I told her.

Once we'd dragged the suitcases to her Camry, we did a final walkthrough of the house to secure it. In the living room, I looked to be sure I wasn't leaving behind anything I'd need. On the way out the door, I retrieved the spare key we had hidden under our mat. "I should probably take this," I said. Amelia nodded.

Just before we got in the car, Gloria drove up. She got out, ran over to me, and we hugged. Amelia told her she'd heard from Papi. "She'll stay with me for now," Amelia told her. "I'll look after her." Gloria thanked her, and we parted.

Amelia's home in Roslindale was only ten minutes from us. She shared a small house with her son and two daughters; Gabriela was the youngest. My best friend helped me lug the bags into the bedroom we'd share. Because I'd spent so much time at Gabriela's, it thankfully felt familiar. Comfortable. Safe. Amelia also did all she could to welcome me. "Here you are," she said, giving me fresh linens and towels. "Make yourself at home."

After showering and putting on my PJs, I called my aunt and uncle in New Jersey. In utter disbelief, they listened as I recounted the day's horrors. "What are you going to do?" my aunt Milly asked. "Well," I said, "I'm going to stay here for now. Papi asked Amelia if I could." Only hours had passed since my parents had been detained, yet I'd already resolved something in my heart. I would not leave Boston. I would not throw away the miracle I'd been given to attend Boston Arts Academy. Getting into that school had been the greatest thing that had happened to me—and I was not willing to give it up. Whatever I needed to do to stay, I was ready to do that and more.

That evening in the dark, with Norma Jean at my side, I stared up at the ceiling from my twin bed. I thought of how the week had begun, with Mami's bizarre dream. I thought of my father's exuberance, the delight that spread across his face upon winning the money. I thought of the thousands of moments, large and small, that had led me to this house. This bed. This life. I tried not to cry, because I didn't want to wake Gabriela. But I couldn't help it. She heard me sniffling and sat up.

"You scared?" she asked.

"Yes," I answered.

"I know," she said. "What you're going through is scary."

A wave of comfort washed over me. My friend hadn't urged me to be strong. She hadn't told me to stand tall or soldier on. She hadn't uttered the shallow reassurance that I'd get through this. Rather, she'd given me permission, right before sleep, to be the frightened little girl that I was.

* * *

The morning after the nightmare, I opened my eyes and looked around slowly. *Where am I?* And then all at once, the horrible memory of the day before came flooding back. *Yes*, I thought. *It really happened.*

I went to school that day. Amelia, a nurse's assistant, dropped me and Gaby off on her way to work. I was physically present, but my head was on another planet. I basically sleep-walked through my classes and tried to forget the devastation, to tuck it away behind some secret door of my heart. As out of it as I was, I was glad I'd come to campus. Being there was a distraction from the trauma. And with Springfest on the way, I didn't want to miss rehearsal.

That afternoon during chorus, Mr. Stewart sensed something was off with me. "You okay?" he asked. I nodded and mustered a fake smile. He likely knew I was hiding something, but he didn't pry. I was as humiliated as I was heartbroken. Now, years later, some of my former high school classmates have said to me, "I had no idea you were going through that. You didn't talk about it." Exactly. The last thing in the world I'd ever do was talk about it. What child wants the world to know that her parents have been forced into custody and thrown into a detention center? It is mortifying.

Over the next week, I had short conversations with Mami and Papi. The calls were all the same—tears, a string of apologies from both, instructions on what to do, who to call. I was exhausted and just wanted to be a kid. They'd each been appointed lawyers, but as they'd suspected, their chances of remaining here were minuscule. Because my parents couldn't speak to each other from their facilities, I became their go-between.

"How's your mother holding up?" Papi asked.

"Okay, I guess," I told him, not sure how to answer that question. I wasn't exactly taking notes on Mami's emotional state, with my own in such shambles.

"Has anyone from immigration tried to contact you?" my father asked.

"No," I told him. Not only had US Immigration and Customs Enforcement been silent, I also hadn't received a call from Massachusetts's Child Protective Services. At fourteen, I'd been left on my own. Literally. When the authorities made the choice to detain my parents, no one bothered to check that a young girl, a minor, a citizen of this country, would be left without a family. Without a home. Without a way to move forward. I'm fortunate that Amelia agreed to take me in temporarily, but no one in our government was aware that she'd done so. In the eyes of the ICE, it was as if I didn't exist. I'd been invisible to them.

Two weeks after my parents were sent to prison, I received word that I could visit Papi. By then, both he and Mami had been transferred from jails in Boston to detention centers in New Hampshire. One part of me longed to see my father, but another part, the part that needed some distance from the ordeal, dreaded the visit.

Amelia drove us there. "How about a little music?" she offered, trying to lighten the mood during the two-hour trip. "No thanks," I muttered. Along the highway, I brightened up upon spotting a Wendy's billboard.

"Can we get some lunch there?" I asked Amelia.

"Of course," she said. I had fond memories of going to that restaurant with my dad when I was a kid. I loved the Frosty shake, the chicken nuggets with all those sauces, the red and yellow walls and tables. Our stop brought me a little consolation ahead of what I was about to face.

We at last reached the prison, a set of brown-brick buildings in the middle of nowhere. Barbed-wire fence surrounded the facility. We drove through a few security checkpoints, including one with barking Dobermans. I couldn't believe that my papi, a man who'd never jaywalked or run a red light, had found himself in a place like this.

Inside, our purses were thoroughly searched. A guard instructed us on a list of visitation rules; no articles or gifts, for instance, were to be directly given to the inmates. Once we'd made it through the metal detector, we dropped off the suitcase I'd packed for Papi. We were then led to a large, windowless area where about fifty others were waiting. I scanned the room. A few people were alone. Others were in groups. Some had small children with them. All were there for the same reason I was—to spend a few minutes with someone whose status was up in the air. A thin, blond guy, another guard, addressed those assembled. "The inmates will be escorted here shortly," he announced. "Please remember to observe all facility regulations. Any violation may result in the future suspension of visitation privileges." Amelia and I locked eyes.

A door opened at the room's side. In single file behind two guards, the male prisoners entered. All wore orange jumpsuits. Amelia and I rose in anticipation of finding Papi. *One prisoner. Two. Seven. Ten.* Inmate after inmate emerged, but we didn't see my father. Others were hugging their loved ones and settling in to talk as we continued to wait. At last, after about thirty men had come in, I spotted Papi. He noticed us, and with his face down, he shuffled in our direction.

I hardly recognized my father. His chin and neck were covered in stubble. His hair was unkempt, his teeth yellow. He'd lost at least fifteen pounds. Months before, in that lawyer's empty office, I'd seen my father at his most powerless. This was worse. In his eyes, I saw the look of defeat. Despair. Resignation.

We hugged. "Forgive me," he told me once he'd let me go. "I don't have any toothpaste in here." My father, so meticulous about hygiene, was self-conscious about his breath and appearance. He cupped his hand over his mouth in shame.

I glanced around nervously, unsure of what to say. "How are you, *hija?*" Papi asked to break the ice. I started to cry. "Don't cry," he told me. I could tell he wanted to hug me, but he couldn't. One of the rules was limited contact. "We talked about this," he told me. "You knew this could happen."

A shot of anger surged through me, which caught me by surprise. My father was right: I'd been aware I could lose him and Mami. Maybe. One day. Some other time. But as the seasons rolled on and my fear hadn't yet come true, I'd been lulled into thinking it wouldn't happen. Life does that to us. Deep down, we know what may come to pass, but we hope that what we dread can be permanently put off. We convince ourselves it may never occur, because if it were going to, it would've already. Then without warning, reality socks us in the face and we realize how foolish it was to believe we'd been spared. And however many years we spent agonizing about what tragedy may come, the sting is no less severe when it does. I knew all along that my folks could be taken—and it still hurt like hell when they actually were.

Amelia opened her purse, handed me a tissue, and we all sat down. "So have you been keeping up with your schoolwork?" my father asked.

"Yes," I said, gripping the edges of the hard plastic chair so tightly that my knuckles turned white. Small talk—that's all we could manage in a situation like this. Anything more would involve addressing the gigantic white elephant in the room, the inevitability that we'd soon be forced apart. Since my father didn't have the heart to go there, he initially kept the conversation light.

"Have you been eating?" my father asked.

I looked over at Amelia. "Yes, everything's good, Papi," I told him. "I'm sharing a room with Gabriela. It's nice."

My dad turned to Amelia, who hadn't spoken a word. "Thank you so much for taking her in," he told her. Amelia nodded. "Maria and I appreciate it. We really do. We can never repay you." My father would, however, try. The two agreed that, from Colombia, he'd send some money each month to cover my basic expenses.

Papi looked at the floor, then up at me. "I want you to know how badly I feel about all of this," he told me. He sighed deeply. "We have to move forward." His eyes looked tired from lack of sleep. He was scared.

Near the end of the visit, my father stood, placed his hands gently on my shoulders, and leaned as close as he could to my right ear. "*Te amo*," he whispered. "I love you. *Se fuerte*. Be strong. Don't forget that." He kissed my forehead and backed up a bit before the guards could call him out for getting too close.

A bell rang to end our time. All the inmates stood. "No, Papi!" I called out, but before I could really flip out, my father shushed me with a hand gesture. Even in prison, he didn't want to cause trouble or bring undue attention to us. Watching my daddy, my beach bud, my friend walk away in that orange jumpsuit was one of the hardest moments I have ever endured.

The ride home was even quieter than the one there. Through mile after mile of freeway, I recalled the years my family had spent worrying about this day, the energy we'd expended fearing my parents' arrest. I now wished we'd set aside the anxiety, refused to let it invade our every interaction, fully enjoyed one another's presence. Instead, we'd allowed ourselves to be robbed twice. We'd trudged through our days with our stomachs in knots, our lives on hold, our hearts in our throats—and yet our worry hadn't changed the outcome. I was still on my way from New Hampshire to Boston, facing a life I never wanted. If there was to be no happily ever after for my family, if we'd find no pot of gold at the end of the rainbow, then we should've lived as if the happiness we'd shared with one another was itself the prize. The dream. The Promised Land.

Amelia made supper for us that evening, my favorite Colombian stew. I ate in silence. In the coming weeks, I'd need to write a paper for my history class. Help with the chores around Amelia's place. Polish my solo for Springfest. Return to New Hampshire to visit both of my parents. And keep quiet about everything that had just happened.

Hey, where are you taking my parents? I'm the one in stripes, take me! Take me!

CHAPTER 8

Left Behind

In every life there is a turning point.
A moment so tremendous, so sharp
and clear that one feels as
if one's been hit in the chest, all the
breath knocked out, and one knows,
absolutely knows *without the merest*
hint of a shadow of a doubt
that one's life will never be the same.

—Julia Quinn, novelist

I will always remember that prison waiting room: Hot. Crowded. Musty. Several rows of attached metal chairs, the kind you see in airports, lined the cement walls. On my row, a teenage mother tried to calm down her screaming baby; two seats over from her, an old man dozed off with his cane at his side. No one spoke. Amelia leaned toward me.

"You ready, hon?" she asked.

I shrugged. "I guess," I said, although I knew that wasn't true. I don't think you're ever actually *ready* to see your own mom locked up. And definitely not when you may never see her again. But I couldn't say that out loud. Not to the one person who'd been willing to take me in.

I'd been to a prison when I was small. A few times, my mother took me to an immigration detention center so we could see some neighbors of ours who were fighting deportation. "We need to go and lift their spirits," Mami told me as she fastened the back buttons on my pink cotton dress. "They need us right now." This is going to sound nuts, but I actually looked forward to going. The guards were so nice to me. My mother, who knew how much I loved sweets, bought me a big chocolate-chip cookie from the vending machine. At age six, the whole experience felt like a fun field trip. At fourteen, it was the most terrifying day I'd ever faced.

The guard, a tall black man with dreads, lumbered into the doorway. "Ladies and gentleman," he announced in a Jamaican accent, "sign in and line up here." He held up a clipboard and nodded toward the entrance to a metal detector. The room stirred as the fifty or so people gathered their belongings. "Your bags will be thoroughly searched," he said. "No cell phones are permitted in the visitation area with the detainees."

The detainees. His words hung there, thick and heavy. Just weeks earlier, my mami had simply been my mami. The loving mother who combed my long, black hair into a ponytail. The mom who made sure I brushed my teeth and finished my homework. Then on an afternoon I've spent a decade wishing I could undo, Mami had been suddenly labeled an inmate. A prisoner. A "detainee." After spending two months in the New Hampshire facility where I'd already visited her twice, she'd been moved to this jail in Boston. And in less than one hour, she'd be forced out of the country.

"Take off all of your jewelry," instructed the guard, "and remove any coins from your pockets." I swiped my fingers through the two back pockets of my jean shorts. Empty. I reached up to unfasten my gold necklace, the one my parents had given me for my tenth birthday. I lowered the chain into the guard's plastic bowl and stepped through the detector. Amelia followed.

We made our way down a hall and into a second waiting area, more depressing than the first. The guard rounded the corner into the room. He was holding the clipboard. "When you hear your name," he barked, "please stand and follow me." I held my breath as he read off the first name. Then the second. Then the third and fourth. Ten names in, I heard what I'd been listening for but dreading: "Diane Guerrero," he announced. Amelia and I took our places among the others. I felt like I could throw up.

The group filed out behind the guard. Halfway down the hall, he stopped in front of a steel door. Above it hung a sign: INMATE VISITATION AREA. With the full weight of his right shoulder, the guard leaned into the door and swung it open. He motioned for us to walk through.

The room smelled like cleaning products. Under fluorescent lights, about twenty inmates sat lined up in booths. Each of them was on a stool behind a giant plastic barrier. Every booth had one of those old-school phones in its upper-left-hand corner. Five or six guards milled around, just watching. As the other visitors scattered to find the prisoners they'd come to see, I stood there and scanned the row, one booth at a time. There, in the middle, I saw Mami. I walked slowly across the linoleum and slid into the chair facing her. Amelia reached up and handed me the phone.

I studied my mother's face. In the eight weeks since her arrest, she looked like she'd aged twenty years. She seemed tired and frail, like she hadn't slept for days. I'd never seen her so skinny. Her eyes were glossy, her skin pale. Her hair was disheveled, frizzy, and in a messy bun. Her wrists were handcuffed together and resting in her lap. A guard on her side of the barrier placed the phone in her hands. She lifted it to her ear and held it there for a long moment.

"Hello, my princess," she said. Her voice was so soft and feeble that I almost couldn't hear her. "How are you?"

My fingers trembled as I stared at her through the scratched plastic. I'd promised myself that I wouldn't get choked up—that I'd hold it together for my mom's sake. But I could already feel the tears building up.

"I'm okay," I said. I bit down on my lip to keep the tears from escaping. It didn't work. "I'm, uh—I'm fine," I stammered.

Mami dropped her head. "Don't cry, baby," she said, her own eyes brimming with tears. "Please don't cry."

All around the room, different energies collided. To my right, an Indian woman laughed hysterically; to my left, the elderly man who'd been asleep in the waiting room now shouted obscenities. I inched closer to the barrier so I could concentrate.

"I'm really sorry about this whole thing," my mom said. "I'm so sorry, Diane."

She didn't mean for her words to sting, but they did. She was sorry. My dad was sorry. The whole world was sorry. But none of it changed my situation. None of it altered the fact that, by dusk, my childhood would be over. This time for real.

My mother sniffled. "Did you bring the suitcase?" she asked.

I nodded. At the prison's entrance, Amelia had already given the bag to the guards.

My mother looked intently at me. "What are you going to do, Diane?"

It was an odd question for a mother to ask her own young daughter—and yet it was the one question I'd been preparing to answer since I was a small child. My parents had always had one set of realities; as their citizen daughter, I'd had a very different set. We'd lived with the daily worry that we'd eventually have to separate. Our fear was at last coming true.

I sat forward in my chair. "I'm staying, Mami," I said. "I've gotta stay."

I'd somehow always known I'd remain. What would I do in Colombia, a place I'd never even been to? What kind of life could I have in a place that my parents had risked everything to escape? Besides that, things were looking good for me for the first time in years. So as far as I was concerned, I didn't have a choice. I needed to stay.

"You see that guy?" my mother asked. She tilted her head toward a Dominican-looking guard on my side of the plastic. He must've felt us staring, because he looked over at us. "He's a nice guy," she said. I wasn't surprised she'd made friends with a guard; my mother has always been social like that.

"You know what he told me?" she asked.

"What?" I said.

She moved the receiver as close to her mouth as she could. "He said immigration only goes after people if they get a tip."

"What do you mean?"

"I mean they're not going around looking for random janitors," she told me. "Someone had to inform them about us."

I gazed at her. "But who would've done that?"

"I don't know for sure," she told me. She inhaled and then slowly released her breath. "That's why you have to keep your eyes open," she said. "Be very careful, Diane."

I started to cry—and this time I didn't hold back. Enormous tears rolled down my cheeks and dripped from my chin. I pulled up the edge of my T-shirt and tried to wipe my face. Amelia, who'd been standing beside me the whole time, began rubbing my back. The Dominican guard walked in our direction.

"Are you her daughter?" he asked me. I nodded my head yes.

"It's okay, sweetheart," he said. "We're not going to hurt your mom."

For some reason, that made me cry even louder. "So why does she have to wear those handcuffs?" I shouted. I could feel myself getting hyped. "Can't you take them off? She's not going to do anything!" Several people looked over at me.

"I'm sorry, but she has to have those on," he told me. "That's the rules."

Soon after, a guard on my mother's side yelled, "Wrap it up! Five minutes!" Mami scooted to the edge of her stool, cradling the receiver between her neck and shoulder. She put her face right up to the barrier.

"*Mi nina, no llores mas,*" she whispered. She paused, stared down at the floor, and then looked back at me. "Never forget that. I'm so proud of you. Be a good girl, okay?"

I let go of the receiver and cupped my hands over my eyes. There were so many things I needed to tell her, so many words I'd stored away. I wanted to stand up and scream, "My mother is not a criminal! Don't you people understand? You've got the wrong family! Please—let her go!" But as the phone dangled by its cord, all I could do was wail. "Bye, Mami," I said between sobs. "Good-bye."

Our time was up. When the guard with the dreads gave the last call, the Indian woman pressed her palms against the plastic, like she was trying to touch the person on the other side. The old man stumbled to his feet, using his cane as leverage.

"You ready?" Amelia asked. I stood and pivoted so I could avoid Mami's face. As much as I'd longed to see her, I also didn't want to remember her like this. Not with her wrists chained up. Not in an orange jumpsuit. The person behind that barrier wasn't my mother. She was a stranger to me.

With hardly a sound, the group shuffled back down the corridor. Amelia held my hand while we walked. "This isn't the end for you, Diane," she said as she tried to reassure me. But it felt like the end. As devastated as I was for my mom, I was even more scared for myself. She and my dad were going home to family. I was stepping into a future I'd prayed would never come.

Outside, Amelia peered out over the lot, trying to recall where she'd parked her Camry. A few hundred feet away from us, near the prison's side entrance, a white police van pulled up. Amelia and I exchanged a look. Seconds later, two guards herded some inmates out onto the curb. My mother was among them.

Just as my mother was stepping into the paddy wagon, she turned and caught a glimpse of me. She froze. I could tell she wanted to say something, to run to me. But before she could make a move, a guard rushed her into the van. "Let's go!" he snapped.

The engine rumbled on. From her seat in the rear, Mami twisted herself around so she could see me through the bars on the windows. She was trying to tell me something, but I couldn't figure out what it was. Then all at once, I understood. "I love you," she was mouthing. "I love you. I love you. I love you." She repeated the three words until the van turned from the lot and disappeared. I smiled. That was the one thing I could be sure of, that my mother loved me. Fuck anyone who tried to come between us.

The summer I lost my parents, it was the strangest kind of heartache. No friends gathered to grieve over the departed. No flowers were sent. No memorial service was planned. And yet the two people I'd cherished most were gone. Not gone from the world itself, but gone from me. We'd find a way to move forward, to carry on. Just not with the promise of one another's presence.

With all of my heart, I wanted to reverse time. Rewind the months. Go back to those days, warm and innocent, when I felt safe. When the smell of Mami's freshly cooked rice and plantains greeted me at our front door. When the sound of Papi's laughter made me feel like the most precious girl in the world. When everything still made sense. But I couldn't go back. The only way out was ahead.

Amelia spotted her car in the lot. On the drive to her house, I stared from my window in silence. My mother's warning, the haunting admonition, echoed through me. *Be careful. Be careful. Be careful.* Tomorrow, I'd begin a new life, one uncertain and frightening. A makeshift family. A different home. A path I'd prayed so hard that I'd never end up taking. I glanced over at Amelia, settled back into my seat, and watched the sun descend over Boston Harbor.

Me and Gaby, sophomore year, in the BAA music room. This picture hung all year in our humanities teacher's room. As you can see, some hater vandalized it. Joke's on you, pahtna!

CHAPTER 9

Second Family

If you go anywhere, even paradise,
you will miss your home.

—MALALA YOUSAFZAI, Pakistani activist
and 2014 Nobel Peace Prize recipient

On the afternoon my father was deported, I didn't get to visit him. Immigration officials hadn't told us exactly when they'd send him off, and since they deported him in the middle of a workday, Amelia couldn't take me to the detention center. I was relieved to miss the final meeting. Seeing my parents with their spirits broken, their heads dropped, had brought almost more sorrow than my heart could hold. Following any loss, there comes a moment when you shift from mourning; if you continued to linger in the grief, you couldn't function. So a little at a time, you create a so-called new normal, although there's nothing normal about it. With a gaping hole in your life, you move on. And it's impossible to do that if you keep peeking over your shoulder. I needed to look ahead.

Amelia was wonderful to me. She, Gabriela, and her other two children, both of whom were in their twenties, made me feel part of the family. They were beyond hospitable—and yet I knew I was a guest. *"Mi casa es su casa,"* any polite Latino host will tell you. But everyone understands the truth: Remaining welcome means abiding by the rules. I found it hard to relax. I had this nagging fear that I might do something to get myself thrown out. Amelia didn't hint at such a thing; but I, aware of the major sacrifice she was making to have me there, became vigilant about respecting boundaries.

Perfect example: I minimized the space I took up. I stuffed my few belongings into a couple of bottom drawers and one area of the closet. I stored my toiletries inside a travel bag rather than on the sink top or in the shower. With five people in the house, things were already cramped. I didn't want to make Amelia or her children regret her choice to take me in. I also recognized how much responsibility she had as a single parent and as a hardworking nurse's assistant. I did all I could to lighten her load.

I'd been around Amelia's home so much that I'd caught on to the way she ran things. Without her having to ask, I helped with the chores. Each time I used a plate, I washed it, dried it, and put it in the cabinet. While I was with my parents, I'd been going through a no-meat phase. I got over that real fast. A permanent boarder can't be picky. I mean, I'm still pretty picky, but maybe less so because of my experience, which, in retrospect, is probably a good thing. My parents had babied me when it came to food. Between meals, Gabriela would sometimes grab a snack from the fridge; I got Amelia's permission before I ate anything. "You know," Gabriela would tease me, "you don't have to ask my mom *every* time." But I was reluctant to be so free. She was the daughter; I was the company. She could get away with things I wouldn't try.

I was so mindful of not rocking the boat that you can imagine how upset I was if I somehow did. Several weeks into my stay, Gabriela pulled me aside.

"Um, can I talk to you for a sec?" she asked.

"Sure," I said. My throat tightened.

"I know you don't mean for this to happen," she continued, "but my sister has been finding a lot of your hair in the bathroom."

I wrinkled my forehead. "*My* hair?" I said.

"Yep," she answered. "It sheds. Before you leave the bathroom, can you please clean it up?"

"Uh, okay," I said, the tears welling up. "I'm so sorry, Gabriela. I promise I'll do that."

From then on, I was OCD about my hair, which was immediately identifiable as mine since I was the only one with a straight, long black mane. After untangling my tresses, I'd thoroughly wipe down the sink and pick up every. Single. Strand.

At Amelia's place, cash was tight. Papi sent money as promised. He'd gotten a friend to sell his and Mami's cars; that cash, coupled with his lotto windfall, had to be split between providing for me and settling into his new life. If Amelia gave me a few dollars, I held on to it; I could make fifty bucks last for weeks. I loved being able to buy small things for myself. If I wanted a bottle of juice or something from the drugstore, I could pay for it without having to involve Amelia. I was smart and careful about my purchases, which pretty much limited me to buying tampons and dollar pizza. I couldn't wait to turn sixteen so I could get a job. Financial independence—that's what I wanted to create. While many girls my age were poring over fashion magazines or giggling about crushes, I was figuring out how I could make it on my own. My parents' deportation had thrust me, headfirst, into the world of adult worries.

Mami and Papi vanished from my life at a critical juncture—as I was navigating that tricky passage between early and middle adolescence. My relationship with my parents had been changing. One minute, I wanted to be with them; the next, I was pushing them aside to hang with my pals. But once I no longer had access to them, I longed for the simplest experiences with them. Like watching a silly movie with my papi. Or having Mami bring me a cup of hot tea when I had cramps. In my mother's absence, I learned to pop an Advil and keep moving. And although Amelia tried to fill in, it wasn't quite the same.

I missed my parents most on one night in particular—Springfest. I'd nearly decided to pull out of the duet; I was so shaken up by my parents' arrest that I didn't know if I could get myself together. Then again, I didn't want to disappoint Mr. Stewart or Damien. And I owed it to myself to go out there and do it. We'd worked hard. It would've been a shame to let our song go unsung.

The night of the concert rolled around. Amelia and Gabriela came to support me; so did Sabrina and her mom, Eva. "Dude, you're going to be fantastic," Gabriela told me before I went backstage. "We'll be cheering you on."

The show was filled with various performances, from opera, jazz, and contemporary to string ensemble and choral pieces. Everyone had a part in this thing; it was the one time of year when we could show our parents what we'd been working so hard at. Mr. Stewart gave Damien and me our cue, and we strode to our microphones. I peered out across the audience. It was packed with parents. Teachers. Administrators. People from the community. Even as I was about to perform, I was pinching myself that I'd been chosen.

Damien delivered his opening lines beautifully. Then came my turn. I closed my eyes. "'In a world that's moving too fast,'" I sang softly, "'in a world where nothing can last, I will hold you . . . I will hold you.'" I was so nervous that my voice shook. And the words I'd practiced over and over now suddenly seemed new. Different. "'So stay with me and hold me tight,'" we sang in unison, "'and dance with me like it's the last night of the world.'"

At the close of our piece, the room erupted in applause. Damien and I linked arms and bowed. I peered out again over the scores of faces, praying that, by some miracle, I'd spot Mami and Papi. Amid the bright lights and magic of that stage, the impossible seemed possible, even for the briefest of moments. Yet off the stage, with the curtains lowered and the auditorium empty, the cold truth remained. My parents, who for weeks had awaited their fate in a pair of New Hampshire jail cells, had already been sent to their homeland a world away.

* * *

I'd never been to Colombia. Yet in a way, I felt like I'd gone a dozen times. That's because my parents kept Eric and me connected to their homeland. They played the music, prepared the foods, told us stories from their childhoods. We also talked frequently to our many aunts, uncles, and cousins there; and over the years, a few visited us. But in our culture it doesn't matter if you've never met family; they are blood, and therefore you are connected by something greater. I didn't have to see my relatives to know they cared for me; their love came through over the phone, and in the birthday cards and letters they always mailed us. Even still, since I hadn't actually set foot in their country, it remained a kind of mystery to me. That changed in July 2001.

About three months after he'd returned to Palmira, Papi arranged for me to spend a month with him there. In the days leading up to my departure, I was eager and, yes, a bit apprehensive. How would it feel to see my parents again? What would their living conditions be? And was it safe there? As soon as my relatives heard I was coming, they began putting in requests for me to bring items that are hard to get or doubly expensive in Palmira, such as Victoria's Secret lotion and Snickers candy bars. "Keep a close eye on your bags," Papi warned me. "People steal."

As if my blood pressure wasn't already high enough, Papi hit me with some tough news a week before takeoff.

"Your mother and I have decided to separate," he told me.

I pressed the phone closer to my ear. My heartbeat sped up. "What are you talking about, Papi?"

"We're no longer speaking to each other," he said. "When you come here, you can spend time with each of us. But don't expect us to do things together."

I nearly dropped the phone. All the bickering, the blaming each other for their circumstances, had threatened my parents' connection for years. Deportation had apparently been the final blow. Once in Colombia, they went their separate ways. Mami moved in with her brother; Papi stayed with his sister. They lived minutes away from each other, but emotionally they were worlds apart. This trip was beginning to sound like one I'd rather not take.

I set out for Palmira on the eve of my fifteenth birthday. "Be careful," Amelia told me as she dropped me off at Logan. "And call me once you're there." The flight from Boston to Cali's Alfonso Bonilla Aragón, the closest international airport to my parents' region, is long. Very. Especially if you throw in a layover in Miami. And especially if you're uncertain what you'll face upon landing. Mami and Papi had told me they'd meet me in the airport lounge. What they failed to mention is that they'd bring company. Oh my Lord.

When I entered the lounge, a band began playing a loud song. *Oh no, please don't let that be for me*, I thought. *Please don't let that be for me.* Yes—my mother had hired a full band to celebrate my arrival! Balloons, flowers, and a sign that read WELCOME TO COLOMBIA, DIANE! filled the waiting area. Several members of my extended family, as well as a bunch of neighbors my mom had rounded up, cheered, called out my name, and snapped random photos of me. I was so stunned that I couldn't speak. I met eyes with Mami and Papi, both of whom were waving madly at me. My look of astonishment probably spoke volumes. I wanted to scream, "What the hell is all of this?" Instead, I put on a half smile. After all, it's not every day that you get serenaded. The whole thing was pretty funny. Well, sort of.

"You're here!" Mami shrieked. She rushed toward me with a hug. Papi stood aside as we embraced, and then he leaned in and kissed me on the forehead. "Hello, *chibola*," he said. "I'm glad you made it." Meanwhile, the band played on. People I didn't know pushed bouquets into my hands. Finally, we all made our way out the sliding doors and into the sauna. The humidity immediately turned my straight hair into a puffy Colombian 'fro.

First stop: a party at my aunt's place. Among a caravan of cars, my uncle drove Mami and me there. As you know by now, my mother can be chatty, but on this day she was completely wound up. She hurled question after question at me. "How's Amelia?" she asked. Before I could answer, she was on to the next topic: "Did you bring the lotion and all the other gifts for the family? And how did Springfest turn out?" I sat dazed and silent. I couldn't believe I was in Colombia. I'd always thought I'd come for the first time with my folks, once they'd been granted citizenship—once "*nuestra situación*" had at last been settled. Everything had happened so quickly. One night, I was cheering with Papi over his lucky win. The next night, my parents were wearing orange. And now I was standing in the nation they'd once escaped. A serious whirlwind.

I stared from my window. In downtown Cali, locals on bikes weaved in and out of traffic. A lot of motorcycles and old cars, models I hadn't seen in America, honked and switched lanes without signaling. Teen girls strutted by in booty-hugging dresses; some girls wore tiny, midriff-baring stretch tops and jeans that barely covered their butt cracks. Music rang out from all directions. Then on the road into Palmira, throngs of barefoot children begged. When we stopped at an intersection, some of the kids wandered right up to our car and pleaded for money or food; many were juggling limes, trying to earn cash from passersby.

"Mami, why are there so many children on the streets?" I asked.

My mother sighed. "Diane, they're homeless," she told me.

"Where are their parents?" I asked.

"I don't know," she told me. My eyes filled with tears. I couldn't imagine what it would be like for a five- or seven-year-old child to be left on their own. The entire scene was chaotic. Colorful. Exotic. Wild. And, because of the straight-up poverty, it was also a bit unsettling. In the States, I hadn't witnessed that kind of hardship. I was struck with a realization: This could have been my life. *OMG, would I have been juggling little limes too? WTF. This is not okay. What is going on? Save the children!*

We pulled up to the house. My aunt and a slew of excited relatives filed out of the front door to greet us. Among the faces, I saw Eric. I lit up. I hadn't expected to see my brother because I'd heard he was away in Santa Marta, a city in northern Colombia. He'd come home early.

"How are you, sis?" he said, picking me up and twirling me. "You're so big now!"

"I'm good," I said shyly, probably because I hadn't seen him in so long. He looked different. Better. His face was clean-shaven, his complexion bright. During his first months in Colombia, he'd struggled to find his way; he floated from one family member's home to the next. But he eventually found work as an English teacher. On the day of our reunion, he seemed happy.

After a bash that went on for hours, Mami and I left for her place. I'd stay with her first. Both of my parents' homes were in working-class areas. Many of the residents had only cold water; you had to be wealthy to afford hot. Rows of cookie-cutter homes, most made from adobe, were as basic as basic can get. No bells. No whistles. No fancy interiors.

"Come on in," Mami said as we walked through the door of my grandfather's house. "Make yourself comfortable." I rolled in my suitcase, set it aside, and began glancing around.

I followed my mother into a rear bedroom. There, she shared a tiny space with my young cousin. He slept on the top bunk, she on the bottom. At the foot of Mami's bed, her suitcase lay open. Because she had no dresser, she lived from her bag—the one I'd hurriedly packed for her. She reached down, pulled out a coat from her luggage, and chuckled.

"So why'd you put *this* in here?" She smirked. "In this climate, I certainly didn't need a coat." I rolled my eyes. She went on to mention that I'd accidentally given her mismatched shoes. I knew my mother was half-joking, but her complaining annoyed me. How the heck was I supposed to know what to pack? Didn't she understand the stress I'd been under just trying to keep our neighbors from looting? "I did my best," I muttered. "At least you got a bag."

That exchange set the tone for our visit. Day after day, Mami talked constantly about how sad she was, how excruciating her split from my father had been. Through the eyes of adulthood, I now understand that my mother was still reeling from all she'd been through. And if I found her new lifestyle difficult to accept, she must've found it incomprehensible. She was also recovering from the heartache of separation, because make no mistake—she was going through one. She and Papi hadn't married, but their breakup was as devastating as any legal separation. At the airport and party, the two had been cordial for my sake. But all they wanted was to steer clear of each other.

I felt sorry for my mother, yet, at the same time, I blamed her for our predicament. By reopening the case in New Jersey, she made herself susceptible to deportation. On the one hand, I didn't fault her for trying to shake things up—she was desperate to move forward in her life, to finally call this country her legal home. Even still, I blamed her for the haphazard way in which she handled the situation. She never tried to get confirmation about whether her application had indeed been handed over to the feds. Instead, she got scared and just let everything fall apart. And because she didn't resolve it, because she didn't see the process through to the end, she'd left our future up to chance. She'd also left us susceptible to people who wanted to do us harm.

I dealt with my resentment by leaving the house. I went out a lot, mostly with my other family. I'd clicked with three of my cousins, Raul, Fernando, and Liz; all were within a couple of years of my age. "Wanna go out tonight?" Fernando would swing by and ask. "Sure," I'd say, glancing at Mami's face to measure her degree of disappointment. To her credit, she didn't hold me back. Even before she left Boston, I'd started spending more time with my friends and less with her and Papi, so this wasn't new. The difference was that, rather than hanging with my friends in the neighborhood, I was stepping out into the unknown.

With my cousins as my tour guides, I experienced a side of Colombia I absolutely loved. There, teens generally have a lot more freedom than they do in America, so we'd be out for hours at a time. We sampled all kinds of foods. We hit the movies, the park, the mall. We danced all night at salsa clubs. It was a way to escape my reality. You name it, we did it, and I enjoyed all of it. Even with its many societal challenges, the country has this amazing energy, an irresistible vibrancy, this fervor that draws you in. When I was out with my favorite trio, I was shuttling between my relatives' homes. From day one, people were all over me. I felt like a celebrity. "Can Diane come over for lunch today?" one of Mami's brothers would call and ask. An hour later, the phone would ring with an additional invitation. Everywhere I went, people wanted to feed me, talk to me, hug me, dance with me, or introduce me to their friends and family. I got all of this attention because others saw me as unique. I was this young American girl who was still totally down with my Colombian roots. I was connected to the culture. I appreciated all the fuss, but it was easy to OD on it.

My last two weeks were spent with Papi. His surroundings were as modest as Mami's, but he was chill about it; if his new lot in life was bothering him, he didn't mention it. In fact, he was quiet overall and maybe a little down. At dusk when the humidity had dropped, he'd often take me out biking. One evening as we returned, I struck up a conversation.

"Papi?" I asked.

"Yes, Diane," he said. "What is it?"

"Do you think someone turned you and Mami in?"

He paused. "What do you mean?" he asked.

"One of the guards at the detention told Mami that someone probably snitched on you guys."

"I don't know, Diane," he said. He looked away from me. "And at this point," he went on, "I guess it doesn't matter. We're here now. There's not much I can do about it." I shrugged, wheeled my bike into the garage, and left the mystery at that.

On the Sunday of my last week, Papi surprised me. "I want to take you someplace special for your birthday," he said. "Just the two of us." In Latin cultures, turning fifteen is a big deal for a girl; it marks the beginning of womanhood. Years before, I'd told my parents I had no desire for a *quinceañera*, the traditional ceremony complete with white gloves and ball gowns. Not my thing. But I did want some kind of party, and, in fact, I'd already had three—one thrown by my mother, a second by my father's sister, and a third courtesy of my cousins. So when Papi told me he'd top all that off with a vacay, I was thrilled.

"Where are we going?" I asked.

"I'm taking you to Cartagena," he told me.

I raised my eyebrows. "Really, Papi?" I squealed. I'd heard that the historic city on the Caribbean coast was one of Colombia's most gorgeous.

"Yes, really," he said, laughing. "I used some of my savings to buy our tickets. We'll go this week."

I wasn't just excited. Given the scarcity of cash, I was also grateful. Papi's generosity made the journey so sweet as we strolled through the streets of Old Town, savored ceviche at a quaint restaurant, and watched the red-golden sunset over the silver waters. The getaway was perfect.

The magic ended as soon as I returned to Palmira. When I mentioned the trip to Mami, she teared up. "Wow," she said, "it would've been nice to be there with you." Hearing that we'd gone away without her brought up all the pain of her split from Papi. The sadness in Mami's eyes reminded me of how wacky our lives had been.

Both of my parents went to the airport to see me off. "Why don't you come live here?" Mami said. I didn't respond. As much as I relished certain things about the trip, I knew there was no life for me there. Mami knew it too. Papi stood quiet. In fact, he'd never said one way or the other whether he wanted me to move there. He probably knew it was pointless to give his opinion, because I'd clearly made up my mind. I heard my call to board. I kissed each of them good-bye and set off for the one homeland I'd ever truly known.

* * *

More change awaited me in Boston. That July, Amelia had relocated from Roslindale to a two-bedroom in Roxbury. Gabriela's brother had moved out, so although the new house was smaller, there was one less person sharing the space. Gabriela and I shared one room; Amelia and her oldest daughter were in the other.

I began my sophomore year—no longer a newbie. I was still finding my way in the music department, and I loved it. I was into my classes. And I was excited about developing as a student and an artist. That fall semester also came with a bonus: Gabriela became my classmate. "You'd like it here," I'd repeatedly told her the year before. "You should audition." She did, and a few weeks later she received the same letter that once gave me a reason to keep going.

The only thing better than being at Boston Arts was having a close friend there. After eighth grade, Dana had moved to Florida with her family, and Sabrina went to a different high school. Still my homies though—don't get it twisted. It was great to have a familiar friend in high school, and even better to know that my other girls would be friends forever.

Following that huge taste of freedom in Palmira, I returned ready to spread my social wings. At a movie theater near campus, a bunch of my friends and I would hang out after school. We'd play around, snap photos of each other (the old-school kind that you have to get developed at

Walgreens, lol), and just be ridiculous. That year, we were obsessed with John Leguizamo, the Colombian-American comedian. He'd released his HBO special, *Sexaholix*, and we'd memorized all of it. We got really annoying after a while, but we were so excited to see a Latino on TV. He was speaking our language and bringing up issues we cared about. Finally, someone we could relate to. We'd entertain ourselves by reciting every joke the guy had told. It was the best time. And then 9/11 hit.

Along with the rest of the nation, I watched in horror as the hijacked planes hit the Twin Towers. American Airlines Flight 11 and United Airlines Flight 175 had originated in our backyard, at Logan. Both planes were filled with Bostonians, adding to the death toll of those lost in New York and Pennsylvania. The day was terrifying. We all held our breath, uncertain whether more attacks were coming. Amelia rushed home early from work to pick up Gabriela and me; the next two days, we stayed home. Even once we returned to school, a funk lingered in the air. What was true in my own life became true for our nation: You can quickly get back on your feet right after disaster, but real healing takes longer.

The year progressed, and as it did, I became super-focused on my studies. For the first time, I fully understood why my parents had put so much on the line to come to the States, and I intended to make good on that opportunity. Not only did I buckle down in school, I became even more conscientious around Amelia's house. I was determined to keep my spot. My chance.

One evening that December, I called Amelia on her cell. She and Gabriela had gone out to run some errands. I was studying.

"May I please walk to the store down the street?" I asked her.

"Why don't you wait until later?" she said. "We'll be there shortly. Gabriela can go with you." But I persisted. I wanted to buy some colored pencils for an art project.

She gave in. "Okay, but don't be gone for long."

I knew the route well. Gabriela and I passed the store every day on our way to the T. I pressed the crosswalk button. The go signal appeared. So I looked both ways and began strolling across the street. When I was about halfway to the other side, a green Mazda swerved out in front of me and—*boom!*—crashed into the right side of my body. The driver, a young white woman, hurried from the driver's side and over to me. I laid sprawled out on the pavement, moaning.

"Miss! Miss!" the lady screamed. "What the hell were you doing crossing the street like that?" She reached down and took my hand. With her help, I slowly stood. I looked down to notice that my knees were bloody. My right arm throbbed as if it was about to fall off.

"Let me call 911," she said, searching her pocket for her phone. I grabbed her arm. "Please don't!" I screamed. "I'm fine!"

"But, miss," she said, "you're hurt!"

"Go, go, go!" I begged, tears flooding my face. "I'm okay!"

I'd just gotten the crap knocked out of me, and yet one thought reeled through my head: *Do not cause any trouble.* If the police showed up, they might realize my parents had been deported and throw me in foster care. Aside from that, I refused to hassle Amelia.

In fact, I didn't want anyone to know I'd been hit. I planned to stay as far under the radar as my family had always been. Rather than calling for help, I hobbled to the house, cleaned myself up, and came up with a story about how I'd hurt myself.

"Oh my God, what happened?" Amelia said the second she opened the door and saw me limping. She put her groceries on the counter and rushed to my side of the sofa.

"Oh, it's nothing," I lied. "I fell on the street."

"You did?" she said. "Why didn't you tell me? Are you okay?"

"I'm fine," I assured her. "It's not a big deal."

But of course, Amelia insisted on taking me to the ER to be checked. Once there, doctors discovered that I'd cracked my wrist. Hours later and a few weeks before Christmas, I left the hospital in a cast I'd have to wear for six weeks. I spent the final days of 2001 recovering from a broken arm. Regretting the deep fracture in my family. And hoping I'd wake up to discover that the last four months had been only a bad dream.

Bright and early and hard at work at Barnes & Nizzles.

Senior recital day with friends from the music department at Boston Arts Academy.

Me on graduation day from BAA. Of course, I thought I was the only one graduating.

CHAPTER 10

Butterfly

Artists are the emotional historians
of the world.

—RICHARD BLANCO, first immigrant and
Latino to be a US inaugural poet

"**H**ello, Diane?"

"Hi, Papi," I said. I'd been chilling on the sofa, listening to India Arie's song, "Ready for Love," when my dad's name popped up on the caller ID. He usually rang on weekends. This was a weekday.

"What is it?" I asked.

He paused. "I got a call from Amelia today," he said.

"You did?" I asked. My pulse quickened. "Everything okay?"

He stopped. "She cannot have you there any longer."

I got up from the couch and walked out toward the balcony to get some privacy. "But, I mean, why?" I stammered.

"Because her oldest daughter just found out that she's pregnant," he told me.

"She is?" I said. I'd seen Gabriela's sister every day that week and hadn't noticed any change in her mood or demeanor.

"Yes," he told me. "And with the baby coming, there's not enough room for you."

My mind scrambled to process what he'd told me. *Did I cause this? What did I do? What makes them want to get rid of me all of a sudden?* Things seemed pretty perfect between Gabriela and me, but earlier that week we had argued; nothing major, just a tiff between friends. But upon learning this news from Papi, I concluded that our disagreement must've prompted Amelia's decision. I pressed my father for information.

"So did I do something wrong?" I asked. My voice shook. "Are they upset with me about something?"

"No, *mija*," he told me. "It's not about anything you did. Not at all. It's only because the house is too small."

I wasn't convinced that was true. I'd made it all the way to the end of my sophomore year with no big dustup. There had to be something that brought this on now. I must've recently slacked on my chores without realizing. By my silence, Papi could tell I wasn't buying his explanation. My eyes welled up with tears. Amelia and Gabriela had become like family to me, and I didn't want to feel lost again.

"Look," he went on, "Amelia was only supposed to have you there for a few months." *A few months?* Until my father said that, I hadn't known he and Amelia had ever agreed on a timeline. "You've now been with her for over a year."

"So what am I gonna do?" I asked.

"Well," he said, "I've spoken to Sabrina's parents." Upon the mention of my pal's name, a weight lifted from my shoulders. Huge exhale. "They said that they'll take you in," he assured me. He then spent ten minutes promising me that all would be okay.

I didn't want to move again. I'd gotten close to the family and didn't want to let them go. Despite Papi's reassurances, I felt lost. At a moment's notice, I could be asked to leave. That's the reality when your own family, your tribe, isn't there to keep you grounded. I was grateful that Papi had lined up my next move, and what better move than with my homie Sabrina and her parents, Eva and Don Federico. They'd come from Colombia years earlier, been granted citizenship, and owned their home. They lived upstairs. Sabrina's aunt and elderly grandmother lived downstairs in the other part of the two-family. Because we'd all been friends for so long, I'd practically grown up there, like I had at Amelia's. All good. Even still, this is the truth: I was sick of all the changes. I wanted one thing in my life to be steady for longer than five minutes. I craved stability.

Amelia heard me sniffling and knew why. Papi had told her he'd talk to me that evening. She wandered onto the balcony, sidled up beside me, and placed her hand on my shoulder. "I just want you to know something, Diane," she said softly. "You didn't do anything wrong." She must've read my mind. "My daughter is having a baby," she went on. "That's it. That's the only reason." From the compassion in her eyes, I knew she was sincere. That eased the sting a bit.

Once Amelia left the balcony, I wiped the tears from my face, pulled my act together, and dialed Sabrina. "Hey, guess what?" I said, trying to seem upbeat, although my heart was in my stomach.

"What?" she said.

"I'm coming to your place," I told her.

She giggled. "I know!" she exclaimed. "My mother told me. But I couldn't say anything to you about it yet."

A week later, I packed up. Gabriela helped me gather my things and saw me off. "Sorry, dude," she told me. "I hate to see you go." Amelia placed my bag into her trunk and drove me to Sabrina's home, which was in my old stomping grounds, Roslindale. Sabrina and her parents welcomed me warmly. "Come on in," said Eva. "You'll be in Sabrina's room." And that's how the summer before my junior year began. Another house. A whole new family. And a new reason to lament that my parents had been forced out of the country. Sigh. Here we go.

* * *

I got a job. Sabrina had been working at iParty, this party supply store in West Roxbury. They sold everything from streamers, balloons, and Halloween costumes to paper plates and cups. "Can you get me in?" I asked her that August. "I'll try," she said. A few weeks later, as the fall semester got under way, I was hired as a cashier at $5.15 an hour, minimum wage then. I put in twenty hours a week, mainly on weekends and a couple of days after school. "Can I catch a ride with you?" I'd ask Sabrina if our shifts overlapped. "Yep," she'd say. She had this little green Jetta. She drove that thing into the ground.

When Sabrina couldn't take me to iParty, I relied on the bus for the hike across town. The new responsibility was a lot to juggle with my studies, but it was worth it to me. Papi continued to send money, but his resources were dwindling; that Powerball money was long gone. If I requested cash for, say, school supplies, he'd scrape it together—but I'd then later discover he was running short on grocery money. So I stopped asking. Landing the gig meant I didn't have to depend on him or anyone. And bonus: If I wanted a cute shirt from H&M or a tube of MAC lip gloss—*boom!*—I could purchase it for myself.

It's tough to imagine that my time at Boston Arts could have gotten any better, but during my junior year, it did. That fall, Ms. Jackson became the head of the vocal department. Her specialty was jazz. She encouraged us to study the greats, and she underscored the importance of good musicianship. I'd been bitten by the blues bug all those years earlier in elementary school, so I knew this was going to work out great. I immersed myself in all things jazz and listened to Miles Davis, Roy Haynes, and Nina Simone. In the middle of the semester, Ms. Jackson even gave me one of the best gifts I'd ever received—a Sarah Vaughan album.

From the first note, my life was forever changed. There's something in Ms. Vaughan's voice that just takes me away. I could listen to her for hours. I admired her power, her vocals, her elegance, and her ability to make me recognize both pain and our capacity for love. I studied the history, the evolution of the genre, the lyrics. Healing power lived in that music. With each note I memorized, I felt less alone. Others had been through far more than I had, and they'd channeled their pain into their art. From devastation, they'd created something beautiful. I wanted to one day do the same.

Then again, I had my doubts. My insecurities. My secret fears that I'd never make it as a professional artist. Aside from that appearance at Springfest, I'd rarely sung duets, much less solos. I didn't want to be too showy; staying in the background, as a member of the chorus, was safe. When I did step up, I thought I had to sing like someone else in order to be good. Some of the other kids at BAA were very talented—I'm talking Whitney pipes. Instead of appreciating my unique sound, I questioned my own talent because I didn't sound like them. I didn't yet have the confidence to be myself.

Another concern also nagged at me: If I pursued a career in the arts, how the hell would I pay my bills? Could I fully support myself after I left Eva's? Once I was eighteen and on my own? At the time, that survival instinct was strong—so strong, in fact, that it made me second-guess my dreams. Let's not get it twisted: Those dreams were alive and well inside me. I was the same girl who'd laid atop my twin mattress and fantasized about taking on Broadway. Yet as graduation inched closer, I got more convinced that I didn't quite have the chops to earn a living as a performer.

And then there was the turmoil in my family. Between school and work, I kept myself insanely busy so I wouldn't have to think about all that had happened. Buried beneath all my activity was a broken heart. I became a classic avoider, talking to my mother and father only if there was no way out of it. Whenever Eva wrapped up a chat with my mother, she'd hand me her phone and say, "Your mom wants to speak to you." I'd take the phone and think, *Here we go again.*

Mami's life was one never-ending *telenovela*, complete with full-length episodes of drama, hardship, and agony. During our calls, she'd recount all her difficulties and even those of our relatives. By then, she'd moved into another family member's house and had her own bedroom, so that was an improvement. Yet for the most part, her calls were filled with doom and gloom. This aunt or uncle had lost a job; someone had been mugged on the way to the grocery store; and of course, she'd end up sobbing over how much she wanted us all to be together again. So did I; I just saw no point in rehashing it. "Okay, Mami, I've gotta go," I'd say to rush her off the line. It was my sixteen-year-old's way of shouting, "I can't effing deal with this anymore!" My poor mother. I now realize how difficult it must have been for her. But I was still sixteen and cranky.

Meanwhile, I'd lost touch with another family member—my niece. I seldom saw Erica. With my parents and Eric away from Boston, the drifting apart happened naturally. I did once run into her and her grandmother in the park. Erica spotted me in a crowd and yelled, "Aunt Diane! Aunt Diane!" When I turned to notice her running toward me, the world stopped for a moment. In the middle of the loud music, the screams, the children begging their mothers for cotton candy, I stood there dazed. She was about seven and had gotten so much taller. It made me suddenly aware of how our lives had moved on, how quickly time was passing.

"How are you, sweetie?" I said, giving her a big hug.

"I miss you!" she squealed.

"I know," I said, still stunned. "Me too."

If I was struggling, at my age, with my parents' deportation, it must have been crushing for her. She'd lost her father and two grandparents she'd lived with, all before her fifth birthday. I'd at least had my parents until I was fourteen. Although the circumstances were out of my control, I felt like I'd abandoned Erica. Just thinking about that broke my heart. Following our reunion in the park, Gloria occasionally brought my niece to Sabrina's place. But between her busy schedule as a single parent and all my responsibilities, our visits petered out.

By that spring, my parents had taken to leaving angry messages on my voice mail; that's how infrequently I'd reached out to them. I loved and missed them as much as they did me, but talking to them was a reminder of everything I was desperate to forget. "Please come here, sweetie," Mami would weep. "I need to see you."

My parents persisted so much that I finally agreed. I was also well aware of the need to give Sabrina, Eva, and Don Federico a break from me, because let's face it, after a year, even the nicest hosts want a little break. So during the summer after my junior year, I booked a ticket for four weeks in Colombia.

The trip was a blur. I may have gone there to spend time with my folks, but I didn't see much of them. That's because I was out chilling with my cousins. Dancing at salsa clubs. And basically having a blast. It was my chance to let loose, to set aside the pressure of being a good girl, a perfect houseguest. Every weekend, I hooked up with a bunch of other teens and went to *fincas*, these summerhouse estates where wealthy kids hang. We'd camp there all night, make fires, play in the pool, and drink. (You've gotta be eighteen to consume liquor in Colombia, but courtesy of my older cousins, I had my first shot of *aguardiente*, a Colombia liquor with a name that means "fire water." One shot soon became two.) Oh, and yes: Let's not forget the tragic belly ring I got. They were the shit at the time. So early 2000s. I thought it was cool—that is, until mine got infected and began oozing.

I brought the party home with me—senior year is when I blossomed socially. My self-doubts hadn't magically melted away, but I was becoming more sure of myself. I'd saved up a few hundred dollars, which gave me a sense of power. I threw myself into even more extracurriculars. In class and out, I was learning to express my opinions. And rather than heading straight home after work, I wanted to have a life. I started hanging with my friends on the weekends, socializing and going to dinner, but I didn't get crazy or anything; I loved it that Eva trusted me and I wanted to keep it that way.

I never went buck wild or got rebellious. When my classmates who had their parents here would get into trouble for no reason, I thought it was pathetic. That probably seems judgmental, but I couldn't understand it. They had so many great things going for them and yet were willing to ruin it. In a way, not having Mami and Papi close led me to give myself rules. Structure. Boundaries. I wasn't conscious of it, but it's like I was parenting myself in their absence. I wanted to show people that even without my family here, I could remain on track.

In the fall, I traded in my job for another near campus. My friend Sophia, a theater major and incredibly talented poet, got me in at the Barnes & Noble Café in the Prudential Center. She and my girl Sasha were always talking about how much they loved it there. Once I got hired, the three of us became our own little club. We called each other *habibi*—an Arabic word that means "my darling"—because we'd heard it in *Bend It Like Beckham*, which we'd seen like a million times. We usually worked from five p.m. to close, or at the ass crack of dawn on weekends. It was fun. And I was growing up.

When I wasn't whipping up cappuccinos or sneaking broken cookies into my mouth, I was hitting the books hard and prepping for SATs. With only months left until graduation, it was time to figure out my path. I really wanted to do work that made some kind of difference. Media was one idea I had. On campus, I was part of a literary and visual arts magazine called *SlateBlue*; Gabriela, several other students, and I would gather our classmates' short stories, art, and poetry and choose the best to include in an annual collection. As part of our participation in the group, we took a field trip to the offices of *The Improper Bostonian*, a glossy lifestyle publication. The editors there taught us the ins and outs of the magazine.

While there, I daydreamed about how cool it'd be to appear on the magazine's cover. But the trip did spark a thought: Maybe I could be a television news anchor, a job that would bring together my love for performing and my desire to make a contribution. A teacher had once told me I had to be very knowledgeable about politics and current events in order to be a good reporter, and that made a lot of sense. So I began exploring the possibility of studying political science and communication. To be honest, I had no friggin' clue what I'd do, but I did know I'd apply to college. The staff at BAA had ingrained that in me from the get-go.

My spring semester, I was heavily committed to the dopest ensemble in school—rhythm and voice. The whole semester was all about preparing for my senior recital, the final evaluation. We got to choose our own songs. I picked "Funny Honey" from *Chicago* and a classical French piece. I also chose "Poor Wandering One" from *The Pirates of Penzance*. And of course, there was my personal favorite, Sarah Vaughan's rendition of *Poor Butterfly*. Two afternoons a week, a voice coach came in to work with us one-on-one. I spent literally hours rehearsing, often even in my head while brewing coffee at Barnes. I intended to be ready.

In March, many of my classmates began receiving acceptance letters from universities all over the country. I hadn't yet applied. Why? Because I was terrified that I wouldn't get in. "It's not too late, Diane," my guidance counselor, Mr. McGillen, told me. "I can help you with the paperwork."

In response to his nudge, I made a list of women's colleges. I had this notion that in an all-female environment, I'd be able to focus. No boys to distract me. Up to then, I had had a serious boyfriend. He was a boy whose name I will not mention. He broke my heart into a million tiny pieces. (You know who you are! I thought I *loooooved* you and you loved *meeeeeeee*! Insert the ugliest cry face you will ever see in your life.) I'm sure every girl has come across a fuck boy or two in high school and beyond. It hurts. Anyway I digress. I'd experienced enough to realize that even puppy love can pull your attention away from your studies; I didn't want even the possibility of nonsense. Also, I'd been reading a lot that year about Simone de Beauvoir and many other incredible feminists. Who knows why I connected my interest in feminism with going to a women's college, but I did.

I applied to five programs in New England—and only the five I thought I had a shot at. Some of my friends were aiming for Tufts and Northeastern. Not me. As hard as I'd pushed to overcome my learning disabilities and get good grades, my GPA was average, not stellar. I knew I had to be realistic. I didn't have the guts, the money, or the test scores to aim for prestigious schools. I was also fearful of leaving Boston, the only city I'd known. Even if, once in college, I wouldn't see as much of Eva or Amelia as I did during all of high school, I still wanted them nearby as my security blankets.

That April, I got called in for a few interviews, and one of them was at the school near the top of my list: Regis College, a private Roman Catholic university a few miles outside of downtown Boston. Eva drove me to the small campus. It was gorgeous. Lush, green lawns that were flawlessly maintained. Massive trees. Historic brick buildings. Just being on campus, I felt like I was finally realizing my fantasy of living in a white suburban town. I sat in on a few classes, and the vibe was wonderful; it seemed like I could really make a path for myself there, grow as a student, and make lifelong friends. Everyone was so chill. And the teachers, some of whom were nuns, seemed to care about the students. Things were looking up.

I knew what I'd come there to do: sell myself. Much of what I've gotten in my life has had nothing to do with what's on paper. Put me in a room, and I can talk myself into or out of anything—it's called the gift of gab. I went wearing a cute dress and my strand of fake pearls, and I made my case to the admissions team as strongly as I could. "I would be a great addition to your school," I told them passionately (I was probably the worst choice, but I wasn't about to tell them that). "If you give me this opportunity," I continued, "I will do everything possible to excel." A month later, *boom shakalaka*—I was accepted. What did they get themselves into? Whatever—I was going to college, bitches!

I got into one other school but I settled on Regis right away. It didn't hurt that they offered me a financial aid package that covered the majority of my first-year costs. I did have a moment of panic, however, when I realized I'd still have to take out some loans. Who could sign for me? No one—and I thought it was too much to ask of Eva or Amelia. So I blundered my own way through the forms and somehow got funded. I didn't understand a lot of what I signed up for, and years later I'd pay dearly for some of my choices. Let's just say Sallie Mae and I have had words over the years. Okay fine—we basically stopped talking after she accused me of being a thieving bitch, and I accused her of being a money-grubbing whore. Oh, but don't worry, Sallie—you'll get your money.

A couple of weeks before the end of the term, my senior recital came around. I arose early that morning, and, while showering, I warmed up my voice with some scales. I wore a beautiful pink strapless dress, one I'd picked out at Charlotte Russe, and pink flowers in my hair from my other favorite "designer," H&M. I wore my mother's shawl as a good luck charm; I could still smell her perfume on it. When I arrived in the music room (which was called the Boston Conservatory), Ms. Jackson, my voice coach, and a few other teachers were waiting.

"You ready?" asked Ms. Jackson with a smile that told me she knew I was.

"Yes," I said with assurance. "I am."

The next hour was one of the most special of my life. This was my night. It was my time to shine. As I sang the pieces I'd worked so hard to polish, the music transported me somewhere else, a place where sorrow and heartache and misery do not exist. I didn't try to pull myself back into the present; rather, I gave in to the feeling, allowing it to carry me off. I ended with a jazz standard called "Poor Butterfly." It's about a Japanese girl enchanted by an American man who never returns to be with her; John Raymond Hubbell wrote the song about the main character in Puccini's *Madame Butterfly*. I'd chosen it because it struck a powerful chord in me. The abandonment. The hoping and waiting and yearning for something that doesn't happen. I'd been so moved the first time I heard Sarah Vaughan perform it. Now it was my turn.

At the end of my concert, the room went wild. Ms. Jackson and the other teachers all stood and clapped, a long round of applause that meant more to me than any I've received since. Sabrina, Eva, Gabriela, and Amelia all sat beaming and clapping in the front row. I was so appreciative of their support, even though I missed my parents. I had done it, and it was a feeling better than any I'd experienced. It took so much courage for me to put my voice on display, to let myself be seen and heard as I am. And for once, I was not afraid. Someone wise once said there are really only two emotions—fear and love—and it's impossible to feel them at the same time. On that morning, in that room, I was surrounded by an overwhelming spirit of love alone.

The recital went so well that I began to regret not applying to a conservatory. But I'd placed a foot on the path toward Regis in the fall of 2004, so in my mind, that meant it was too late. Someone should've talked me out of that.

That entire school year and all the way up through graduation, my mami and papi called. And called. And called. It was as if they could sense I was drifting further and further away from them, and they were grasping to hold on to something, anything, that would keep our relationship intact. They'd missed a lot. Proms. Recitals. Birthdays. Think about all the big things that happen between ages fourteen and eighteen—all the markers we hit, how we change and develop and step into our personalities. At the end of my years at Boston Arts, I was already a little adult. I'd grown from that girl once frightened and shivering under a bed into a poised young woman, a butterfly, ready to spread my wings and navigate my life. And my parents, as deeply as they wished otherwise, hadn't been there to witness any of the transformation.

Top: Sophomore year at Regis College. The orientation leaders and me. Middle: Junior year study abroad, Roma, Italy. In the back, looking sexy as hell, is a super-old Italian statue. Bottom: Venice, Italy, being the ultimate tourists.

CHAPTER 11

New World

*Life begins at the end of your
comfort zone.*

—Neale Donald Walsch, author

The day I set foot on campus, I knew I'd made a mistake. A big one. It's not that Regis seemed any less ideal than it had during my visit; it was more stunning in fall than it had been in spring, and it was buzzing with the students' energy of a fresh start. But after that memorable recital, my doubts about my direction had grown louder. *Why didn't I try for a conservatory?* I kept thinking. *And why am I not in New York?* I'd rushed to do the whole university thing because it was the next logical step. I now realize I could've taken off a year to get clear about what I wanted. Oh well.

Right away, I had to make a huge adjustment to—how shall I put this?—*Les (White) Girls.* I'd befriended the sprinkles of Caucasians who'd been at Boston Arts, most of them the Jamaica Plain, clog-wearing, crunchy-granola types. But the girls at Regis were different, and those variations extended beyond race. There were hoity-toity suburban girls. Super nerds and super-religious girls. Girls who didn't get into Wellesley. Oh, and lesbians—lots and lots of lesbians. Within a week of being there, I had my first lesbian experience. *Phew—now that I've got that over with, what's next?* There were also quite a number of black and brown girls, but not nearly as many as I was used to. And I didn't find much of an artsy crowd other than the Emo goths in the theater department. No more music and no more fantasy. I was stuck.

I missed my crew. Gabriela had enrolled at Pine Manor College in the greater Boston area. Sabrina was in the city too, attending beauty school to become a hairdresser. Sophia, my Barnes bud, had gone off to Hofstra University in New York. Sabrina, Gabriela, and their moms all dropped me off in my dorm room a week ahead of the fall semester. "You always have a spot in our house," Eva assured me as we hugged good-bye. "You can visit anytime." And I did sleep over on some weekends and holidays. But you know how it goes: After you move away, you often don't keep in touch, even when your loved ones are nearby. That's especially true once you get caught up in your new life.

And soon enough, I did. I immediately clicked with my roommate, Adrienne, this gorgeous girl with auburn hair and green eyes. She'd been raised in a progressive community in the Berkshires. When she pulled out a *Les Misérables* poster and hung it over her bed, I knew she was my kind of roomie. Artsy. Earthy. Cool. A good fit with my Artsy. Cool. Undecided.

As the year got underway, I did make more friends in class and in other school activities and functions around campus. I connected with a group of pals, including Paula, a Puerto Rican Republican in love with

George Bush; Jemma, who was from Maine, super fun, and incredibly diligent and organized; Jenny, who was mild mannered and studying to be a nurse; and Sarah, who was then exploring the goth alternative lifestyle.

Especially during that first year at Regis, race was on my mind a lot because the topic was part of my curriculum. I'd chosen poli-sci and communications as a major. With my eye on a media career, I was hungry to educate myself, to learn all about the various philosophies. I read voraciously. Plato's *The Republic*. Niccolò Machiavelli's *The Prince*. Jean-Jacques Rousseau's *Of the Social Contract*. I'd get so attached to whatever I was reading that I'd switch my view. After some Henry David Thoreau, I'd be like, "Revolution is the only way to achieve justice!" Then following a little Aldous Huxley, I'd start spouting off about pacifism. I wasn't simply reading. I was also carving out a belief system. An identity. A place to fit in as a Latina and a female and a Millennial. Trouble is, from one course to the next, I couldn't decide whether I wanted to be a Black Panther or Mahatma Gandhi. Depended on my mood—#mood.

I'd bug out on certain issues that plagued my mind, things like racial and societal inequality, reproductive rights, and overall injustices. If I talked in class about wealth distribution being our world's only hope, and a white girl then made a snarky remark, I'd snap, "Are you talkin' to me? You fascist right-winged schoolgirl, you! You know nothing!"

Much of my anger was misplaced. I was furious that I'd lost my mother and father. Furious that those around me were from communities where my reality wasn't part of the conversation. Furious that others paid little attention to the existence of undocumented workers. My family's struggle to remain in America had defined my childhood, yet immigration wasn't on their radars. They had absolutely no idea what I'd been through.

That was by design. I shared a lot with my friends, but I initially avoided that Kryptonite of conversations—my parents' whereabouts. "Are you going home to see your folks?" a friend would ask. "Oh no," I'd tell her. "They relocated overseas a few years ago." While that was technically true, I'm sure she thought my parents were in the French Alps or Tahiti, not living hand-to-mouth in the Third World. If she or the others pressed the point, I quickly changed the subject because I was ashamed.

Aside from that, I didn't want to be seen as a victim. I'd done my share of sulking. I was ready to turn the page on the "poor Diane" story.

* * *

For most of my friends, summer break was summer break, that time when they traded their studies for, say, a Tuscany vacation. For me, however, the off-season was a reason to panic. I was worried about where I'd go and how I'd earn money. After freshman year, I headed to Eva's place, but that got old really fast. Not only was I nervous about wearing out my welcome, I also wanted to show that I could at last be independent. Who wants to be a permanent charity case? I didn't. But since neither my parents nor I had the cash to fly me to Colombia, I had to figure out something. So at the end of my freshman year, I became an orientation leader, a job that involved giving tours to prospective students and—bingo—staying in the dorms for free during June, July, and August. Second summer down, one to go.

Holidays were tricky as well. While others were preparing to deck the halls, I was stressing about whether my loans would cover the spring term. "I want you to come here in December," Mami told me. "I haven't spent Christmas with you in four years." In the winter of 2005, her plea got through to me and I arranged a trip. I didn't have the money for the airfare, so God bless Gabriela's sister, who put the eight-hundred-dollar ticket on her credit card. "I'll pay you back," I promised. (Which, by the way, I did; when all you've got is your reputation, you learn to be impeccable with your word. I'm anal about promptly repaying my friends, as well as returning, in pristine condition, any items I've borrowed.)

Christmas in Colombia was amazing. I'd heard about people going from house to house, singing and reciting verses during *La Novena*—exactly as we'd done in Boston, only multiplied by twenty. The stories didn't come close to the experience itself. There were parties all over the place. Homes lit with hundreds of twinkling lights. Parks and plazas aglow with nativity displays. Children playing in the streets. Those who had jobs set them aside for the month. Music and fireworks filled the air. Over the years, one of my aunts had often sent me tapes of pretty Christmas carols.

Some were those we sing here, such as "Silent Night" and "The Little Drummer Boy." Others were traditional choruses like "Vamos Vamos Vamos Pastorcito" and "Los Pastores de Belén." The sounds, the sights, the taste of *buñuelos y massamora*, Colombian pastries and cornlike pudding—it all brought the season to life and created this enormous national fiesta.

Mami and I exchanged gifts. I brought her the usual items on her list: eyeliner, lotion, perfume, makeup. Early that Christmas morning, before I'd gotten out of bed, she came into my room and handed me a package. My eyes lit up.

"Open it," she said. I removed the tape from the layers of pink tissue paper. Inside, I found a stack of seven underwear, one in every color of the rainbow.

"Thank you," I whispered. I was half-asleep, but awake enough to reach over and embrace her. To anyone else, the present would've appeared to be a set of basic cotton undies. To me, it was a symbol of my mother's care. It took me back to those days when I was four and seven and ten, the years when Mami had been there to give me a personal item that often only a mother would buy for her daughter. It probably sounds funny, but I still look forward to receiving panties from my mother.

It was after that Christmas break that I began thinking about how I could eventually bring my parents to the States again. Could I do that? What would the barriers be? Upon completing college, would I be able to lock down a good job, save up, and hire a respectable attorney? I had none of the answers, but my time with Mami had reminded me of how lonely I felt without her and Papi here. How much I needed them. I didn't tell either of them what I was considering. Instead, I stashed the thought away. It gave me something to look forward to, to anticipate, to pray about. We all need that. Dreams are what keep us alive.

You'd think my sweet reunion with Mami would've prompted me to call her and Papi more regularly. It didn't. Same song, seventeenth verse: I would've given just about anything for them to be closer, yet I also needed to keep some distance between a situation I was powerless to alter and myself. By this point, my parents had gotten used to me going underground.

They stopped giving me shit about it. That battle was lost, and they knew it. Which might be why Mami smartly switched her tactic from demanding to guilt-tripping. "Diane," she said on my voice mail that March, "I get so sad when you don't call me." A day later, I returned her call.

Now, years later, I recall that particular conversation. The mother I'd known as a girl, the one who'd gently stroked my hair and tucked me into bed, showed up during that call. This time, Mami didn't mention the heartache of 2001. She didn't speak of how badly she wanted to be with Papi again. She didn't linger on the daily hardships of her life in Colombia. Rather, she asked me a simple question, one I've carried with me since: "How are you, my dear—really?" She then listened, fully listened, as I told her.

I hadn't been there to see all the ways in which it was happening, but my mom was shifting. She was moving past the trauma and the outrage and the grief and settling into a quiet acceptance of things not as she wanted them to be but as they were. We don't do all our growing up between birth and adolescence or even our twenties. If we're fortunate, we never stop.

* * *

My classes were kicking my butt. As hard as I was working I was still pulling only Bs and Cs. That's all good, but I wanted better, and I couldn't understand why better was out of reach when I was making such an effort. It's not like I was partying or procrastinating. So I went in to talk to my counselor. "Have you been tested for a learning disability?" he asked. I hadn't. Once I took the tests and the results came in, we discovered those two culprits I'd been dealing with since elementary school: ADD and dyslexia in both math and reading. I got on medication, requested extra time from my professors to complete exams, and sure enough, the As began to roll in.

With my GPA on the rise—and with a less generous financial aid package for year two at Regis—I searched for work. I landed a gig at Jasmine Sola, a retail store that sold designer denim and trendy clothing. I hadn't ever been in the same room with such expensive jeans, some pairs as much as $250! As I folded and hung them each evening, I drooled. Who had that much loot to drop on clothes? Oh, right—everyone in the store but me.

I did, however, meet really interesting people while on the job. There was this one girl—petite, blond, cute as a button, and a vision in baby pink. I instantly tried to look away. But even after all my crap, weird hang-ups, and promises to myself to have more girlfriends of color, Katie was the one white girl I could not pass up. She was and still is one of the most beautiful and caring people I've ever met. She wasn't afraid to call me out on my bullshit, or to let me call her out on hers. She saw me for who I really was, and she still wanted to be my friend. That kind of friendship has no color and no limits. We would talk all throughout our shifts. While folding clothes and helping customers, we'd plan our futures and pick out clothes in the store we wanted to blow our paychecks on. It was a great time, and nothing could distract me from what I wanted to accomplish.

During one of my shifts, a guy walked in. He was handsome with dark features. About five feet eleven. Well groomed. Broad smile. "Excuse me, miss," he said. I turned, thinking he was ready to be rung up. "May I ask your name?"

I blushed and smiled. "It's Diane," I said.

"I'd love to get your number," he said coolly. I blushed harder. When I didn't answer, he reached into his jacket pocket and took out a pen and paper. "Would that be okay?" he asked. I nodded, grinned, and gave him my digits. "My name is Brian, by the way," he told me. He didn't take his eyes off me.

So much for not being distracted by boys. That weekend, Brian took me out for a nice dinner. And then a second one the Friday after. And then a third the next week. Dating was fairly new for me. The handful of times I'd gone out in high school, the dude and I would chill with a group at the movies or McDonald's. This was different. Brian was already out of college and had a real job. He'd call ahead to get on my calendar, choose a restaurant, swing by my dorm to pick me up, and then wine and dine me. I soaked up the attention. I also loved the freedom of not having to tell anyone who I was with or where I was going. We began seeing each other almost every weekend, and within a couple of months, we were chillin'. I felt like a real grown-up.

* * *

One afternoon, my friend Jemma came into my dorm room, energetic as always and holding a brochure. It was a study abroad application. "Pack your bags," she said in her best British accent. "We're going to London!" I'd heard about the program earlier, and although studying abroad was one of those things I'd dreamt about, I didn't let myself get too excited. "Jemma, I can't go," I told her. "I'm broke as a joke! I can't go sip tea with you and the Queen." I then turned back to my studies. But being the can-do, resourceful person that Jemma is, she completely ignored my whining and pessimistic attitude and said, "It has a great international relations program." I raised an eyebrow and thought, *Well, maybe*, but then the flood of doubt came pouring in. *How could I pay for this? This isn't for girls like me.* I paced and paced, trying to make sense of this crazy idea. *Me? Noooooo, not me. I'm too poor, too brown, too unfortunate.* Then again, I'd gotten this far. Why not me? I looked over at Jemma, and she had this sneaky smile on her face. "See you in London town," she said. She then handed me my application—which she'd already filled out for me. Not long after, I got the news: I was going to the United Kingdom. Jemma and a few of my other friends got in, too.

The Westminster campus of Regent's University London, my college's partner school, could've been yanked off the set of *Downton Abbey*. Old brick buildings around a grassy quad. Cobblestone walkways. Sycamores displaying autumn's red-golden leaves. Adrienne, Jemma, and I shared a decked-out suite with a balcony overlooking a picturesque courtyard while Paula was in her own room on the second floor.

If I had been underground in Boston, I became a friggin' MI6 agent in London. I'd only shared my story with Adrienne. One night when I was being particularly difficult to deal with, she said, "What is your deal?" So I spilled the beans. "Oh, it all makes sense now," she said. "What?" I asked. She just hugged me and told me I was safe. From then on, I didn't tell another soul about my background.

"Where do your parents live?" some people would ask me. "Oh, they passed away," I said. Other times, I claimed that my mother and father had returned to Colombia to run their own business. "They're retired," I explained. I had so many different tales going around that Adrienne was like, "You'd better keep your lies straight. You're losing your shit out there. Pull yourself together. cap'tn! Arrr." The way I saw it, this time in London was my opportunity to become someone else, to take on an identity in a plot of my own creation. If I'd revealed my tragic past, others would've pitied me—and I was so over pity. What I wanted was to be normal. I now get it that normal is relative, and even the person who appears so together is dealing with something. *Así es la vida.*

During my entire time away, I talked to Mami and Papi only a few times. In one of those calls, Mami dropped some news. "I'm moving to Madrid," she said. I gulped. *Madrid? Why?* "I need to start over somewhere new," she said, as if she'd read my mind. Years ago in the seventies, my mother's brother had relocated to Spain to pursue his dream as a bullfighter. Even though jobs were scarce in Madrid, there was still more opportunity than Colombia had to offer. "That's nice. Mami," I said. Wow. I didn't have much to say because I was stunned. Also, I was so immersed in college life that I'd really ignored the fact that my parents were still living their own lives without me. No time to be sad, I told myself. You've gotta keep it moving. "Good Mami, that's great," I said. I didn't ask whether she'd be there before I left the region. I was too focused on pretending I wasn't her daughter, acting as if the life we'd shared hadn't existed—and that she was retired and/or deceased.

Even with all this pretending, I still managed to fulfill my duties as a responsible college student. My time in London was amazing, an experience I thought a girl like me would never have. I loved my classes and was thriving in a foreign land where people had accents! On breaks and on weekends I traveled with my gals all over Europe, seeing things I hadn't imagined in my wildest dreams. I was living on bread, tomato, crisps, but my God, it was a dream. The worst thing I could've done would have been to deny myself the opportunity because of fear or feeling like I didn't deserve it. It was one of those times when I really saw the power of having a dream and making it come true, no matter the obstacles. The only thing

I would've changed would have been to have lived that dream as myself, and not someone else.

I returned to the States, but not to Regis right away. I'd enjoyed my experience abroad so much that I decided to spend the spring semester in the field, this time at American University in Washington, DC—another of my college's partner schools. Ahead of my program, I spent the holidays with Brian in Boston. When I told him about DC, he wasn't too keen.

Why can't you go *next* year?" he shouted. "You've already been away so long!"

"I don't want to go next year," I shot back. "And why are you flipping out? I'll be in DC, not Europe. We can take the train to see each other."

The argument certainly clouded my decision and made DC a little gloomier than I'd hoped. In retrospect, I should have nipped that shit in the bud and kicked him to the curb. But alas, the heart wants what it doesn't need sometimes. I realize this wasn't the healthiest of relationships, but fuck—it's not like I had anything else super-important going on, right?

Despite Brian's objections, I set off for my program in the nation's capital. I'd chosen foreign policy as my concentration (at this point, I was thinking about a career as a diplomat). "Why aren't you doing American policy?" Adrienne asked me. She knew I preferred debating this country's social issues. As it turns out, my friend was right. The topics we discussed in class, though important, put me to sleep. US-China relations. Free-trade agreements. United Nations resolutions. Snore.

College is a chance to explore, but even by the middle of my junior year, I was no closer to figuring out my path. I wanted to serve others and to do work that had meaning. That I knew. What I didn't know is how to end up there. I had no one saying, "Hey, Diane, what are you going to do with this degree?" I was just drifting—and praying the wind would carry me in the right direction.

* * *

My time in DC was pure misery. A month into my coursework, my financial aid collapsed. I discovered (too late) that my federal student loans couldn't be transferred to cover my costs at American. In desperation, I applied for private loans with high interest rates. I put my signature on agreements I had no business signing, but it was the only way forward that I could see. Those loans didn't come through immediately, so in place of studying, I was agonizing over whether I'd be booted out on my behind. I got called into the financial aid office on several occasions. Things got so tense, in fact, that I considered quitting altogether and booking a one-way flight to Colombia. But I knew that wasn't an answer; you can't run away from your problems. College gave me a shot at a future.

I fell into a depression. I'm not referring to a little case of the blues. I'm talking about a dark, heavy fog that kept me in bed for days at a time. I skipped classes. I stopped socializing. My appetite disappeared and I dropped twenty pounds. From Boston, Adrienne checked on me. "Diane, what's up?" she'd call and ask. "I haven't heard from you. You okay?" I put on a brave voice and reassured her I was fine so I could get her off the line. The pain, for me, was beyond emotional; it was physical. I literally felt as if I was about to burst. My whole body ached.

I'd been low before but never *this* low. Which is why I decided the meds were contributing to my mood. So without consulting a doctor, I stopped taking the pills—and the impact on my grades was immediate and disastrous. In a month, I went from excelling to nearly flunking out. Things unraveled further from there.

The combination of everything—my disastrous loan situation, my plummeting grades, my souring relationship—overwhelmed me. I had a lot riding on this grand plan to make it through school, land a job, and bring my parents back here. None of it was falling into place. *I should go back to Regis,* I kept thinking after I realized the financial hot mess I was in. *Where did I go wrong?* My life was a big unfinished project, one I feared I'd never complete. I was disappointed in my choices. How could a school year that began on such an amazing high in London end up in the ditch?

When that attorney duped my father out of his life savings, Papi wanted to give up. That is exactly what I wanted to do. I was so burdened and exhausted that I hardly had the will to carry on.

At the close of the semester, I dragged myself back to Boston and moved in with Brian. Again. I knew the relationship wasn't the smartest choice, but it was all that I knew. I had come to rely on him.

Depression can take various forms, and mine showed up in new ways that summer and into the following fall. I loved to P.A.R.T.Y., and I went out a lot with the girls from work. I'd crawl home drunk at three a.m., and then awaken the following afternoon, dizzy and dry mouthed. I didn't give a rip about missing class. Several times, I got so wasted that I passed out, and my friends had to lift me into a cab and escort me to the house. Even now, years later, there are periods of that time that I cannot recall because I blacked out.

I pushed everyone away. "Please call me!" Gabriela pleaded on my voice mail. "Please tell me you're okay." Sabrina, Eva, Amelia, and my aunt and uncle in New Jersey all rang as well, but I wouldn't call back. Adrienne once came by my apartment and banged on the door. "Hey, Diane!" she yelled out. "Are you in there?" I ignored her. I had no desire whatsoever to discuss what was happening to me or to reveal the tightrope I was on. So I tuned out my loved ones, and the more I rejected their help, the more isolated I became.

And the more I drank and socialized. I didn't simply want to take the edge off; I wanted to be numb. In most weeks, I couldn't have told you whether it was a Monday or a Thursday. Every day felt the same—like one I'd rather sleep through. It was wash, rinse, repeat: Depression. Drunken revelry. Fighting with Brian. Shame about my behavior. And then always—always—another round of liquid anesthesia.

* * *

"Diane?"

My eyes fluttered open. Brian stood at my hospital bed, looking down over me. Around us was a blue curtain, one of those fabric partitions used to separate one patient from the next. My head throbbed. The room was blurry. I looked down to notice that my forearms were wrapped tightly in white bandages. A monitor at my left tracked my heartbeat. *Beep. Beep. Beep. Beep.*

"What happened?" I muttered. "Where am I?"

Brian pressed his lips together. "You tried to hurt yourself again," he said. He nodded toward my arms. I peered at them and then back at him. "You know," he whispered, leaning in close to my ear, "You cut yourself."

The cutting. The first time I'd hurt myself was in DC. That morning, I'd received the horrible news about my loans, and by that evening I was inconsolable. I uncorked some Merlot, sat on the floor in the middle of my room, and drank a glass at a time until the bottle was empty. For the life of me, I could not understand what I was feeling. I was uncomfortable, almost to the point of wanting to get out of my skin. I was literally trying to pull myself out of myself. I rolled around, slapped myself, pulled my hair, and dug my nails into my skin. I was exhausted and panicked. I thought, *Do I have to just sit here and feel all this shit? Why?* I looked in the mirror and cried out for my mother. "Ma! Mama! Where are you? Please—Mama, Papa!" Like a child, I wrapped my arms around my knees and rocked my body back and forth, as if doing so would soothe my distress. It didn't. And in an instant I wish I could reverse, I grabbed the wine corkscrew from a table nearby, pointed its sharp tip into my arm, and ripped across my skin. As I saw the blood drip down my arm, my eyes widened. I got up and raced for a towel. *What the hell is wrong with you?* I thought. I did eventually pull it together, and after that episode, I promised myself I'd never do that again. It frightened me.

And yet it also brought a strange relief. For a brief moment, the sharp physical pain blunted all other anguish—a kind of temporary interruption to my despair. It also put me in control. At the time, I saw myself as powerless. Although cutting did not offer a solution to my problems, I used it as a way to calm myself down when I got out of control. With the slight turn of my hand, in the privacy of my home, I could decide how I wanted to feel. I was in charge. I was holding the weapon.

My vow to myself didn't stick. As the sadness intensified, so did my urge to hurt myself. I tried to avoid it by writing letters to myself; I scribbled page after page about how lost I was. But my desire to release grew so intense that it overtook me. Those who've done this to themselves would probably describe that desire the same way I do: It's like suffocating. Hurting yourself is a way to breathe again. So stupid. At first, I would do only little cuts on my arms and thighs where the wounds weren't all that noticeable, since I usually used a sharp razor or kitchen knife. I figured it wasn't a problem and almost liked the sensation and secrecy of it. But after a while, I knew I was fucking losing it. I thought the feeling of wanting to do this crazy thing to myself would go away, but as time went on, I wasn't getting any better. Surprise! I had ended the semester poorly and left DC feeling quite unaccomplished, a fact made worse by my new nasty little habit. As time went on, if I was having an episode, I'd pick up anything that happened to be close. A bobby pin. A metal nail file. A paper clip. The less sharp the object, the nastier the scar.

I was lost, and I was becoming a huge inconvenience to myself and those around me, especially poor Brian. I say poor Brian because no one deserves the kind of crazy I was exhibiting. These tantrums became more and more frequent and scary. I was exploding, and all those years of being "the good girl" and being strong for everyone were going out the window. I couldn't hold it in anymore. I was beside myself.

The curtain swung open. A nurse, a heavyset woman with wiry silver curls and Coke-bottle glasses, marched in with a clipboard. "May I have a minute alone with her?" she said to Brian. He nodded and stepped out.

"You wanna talk about this, hon?" she said. I didn't respond. She scanned my take-in sheet. She paused and looked intently into my face. "We've got social workers on staff here. I'd like to set you up with one. Would you like that?"

"Yes, but please don't take me away," I said, sounding like a child. The trauma I'd lived through with my folks seeped out in so many ways. It was like I was stuck in time.

"No one is going to take you away" she said, reopening the curtain. "Are your folks in the area?"

"No," I answered.

"Well," she told me, "I really do hope you can get some help. You need it." *Ha! Don't I know it, lady.* Maybe I needed someone to tell me that, to take notice of me and the pain I was feeling inside. Or maybe I wanted to be taken care of. Whatever the reason, she was right: I did need help. And fast.

The hospital released me that same evening. The drive home was quiet. "I'm worried about you," Brian finally said to break the silence. "We've gotta figure this out. I want to help you, but I don't know how." It's funny how you can be sitting right next to someone and feel lonelier than you would be if you were alone. That's how I felt.

The hospital stay scared me straight for a couple of months. But like alcohol or drugs, which I was doing a lot of, cutting can be addictive. On the rare occasion when I bothered to show up for class, I'd catch people looking at my arms and then quickly averting their gazes when I noticed their gawking. Their facial expressions said it all: *What the hell is wrong with you?* I felt like a failure and a freak of nature.

Others tried to throw me a life preserver, but in one instance, that seemed like a betrayal. Someone anonymously told the dean's office about my scars, and I got a call from the Regis counseling center. "Diane," said the therapist once she finally got me on the line, "I need you to come in and see me." *Fuck.*

A few days later, I shuffled through the office doors at three p.m. I'd just gotten out of bed after another night of partying. My olive skin had grown pale. My face was gaunt. My eyes were bloodshot. I was skin and bones and wearing a turtleneck in seventy-five-degree weather.

The counselor met me in the waiting room. She was a middle-aged white woman who wore pearls, a Jackie O hairstyle, and flesh-colored nylons. She seemed so perfect—so waxy and plastic. She smiled and extended her hand. I didn't take it.

"I'm glad you came in today," she said. "Come with me so we can talk." I followed her down the hall into a room. She closed the door, and we sat across from each other. I stared at the floor.

"I know you've been having some challenges, Diane," she said. She cleared her throat. "Can you tell me what's been happening?"

To this day, I have no idea what I said to that woman. All of it was BS. I wasn't ready to talk to anyone, especially someone from my school. And the second I'd laid eyes on her, I'd instantly dismissed her as someone who couldn't relate to me. So forty-five minutes later I went back through the center's doors, feeling no better than I had when I entered them. What happened twelve days later still haunts me.

My twenty-second birthday in Boston.

CHAPTER 12

The Edge

*In the broken places, the light
shines through.*

—Leonard Cohen, singer

Forecasters had predicted snow, and on the evening of December 13, 2007, it arrived. Ahead of the downfall, commuters rushed home early from work, bringing gridlocked highways to a standstill. Last-minute shoppers scurried into supermarkets to pick up bottled water. Neighbors emerged from their front doors and scattered salt on their steps, hoping to ease the next morning's shoveling duties. By nightfall, the city's hubbub had quieted to a murmur and Boston slept under a thick blanket of white. I was tired, so I turned in early, at nine, even before Brian had made it home. I was scheduled for back-to-back bartending shifts the next day and badly needed some rest. *Maybe I won't have to go in because of the weather*, I thought. Things seldom went that way, but I could hope.

Buzz! Buzz! Buzz! I lurched toward the alarm clock at my bedside and switched it off. *8:50 a.m.* I glanced over at Brian, who must've come in after I was knocked out; I hadn't even heard him. He stirred, turned over, and looked sleepily in my direction.

"What are you doing today?" he asked.

"I've gotta work later," I groaned. I pulled the comforter up around my neck. *Just five more minutes*, I told myself. When I woke up again, the red digits on the clock read 9:40 a.m. Brian had showered and dressed. He popped his head in the bedroom.

"I have to make some stops on my way home so I'll get in late," he told me. "I'll see you when I'm back." Seconds later, he was out the door.

I stretched to get my phone from the nightstand. *Two voice mails.* I pressed PLAY.

"Miss Guerrero," said a woman's voice, "we have an urgent financial matter to discuss with you regarding your credit card account. This is our fifth and final attempt before legal action will be taken. Please return our call immediately. This is an attempt to collect a debt." *Click.*

The next message followed. "Diane, I'm calling you on behalf of the Regis financial aid office," I heard. "It's extremely important that you come by our office as soon as you can. We need to talk with you about your Stafford loan." *Click.*

I flung back the comforter and went into the bathroom. I turned on the faucet, leaned my head down into the sink bowl, and splashed cold water on my face.

As the holidays had neared, the city buzzed with lightness and joy. I wanted so much to be part of it but couldn't fully do it. Do you know what it takes for a cheery and highly optimistic person such as myself not to enjoy Christmas? A lot, so you know shit had to be unsettled. Everyone seemed so happy; even the usual Grinches chirped hello to passersby. Salvation Army volunteers, with their rosy cheeks and big grins, stood out in front of Macy's and rang their bells to welcome donations. I was like Alanis Morrissette in her "Hand in My Pocket" video, standing naked in the middle of all that Christmas cheer—although I wasn't singing or happy to be naked. I was just dull and blah. In late November, following Thanksgiving, I'd tried to jolt myself into the spirit by window-shopping near Downtown Crossing. I came home more depressed. The crowds, the bright lights, the music, the families strolling gleefully along the boulevards—it all made me keenly aware of how alone I was.

I sleep-walked through my days, all of which looked exactly alike. Home. Drinking. From the time I dragged myself out of bed, I began counting the minutes until I could crawl back under the sheets. I'd lost my grip on everything important to me, and soldiering on was the best I could manage. Here and there, I'd have a halfway-decent moment, a laugh, a little relief while watching TV. But then I'd watch something that made me hate my life and want to trade places with someone else.

Morning turned into afternoon, and before I knew it, it was time for my evening shift; after Jasmine Sola, I'd taken a job at a nightclub. I reached the T entrance, descended the stairs, and began mentally preparing myself for the evening. I was starting to really dislike my work environment. I mean, at first it was fun and easy money. But it was also mind-numbing and superficial. And like every job, it had its share of drama, not to mention the sketchy dudes—like one of the regulars who was seated at the bar stool when my shift began.

"What can I get for you, sir—the usual?" I asked, although I'd started mixing the gin and tonic he typically ordered. When I turned back around, he stared right at my breasts. A real original asshole.

"It's nasty out there, isn't it, sweetie?" he said, keeping his eyes locked on my blouse. He stood, leaned up over the bar, and motioned for me to come closer, as if he was about to tell me a secret.

"How would you like someone to keep you warm tonight, honey?" he said. His breath reeked.

I gave him his drink without flinching. "No, thanks," I snapped, picking up the glass and slamming it down in front of him. "Will that be all, sir?"

He scowled and returned to his stool. "Merry Christmas to you too, cunt," he muttered under his breath.

I endured this sort of sexual harassment a lot. Sometimes it was from the customers; other times, it was from the manager who ran the bar or the guy who owned the restaurant. Not only did it disgust me; it was very upsetting. I was more fragile than I'd ever been, and some jerk was doing all he could to get into my frickin' underwear. Most of the time, I could ignore it, but on this day, the man's insult made me want to climb over the counter and strangle him. The crazy thing is, I couldn't have even worked up the energy for that. I was over it.

I was wiped when I got home. I was coming down with a cold, so on the way back to our place, I swung by a bodega and bought some Tylenol. *I should call in sick tomorrow.* I flopped down on the sofa, flipped on the TV, and surfed through the channels. All news about the storm cleanup.

My phone rang. I could tell by the area code that it was a Colombian number. I let it go to voice mail. A half hour later, I listened to the message.

"Diane, this is your papi," he said with a cracked voice. "Please call me. No one has heard from you in so long. You're not in trouble. I'm not going to yell at you. Please, *chibola.* I just want to know that you're okay." *Beep.*

I hadn't talked to either of my parents in forever. They rang all the time, of course, but like with the creditors, I ignored their recorded pleas. Since Mami had relocated to Madrid, she'd e-mailed constantly and begged me to visit. I didn't respond. In others' view, I'm sure, it seemed as if I didn't care about my mother and father, like I enjoyed seeing them hurt. Not at all. It broke my heart to know that I was breaking theirs. And yet the angst that surged through me whenever I heard their voices was more painful than knowing I was alienating them. When we did catch up, the conversations were stilted and awkward. Where do you begin when you haven't talked to someone in a year? How do you talk through all the moments you've missed? You really can't. And every time I put down the phone after talking with them, I felt as if my own mother and father were strangers to me, people I'd perhaps known in a former life but whom I did not recognize anymore.

I shocked myself when I began dialing my father's number. In the voice mail, he'd sounded more frail than ever. I wanted to check on him.

"Papi?" I said.

"*Hola, hija*—is that you?" There was sleep in his voice. I glanced up at the clock on the living room wall. *Ten p.m.*

"Yes, it's me," I said. "How are you?"

"I'm okay," he whispered. "It's great to hear from you. What's been happening?"

"Nothing much," I said, which was the standard answer I gave whenever anyone probed into how I was doing. I couldn't bring myself to tell him about the train wreck my life had become, which is why I directed the spotlight back onto him.

"How have you been?" I asked. "How's the family?"

He sighed. "Things are the same," he told me. One of his brothers had been robbed while riding his bike to the grocery store; the week before, he'd heard from my mother's sister that Eric had been laid off from his job; and my father, who still hadn't been able to find work in all this time, was low on money. "But I don't want you to worry about me," he told me. "I'll be okay." When Papi said, "Don't worry," it often meant he was down to his last twenty dollars. I had zero money, but I felt so badly for him that I offered to wire him some cash. He wouldn't hear of it. "Use it for school," he told me. "That's your focus right now."

We'd been on the line for less than five minutes, but I was eager to hang up. "I love you, Papi," I told him, trying to end the call.

"I love you, too," he said. "I miss you so much. When can you come here?"

"I don't know," I said. "We'll see. But I'll call you later."

"You promise?" he said.

"I promise," I said, although we both knew the truth.

My papi might as well have been on Neptune; that's how far away he seemed. I knew he and Mami both adored me as much as any parent can cherish a child, and yet I felt like I didn't belong to them anymore. Like I didn't have a home. A center. A base. A foundation. A place where I was from and could go back to when things got rocky. If I had an argument with Brian, for instance, I longed to be able to go to my mother's house and talk it through with her.

At fourteen, I'd somehow been able to stuff down much of what I was feeling. But as I'd gotten into my twenties, that decade when you're figuring out everything, the gaping hole at my life's center had become impossible to disregard. At the mention of my parents' names, I'd get all jammed up. I'd revert to the child I once was, to a girlhood that had been over far sooner than it should've been. I'd at least been able to lean on Amelia and Eva in high school and early college, but that safety net had vanished. I'd wanted so badly to prove that I could take care of myself. That I didn't need anyone. That I was a full grown-up. I clearly needed others, but by the time I admitted that to myself, I'd alienated everyone close to me. That realization added to my sorrow.

School had become a joke. I was pissed at everything and everyone. My grades were in the toilet. In three of my six classes, I was on track to earn a C minus; in one course, I was outright failing. A few of my professors encouraged me to switch from a letter grade to a pass-fail in order to keep from ruining my GPA. I'd been considering graduate school—I had my eye on law—but with such a poor academic performance, I was ruining my chances of being admitted. At times, I tried to keep up with my assignments, but because I hadn't been able to afford my books, I had to borrow them from friends for an hour or two at a time. I needed tutoring but I didn't have the mental energy or the resources to seek it out. And when I did show up for class, I was completely fatigued. I'd either worked late the night before or I had a hangover—and often both.

I was up to my eyeballs in debt. By the start of my senior year, I owed almost eighty thousand dollars. That may not seem like a tremendous amount to some—many complete school with three times as much debt—but for me, it seemed impossible to ever repay. Once I'd taken all the federal financial aid I could get, I turned to credit cards. Within months, I'd maxed out a Visa card and a MasterCard, which is when the creditors' calls became relentless. I shouldn't have applied for the cards in the first place, but I had no other choice at the time. I also had the financial smarts of a three-year-old. When Mami and Papi were deported, I hadn't yet even been taught to drive, much less sidestep ridiculous interest rates. Brian tried to weigh in, but I shut him down.

During earlier difficult periods, I'd looked to the arts; performance had always been my salvation, an experience that buoyed me in the most treacherous waters. That anchor was gone. All through college, I'd had this burning desire to express myself artistically, but there weren't many outlets for that. I yearned to find my way back onto the stage, even in the most amateur production. But because of everything else that was happening—and because I'd sunk so low emotionally—I couldn't seem to find a way to do that. Melancholy can feed creativity; yet it's also capable of killing it.

I said nothing about my condition to anyone. That's the thing about depression: It's not a topic for breezy, polite dinner conversation. It's easier to tell someone, "I have a headache," or even "I have cancer," than it is to say, "The bottom has fallen out of my life." You turn into this helpless mute, wandering aimlessly through a wilderness in search of water, with no ability to scream out that you're dying of thirst. Depression is not like sadness; it's not how you feel after cutting things off with a lover or losing a job. Those things hurt, of course, but even amid the agony, you know there'll come a moment when the heaviness lifts. Despair is different. It's the absence of hope. It's a long, flat road with no horizon in the distance. It's the path my brother once walked.

* * *

My eyes shot open. In the shadows, I reached for my phone, turned it on, and held it right up to my face so the light wouldn't wake up Brian, who'd come home by then. *2:52 a.m.*

For the longest time, I tried to make myself nod off. I couldn't. I kept thinking about all that had happened in the previous eight years. About the day I'd come home to find Mami and Papi missing. About how much effort it took for me to lie there and keep breathing. *This shit is way too hard.*

I slid from beneath the covers and wedged my feet into my white slippers next to the bed. Without turning on the light, I staggered my way to the living room and creaked open a closet door. I pulled out my long, black wool coat and put it on. I then tiptoed to the front door, turned the handle, and stepped out into the hall.

Our building had eight floors; Brian and I lived on the first. I walked over to the staircase that led to the rooftop and slowly climbed. When I emerged onto the terrace, the icy air stung my face; my sockless feet trembled. I zipped my coat all the way to the top and clutched my arms around my chest. Light flakes, a nearly imperceptible twinkling stardust, layered fresh snow over the gray cement. I looked out over the neighborhood. Eerily silent and beautiful.

I shuffled toward the building's edge and stopped when I came within a foot. No wall or barrier enclosed the landing. I lowered myself onto the ground and inched forward until my feet dangled over the side. I poked my head over the ledge and stared down. A parking lot, one with only a few cars in it, was below. I visualized my body, ashen and paralyzed, lying across the gravel. *Am I going to do this?*

I'd come close before to ending it all. Once when Brian and I were traveling out of town together, we had a heated argument. I was so distraught that I dragged a chair up to the balcony wall and climbed atop it so I could hurl myself over. "Nooo!" Brian shouted as he darted from the room to yank me back. "Diane, stop it! You can't do this!" After he'd calmed me down, he tried to reason with me. "Can you imagine how it would hurt me and your family if you took your life?" he asked. "You're fucking crazy if you give up." He had temporarily restored my senses—because when you spiral into desolation, you're no longer rational. In fact, you already feel dead; the suicide act is a mere formality.

This night wasn't like the one on the balcony. I faced a simple choice about whether to jump, and no person was there to pull me back from the brink. *Am I really ready to do this?* The spool of thoughts that had been running through my head for weeks started up. *I'm useless. I'll never amount to anything. I'm not smart enough to get through college. How can I help Mami and Papi when I can't even help myself? The world would be better off without me in it.*

I'd been telling myself that things would turn around, that tomorrow would be brighter. But it wasn't. Maybe if I'd been older, maybe if I'd had a template for overcoming crisis, I might've realized that things would eventually improve. That a better existence was possible on the other side of the anguish. But I didn't yet have the perspective that only years of wading through horrendous circumstances can bring. At twenty-two, all I could see was darkness. I peered down at the lot. As I did, my left slipper fell from my foot. I tried to catch it by squeezing it between my toes, but it got away from me.

As I sat contemplating the end, I wasn't scared. A peace I'd never sensed settled over me along with the snowflakes. My lids grew heavy with exhaustion. With my legs still swaying over the ledge, I lowered my upper body onto the cement and dozed off. I don't know how long I was out, but a strong wind gust awakened me.

Where am I? I pushed up onto my elbows and gazed around, confused about why I was on the rooftop. Then all at once I remembered, and my precarious position spooked me. *My God, what am I doing?* My stomach sank. I scooted backward and tried to get up, but as I rose, I felt disoriented and groggy. I lost my balance and almost fell over. I then slid off the ledge.

My heart hammered away in my chest. I clasped the pavement with my palms and struggled to maneuver my whole body back onto the ledge; it was windy and I was weak. But with every cell in my body, with every ounce of strength I could conjure up, I hoisted myself to safety.

I stumbled to the rooftop's center and dropped down cross-legged. I was breathing heavily. *Holy shit! Did that just happen?* Hours before, I'd been desperate to take my life, but only if I could do so on my terms. In that split second when the decision slipped out of my control, my impulse for survival jolted me from despair. A vision of my mami and papi, doubled over in grief after hearing I was dead, flooded my head. They'd endured so much heartache. They'd put it all on the line to come to this country so I'd have a chance to make something of myself. With another centimeter, with the slight turn of my wrist to the left or right, all they'd given up would've been for naught.

The same deep love that can wound us beyond repair also has the power to preserve us. When we've lost the determination to continue breathing, when we have no will whatsoever to soldier forward, our care for others is the one thing that can keep us marching onward. We stay alive for one another, often with more resolve and fight than we could ever muster on our own behalf. I don't know what I thought I owed myself, but I did know I owed at least two people—my parents—more than this. They'd paid too great a price for me to discard my life so senselessly. It wasn't time for me to go. Not like this.

Makin' dat money.

CHAPTER 13

Turnabout

*A person often meets his destiny on the
road he took to avoid it.*

—Jean de La Fontaine, poet

By some estimates, you and I will cross paths with as many as eighty thousand people during our lifetimes. Many of the folks we'll encounter will be passing acquaintances. Others will be family, friends, and coworkers who remain in our lives for decades. If even one of those people has a lasting impact on us, we're fortunate. Lorraine was my one.

I met my therapist shortly before the suicide attempt. I was still hurting myself, which is what led me to her doorstep. I did most of my cutting in private, but as I spiraled deeper into depression, that shifted. After a horrible fight with Brian, for instance, I'd pull out a blade right there in front of him and drag it across my forearm. "No, stop!" he'd scream, leaping to grab the razor from me. He was terrified.

Though he had his own issues, Brian was a good person. The guy did his best to pull me from my crisis. But it's hard to help someone who won't help him- or herself. Because of the state I was in, I wanted Brian to be more than a boyfriend to me; I wanted him to be my therapist, my savior, my knight who galloped in on a white horse to rescue me, the way it happens in a Disney fairy tale. That ridiculous expectation put even more weight on our fragile relationship. "You need to see someone," he'd tell me. "This shit is getting really scary." I agreed, but I sure as hell wasn't going back to that Jackie O wannabe. So one evening when I was particularly desperate, I Googled "low-cost clinics in Boston." Near the top of the results was the name of a center in my area. I called and made an appointment.

The next day, I showed up at the clinic and took a spot in the waiting room. I sat down next to this young Asian dude who was glued to his BlackBerry; across from us sat a blond girl flipping through the pages of an old *Cosmo*. They both looked normal and cool. I prayed the same was true of this experience.

Seconds later, a Latina woman stepped out of a swinging door. She was around five feet three, probably in her midforties, and rocking cute skinny jeans and a fitted blazer. Ringlets of short black hair framed her round face perfectly. She had on a pair of stylish glasses. *Nice*, I thought. *This might work.*

"I'm Lorraine," she said. Her eyes were bright, her expression warm. She seemed cordial, but not that perky, Pollyanna kind of friendly that makes you want to puke. "You must be Diane," she said. I nodded, stood, and followed her back through the swinging door and down a long hall. We settled into a corner office.

"So what brings you in today?"

I stared at her. The usual crap, the type I'd given the first counselor, swirled around in my head. Before I could dish it out again, I caught myself. No point in yelling for a life preserver if you're not going to take it. I cleared my throat and sat up.

"Well," I said, "things have been tough lately." I glanced down at the rows of fresh cut marks on my brown skin. She looked too.

"What's been happening, hon?" she asked.

"I've been hurting myself," I told her. Before I could continue, tears tumbled from my lids and down onto my shirt. It was the first time I'd heard myself say those words out loud, and as I did, the realization of how close I'd come to dying swept over me.

Lorraine didn't appear to be taken aback or surprised by what I told her. In fact, she scooted closer to me.

"Why do you think you cut yourself, Diane?" she asked.

"I don't know," I sniffled. "I guess it feels better than all the other stuff I feel."

"What other stuff is that?"

"Just everything," I said—and right there, in a torrent of emotion, the whole ugly mess of the previous six years came spilling out: How frightened I'd been in the months following my parents' deportation. The stress I was under to take care of myself. The financial disaster I was in. My crazy relationship with Brian. The class-ditching, the drinking, the partying. The big responsibility I felt as Mami and Papi's only hope for returning to America. The guilt I felt for locking out my parents when they repeatedly tried to connect with me. As I told my story, Lorraine never took her eyes off me. She let me completely finish before she spoke.

"You know, Diane," she whispered, "what you're feeling makes so much sense." She sat back in her chair. "When your mother and father were taken from you," she went on, "you were forced to become your own parent. That's an enormous load that no fourteen-year-old child should have to carry. It's time for you to put down that burden." She handed me a tissue.

At the end of our meeting, she asked me, "Would you like to come back in and see me?"

"Sure," I said, pulling a stray tissue from my purse to wipe down my face. "That would be cool."

"You're going to be okay, Diane," she reassured me as she walked me back out to the lobby.

I'd love to tell you that our session was enough to immediately straighten things out for me. But I still had thoughts. Lorraine couldn't wave some magic wand and, poof, make everything work for me. That's not how it goes for any of us. It's taken years for me to see that, while Lorraine's tenderness didn't keep me off that ledge, it had much to do with why I didn't ultimately jump. She clearly cared what happened to me— and that gave me one reason to carry on.

* * *

On the evening I came so close to ending my life, I crept back down the stairs, tiptoed into our dark condo, slid under the sheets next to Brian, and cried myself to sleep. I never told him what happened. I didn't initially reveal it to anyone. The episode hadn't been a plea for help, a way for me to get the world's attention by screaming, "Look here—please save me!" Rather, it was a quiet moment between God and me when I had to decide whether I would go on. Part of me wanted the pain to be over; that's how much anguish I was in. But a bigger part of me knew that if I remained strong for a while longer, my story could have a different ending.

Christmas Day was a blur. I spent it in my PJs, upset as Brian tried to do things to help, like making me a cup of tea. A few days later, at the start of 2008, I dragged myself back into Lorraine's office and admitted to her that I was still having thoughts of hurting myself; I also told her I'd even been looking at websites that supported such behavior. The whole thing was fucking disgusting, and I was desperate. She listened and offered consolation.

"I'd like for you to go on an antianxiety medication," she told me. "We'd still have to work through everything, but the prescription would get you stable." I refused. Given the problems I'd had with the ADD prescription—not to mention my alcohol abuse—I didn't want to take anything I could get hooked on. I needed to detox. "That's fine," Lorraine reassured me. "So we'll need to focus heavily on behavior changes— because I do believe that you can change, Diane." *Yeah, whatever*, I thought. Even as I doubted that, I hoped that she was right.

After struggling through my last semester and failing some courses, I'd had to make them up during the summer. I was disappointed that I didn't get to walk across the stage with Adrienne and my other classmates. But I did have one thing to celebrate—I'd lived to see my twenty-second birthday.

* * *

They say old habits die hard, but they're damn near impossible to break when you keep yourself intoxicated. Once school was over, I got a new nightclub gig. I'd gone there to interview for a bartending position but the manager took one look at me and said, "Sweetie, you're my newest cocktail waitress." I soon discovered that "cocktail waitress" was code for a skimpily dressed hussy who happens to serve cranberry-and-vodkas. It was the last job in the world I should've had—but it was the one way I figured I could earn fast cash every weekend. I was right on both counts.

Six of us worked the nine p.m. to two a.m. shift on Thursdays through Sundays. There were a couple of white college girls from New Jersey, both in the area to study fashion and PR. My girl Amir was in nursing school at the time. Others just partied for a living. I forget what the others did. My favorite was Luciana. She was a sweet girl from Brazil. She was fair-skinned and athletic and had a tiny waist and an amazing J. Lo booty. Her hair swung down past her waist. The first time I saw her, I was like, "Holy fuck—how on earth do you have hair that long?" Luciana's family had come to the States when she was small, but somehow she still sounded a bit like she'd grown up in the Boston section of Belo Horizonte. Her accent was this weird mix between a Brazilian one and a wicked Bostonian one. She'd be like, "Diane, come out to the *cah*"—as in *"pahk the cah in Hahvuhd Yahd."* Her dream was to become a registered nurse, and she was using the money from this job to pay for school. She was so much fun and a good friend. In fact, she was one of the people who really encouraged me to pursue acting. We were all these young women—at twenty-two, I was the oldest in the group—trying to figure out what the hell to do with our lives.

"You here all weekend?" Luciana asked me one Friday. We were getting dressed in the bar's green room. On one side of the space was a floor-length mirror, the sort you'd see in a dancer's studio. On the other side was a short row of lockers in which we stored our belongings. The space was so tiny that we were basically tripping over each other as we struggled to put on our outfits. Every night, I squeezed into a tight corset that pushed my boobs up to my chin. To top off the look, I wore high heels, fishnet stockings, and boy shorts that were basically underwear. Don't judge.

"Yup, I'm here till Sunday," I told her as I painted on a thick coat of mascara.

"Is Heath-uh coming in tonight?" she asked. I cracked up at the way she pronounced Heather's name.

"I think so," I said. "We're all on tonight."

The doors opened at ten, but the party really began popping at eleven. The house music thumped, the customers clustered around the tables, and we girls sashayed around the smoke-filled room to take orders. Each time I shook up a concoction for a guest, I had one myself. Vodka Red Bulls were my drink of choice—that's how I maintained my energy. It's also how I kept myself from noticing how sketchy this whole scene was.

"Come here and sit in my lap, beautiful," some bald, middle-aged white dude with a huge stomach would slur.

"Well hello, handsome." I'd play along flirtatiously. "Let me know if I can get you a second drink, K?" A large portion of the job was about being super nice to (gross) men who were slobbering all over my tits. Okay—they weren't all gross, and some were young and handsome but had that Christian Bale in *American Psycho* look. They would say "Hello," but all I would hear is "Do you wanna come to my place so I can cut you up into little pieces?" Then there were the few who really were cool, and to be honest, I thank them all—had it not been for their ridiculous spending, I wouldn't have had a way to support myself. You could call it my first acting gig—and let me tell you, I was so convincing that I should've earned an Oscar. Certain dudes would come back night after night and request me or one of the other waitresses. They felt we had a connection with them. Either that, or they were lonely. Or horny. Or just wanted to party. Or all three.

In between pouring cocktails, we'd get up on the tables or stage and dance to entertain the crowd. If you'd asked me then whether I was having fun, the answer would've been yes. Definitely. One hundred and fifty percent. But that's because I was so super-drunk that I had no true awareness of what I felt. Even as we'd get dressed in the back, I'd already have my clear plastic "water bottle" filled with vodka. All of us threw back so many shots that we could hardly stand up straight by closing time. In my heart, I knew this was a terrible environment for me. I made myself forget that by numbing out.

Behind the scenes, there was drama, and plenty of it. For starters, we all competed with one another for Friday and Saturday nights, the shift when you could make the most in tips; things got nasty whenever a new girl came in and tried to get a spot. Aside from that, arguments erupted over pay. Every evening, one server would stay in the back and collect all the gratuities, and then we'd split the pool at night's end. "I saw Heath-uh stuff a wad of cash in her bra," Luciana once whispered to me. "She's gyppin' us." After scoping out the situation for a few days, we realized the others were also pocketing a shit ton of our money. On a night when we should've left there with eight hundred bucks, for instance, we'd ended up with half that. When Luciana confronted a couple of the girls, a fight broke out in the locker room. Like I said—drama.

Outside of my moonlighting, I had a life, and an extremely busy one at that. In the fall of 2008, I enrolled in a one-year paralegal program at Bunker Hill Community College in Charlestown. I'd moved on from the idea of a career in diplomacy and became more interested in law. If I became an attorney, I figured, I could one day represent my parents' case; I could also become an advocate for immigrant families. But law school is such a major expense (hello, more loans) that I wanted to first check out the industry and see if I liked it. My plan was to get certified as a paralegal, work with lawyers, and then decide whether I still wanted to apply to law school. I also took a part-time receptionist position at a law firm specializing in personal injury cases. Between that, my waitressing, and school, I was barely catching any zs.

With so much going on, there wasn't a bunch of time left over for me to see Lorraine. Even so, I fit in sessions every other week. In the first few months, I did most of the talking as she nodded and took notes. But over time, as she got a clearer sense of my issues, she began challenging much of what I told her. Like this:

"I used to think I wanted to be a performer," I said. "I'm now considering law."

"What made you change your mind?" she asked.

"A career in the performing arts isn't practical for me," I told her.

"Why?"

"Because it's too late," I explained. "If I wanted to be in musical theater, I should've gone to a conservatory."

She removed her glasses and placed them in her lap, then looked right at me. "Girl," she said, "Do you think you're just afraid that if you went after that dream now, you'd fail at it? It may be why you set up these roadblocks for yourself."

I squirmed in my chair. "What roadblocks?" I said. "What do you mean?"

"I mean that you get in your own way, whether or not you're aware of it," she explained. "Look at the choices you've made over the last few years. Notice how often you've gotten close to completing a goal that's important to you, and then you've fallen off track. That's probably not a coincidence."

I sighed and tried to wrap my brain around what she was saying. "I guess so," I said. "But I'm not even sure I still wanna be an entertainer."

"Really?" she said, raising her brows. "You light up every time you mention it."

I shrugged. "I don't know," I said. "I may not be good enough."

I may have doubted my own talent, but the girls at work thought I had a knack for performing. Every night as we got dressed, I'd break out my best material for them. I had this one spoof where I'd imitate Britney Spears dancing in the video *Stronger*. I would make my voice sound all high like hers, wildly swing my hair from left to right, and do these insane moves all over a chair the way she does, only I would trip over the chair and make it as unsexy as I could. My friends laughed hysterically. One day, a man walked by and suggested I never do that again because it

indeed wasn't sexy. "Ah shove it, you pig!" I snapped. "What do you know?"

"Diane, why aren't you trying to be an act-ah?" Luciana would ask. "What's with this law thing? You could totally be on TV." That sounded good, and I looked forward to going to work so I could show off whatever new routine I'd come up with. But entertaining my friends was one thing. Making a living and putting myself out there in front of the world was another matter altogether.

My drinking hadn't stopped, but I had been practicing my daily affirmations, courtesy of Lorraine. "Forgive yourself, Diane—today is a new day," I'd say to myself.

"It's okay if you drink, as long as you can get up the next morning and accept yourself." Ha! That's right: I made up the last sentence of that affirmation so it could fit my lifestyle. That worked for the most part, except when I got terribly ☹. When you fling open the closed doors of your heart, it's incredibly painful. You want to escape, and I often did. But at least I wasn't doing that as much by tearing into my skin. "When you have the urge to cut," Lorraine had told me, "squeeze some ice in your hand instead." Believe it or not, that worked for me. That, and a little yoga Namaste, was life-changing. "Be kind to yourself, D," I'd often have to remind myself. I still do.

A session at a time, Lorraine's ideas began to stick. She was right: Most of my moves had been based on the fact that I was scared out of my mind. What if I did everything in my power to become a success, only to fail miserably? What if I pursued a career in entertainment and got booed off the stage? What if people didn't like me? In many ways, I'd been tripping myself up so that I'd never have to answer those questions. It's interesting what you start noticing about yourself when you pay close attention. "You're allowing fear to block your greatness," Lorraine often reminded me. "You've gotta change your mind-set." She had a point. Fear is what had kept me from applying to a conservatory. And fear was dogging the dream I claimed to no longer want—#selfsabotage.

Meanwhile, week after week, I sat there at that desk job, answering phones and filing documents. I absolutely hated it. I have never been more bored in my life. The minutes literally dragged by. And the whole time, this

whisper I'd been hearing, this nagging sense that I was meant to be doing something else, grew louder. I wasn't supposed to be sorting through legal documents. I belonged not in a courtroom but on a stage or on a set. Yet law was the safe option, or so I thought. That's why I clung to it so hard. By then, though, I'd figured out this wasn't the road for me; rather, it was a detour from the route I was too frightened to take.

During our months together, Lorraine gave me many gifts—and one of the greatest came during a session in the summer of 2009. I was telling Lorraine (again) about all the ways I'd dropped the ball. All the stupid decisions I'd made. All the times I'd let myself and others down. Usually, she let me vent fully before she spoke. On this day, she interrupted me.

"You want to know something, Diane?" she said.

"What?" I answered, surprised that she'd cut in.

"You are not your mistakes."

Lorraine stared at me for the longest time as that sentence hung in the air between us. I lowered my head, fiddled with my bangle bracelets, and looked up at her again.

"Your failures don't define you," she continued. "Your worth isn't about what you do or don't do. You have value simply because you're here."

I dropped my eyes to the floor and let that sink in. I'd spent my entire childhood trying to be the good Catholic girl. Trying to earn the approval of others. Trying not to make the mistakes my brother made. Trying to show everyone that I wasn't going to be *that* child—the daughter of immigrants who fell in the ditch. And after all that struggle, I was completely worn out. I didn't have it in me anymore to keep pressing forward. The fact that I'd at last thrown up my hands made me, in my own eyes, a total fuckup. But in Lorraine's view, it made me a human being—one who deserved to be here, whether or not I did another right thing that day. Pick yourself up and try again—what a revelation.

Our lives try to get our attention in countless ways. Through our gut instincts. Through our loved ones. Through our circumstances. And in my case, through an angel God once sent to me at exactly the right juncture. Lorraine showed up in my life when I urgently needed a friend to help me see the truth. She did that—and it was all that she could do. Because I'd reached that place we all get to where no amount of compassion or love or

hand-holding from someone else can change things. It was on me. As I'd done on that rooftop, I had to close my eyes and make a choice that I wanted better for myself. In November 2009, one year after I'd nearly slipped from this world to the next, I made a couple of moves. First, I let go of the delusion of a career in law. I then enrolled in an acting course at Boston Casting. And finally, I got head shots taken.

Peter Berkrot's beginner acting class at Boston Casting.

CHAPTER 14

Stage Right

*When I sing, trouble can sit right on
my shoulder and I don't even notice.*

—Sarah Vaughan, jazz singer

Much has been written about how to find your passion. Your true calling. Your career path. As 2010 got under way, I discovered something: You don't choose your life's work; it chooses you. It's this new love that sweeps you up in its momentum. From daybreak to dusk, you can think of nothing else. You find yourself talking faster, louder, more excitedly upon its mention. When I finally gave in to the major pull the performing arts has always had on me, I felt all of the above.

I began my mornings by scanning the online industry gossip columns. Who was acting in what? What star had landed a big role in a film or TV series? What trends were popping up in theater? I wanted to see what the industry was looking for. Oh surprise, surprise—not me. That was okay, because I was determined to figure out a way for them to get to know me. I searched for any acting classes I could take, and of course, I eagerly clicked on the classifieds and pored over the audition listings to see if I could walk in somewhere and be discovered on the spot. Hey, a girl can dream—but the reality was much different. I had no idea how to break into this business. None. I couldn't try out for anything, because in order to do that, you mainly needed representation by a manager or agent.

At first I kept my mouth shut about my new direction. Brian was aware of it; in fact, he'd been the one to encourage me to sign up for acting classes. He knew it was the one thing that might end my craziness. But I didn't want to discuss my plan with anyone other than him, for a few reasons. First, I thought talking about it might jinx it—I'm a bit superstitious that way. Second, I enjoyed having my own little secret, this thing I could savor in private. And above all, I had zero interest in hearing the (unhelpful) opinions of others. You've gotta be careful who you share your big dreams with. People often piss on them. Some will even talk you out of your aspirations, mostly because they've given up on their own. It's not like I had so many close friends left to shoot the breeze with, but still—I zipped my lips. Plus, I wasn't the type to walk around saying, "I'm an actor and I want to do something special!"

I enrolled in two classes: beginning acting and intro to improv. My teacher for both was Peter Berkrot, who was in *Caddyshack*, a cult classic staring Bill Murray. About twelve of us were in each course, and the students were from all different backgrounds. There was this one lawyer who wanted to improve at litigating by using acting techniques in the courtroom. Another guy just enjoyed being around people and loved the exercises. And there were plenty who, like me, were sticking their toes into the thespian waters for the first time. Yup, a real A-list class. One session was on Mondays, the other on Wednesdays. As the end of each weekend rolled around, I could hardly contain my excitement about taking part in whatever new material we'd cover in the upcoming class. I went from sleeping all day, drinking all night, and not giving a shit about my life, to waking up early in anticipation of all that I could learn. Our passions don't just compel us; they can also heal us.

I absolutely loved Peter's courses, and they loved me back. We did a lot of scene work. At the start of improv, for instance, Peter would throw out a scenario. If you've read Amy Poehler's *Yes Please* or Tina Fey's *Bossypants*, I'm sure you already know what real improv is. For those who don't know, here's how it went in our class: After Peter had set up the storyline, each of us then had to step into a character and situation and run with it. It was liberating to be so spontaneous and to say yes! Yes to myself. Yes to life. It was so much fun! It all just poured out of me. I started to feel like myself again. Happy. For most of my life, I'd been a very happy person, and to be in a space where I wasn't, and for such a long period of time, was driving me nuts. I needed this—an artistic outlet. And Peter was great. He made me feel like I belonged there. In fact, Peter's feedback is what kept me going. Once class was over, I'd often stick around to talk with him, just so I could pick up any extra tips he might have. "You know, you're good, Diane," he once told me. "You'll have to keep working hard at this, but you do have something." I was already singing my rendition of "Some People"—the Bernadette Peters version, of course—from the musical *Gypsy*.

Peter also urged me to be less shy. I wasn't always aware of it, but I am a shy person—and believe it or not, that was a revelation to me; it still continues to shock me. To this day, for instance, I am a socially awkward person who feels weird about hugging. I still have a problem determining if a situation requires a hug or a handshake. I usually end up doing a weird mix of both, which makes people really uncomfortable. Who woulda known? This indecisiveness and insecurity would show up in my work. "Forget about looking silly," Peter often told me. "You've gotta get over your inhibitions so you can fully embody the character." I enjoyed class so much, and as I started to dream again, I began to actually call myself an actor. Not out loud, of course—too soon—but in my head. *Chill, D.*

Although I'd mentally moved on from the whole law thing, I held on to my job at the firm. The longer I stayed, the surer I became that I'd made the right choice to set aside law school. Most of the attorneys in my office were happy doing what they loved, but that wasn't my gig. I can't stay still for too long, or I will turn into stone, melt, or explode. Not sure if this is 100 percent true, but I didn't want to chance it.

My job there might not have been exactly inspiring to me personally (I was answering phones and taking messages all day), but what I earned did pay for my acting courses. And although I missed all the cash from my cocktail-waitressing days, I was thrilled I'd moved on from that. I needed a little break. That job had really drained me. I knew of many girls who worked in that kind of environment for years. *That's not going to be me*, I'd think. It's not a bad thing; some waitresses make a very nice living. But I couldn't handle the constant drinking, the partying, the staying up all night, the entire seedy world. It had carried me down the wrong road.

But then, as usual, real life hit and I realized, *Oh shit—I need money.* I had to earn a second check so I could get the creditors off my ass and pay for acting classes. So I took another nightclub bartending job. At least I wasn't out on the floor—I ended up working behind the bar. And I did love that the job came with a flexible schedule. Because work was at night, I was free during the day to potentially audition. I knew I had to stay available. I was so determined to get even just a foot in the door that I wasn't about to miss an opportunity. If a casting agent asked, "When can you come in?" I'd go, "Today at two is perfect." At this point, most of my auditions were straight off Craigslist (as well as whatever Boston Casting would send me), and you can imagine what kinds of roles were advertised. Some involved no acting at all, but even those were a chance to get on camera. And you name it, I went after it.

I once answered an ad for a foot model. Not that I thought my feet were cute, but like I said, I went for everything. When I showed up on set, the director asked if I felt comfortable being topless. Whoa, whoa—I'm here for a foot audition. I had no interest in going down the Playboy Bunny road. Oh, and I also tried out for countless (no-budget) short films and music videos. Most were produced by students who were completing their senior projects—and few involved pay. I was cool with that, because just getting something onto my résumé was its own kind of payment.

One of my first parts was in a music video called "Faces," with a Boston R & B singer Louie Bello. When I look at the video now, it cracks me up and makes me cringe. All the way through it, Louie and I are basically staring at each other with bedroom eyes! It was all about me trying to look pretty. I was appreciative of the opportunity, but I didn't feel comfortable being the "pretty face." I wanted to fight monsters and solve mysteries instead, but hey—it got me on camera. I had to put myself out there somehow. I was working at it constantly. There wasn't a second of the day when I wasn't thinking about the moves I could make to get closer and closer to my dream. Things seemed slow, but I was just taking in the journey. I was giving myself the space to really try something and either succeed or fail at it; at least I wouldn't die knowing that I didn't make an attempt. I had no illusions of grandeur. I just wanted to throw my hat in the ring.

With every part I took, even if I had only a couple of lines, I pushed myself to make the experience smoother than the last. I agreed to be in a twenty-minute short, a horror indie flick produced by my friend Billy Duefrese, who was excited just to be making movies. Honestly, the film was wacky, and we did all of our shooting in Billy's backyard. I played a girl who'd gotten locked in a basement by some drug dealers; for most of the filming, I waved my arms wildly and grunted and groaned with duct tape over my mouth. As ridiculous as it was, I was doing it—I was in a project and I was acting! I was also healing and learning even as I was experimenting. There was no time to be sad or discontent with life, and no room to judge myself in the process. I wanted something, and I was going for it.

In the beginning, all my parts were nonunion—which meant I wasn't even put in a room with other members of the Screen Actors Guild (SAG), the gold standard membership for actors. You have to work a number of union jobs in order to earn your membership. Starting around June 2010, I got strategic in my search for union jobs. Many actors build up their credits by working as extras in big films. I tried that approach. I eventually scored a job as an extra in the film *The Zookeeper*, the romantic comedy starring Kevin James from *The King of Queens*. A big movie with A-list actors on a real set. Whoa. I was doing this thing.

Or was I? Because long story short, it was pure torture. I was one of a slew of extras dressed to appear at this big party in the movie. My time on set started out cool: I got to see (but not personally meet) Kevin James, who was hilarious and phenomenal in his role. Things went downhill from there. All the other nameless faceless masses and I stood around in our heels and cocktail dresses, holding glasses of champagne that were really filled with apple juice. Every hour or so, the director would yell, "Action!" and the group of us would walk across the room and pretend we were enjoying the shindig. At certain moments, I was supposed to laugh and/or cough. It was tedious. I left the set early without even collecting my voucher. I was like, "I'm outta here. I'm not doing this." Are you kidding, boo? I'm an artiste. I did not, repeat *not*, want to be in the background. Don't get me wrong: It's a fabulous gig for some actors, and you can make decent money at it. But I had a much different vision for myself. I knew I had a long way to travel before I got to my goal, but this gig made me crystal clear on the final destination I had in mind: I wanted to be an actress who could continue refining my craft by working in the front, not the back. From then on, I decided I'd concentrate on getting whatever work I could get, as long as it required me to use all my skills. The SAG membership would come one way or the other.

As my fervor for my work increased, the depression fell away. I continued to see Lorraine, who nudged me toward more changes and set me up with some tools for staying on track. Perfect example: She suggested that I use affirmations as anchors. When the doubts in my head cranked up, when my insecurities popped to the surface, I'd reach for one of the phrases Lorraine had taught me to repeat: "I am an intelligent woman. I am a good person and a loving daughter. I matter, and what I have to offer also matters. I can forgive myself for whatever I did yesterday, because today is a new day. Think: You is smart. You is kind. You is important." Truth? It initially sounded like hokey psychobabble to me; it felt weird to say these things out loud to myself. But I got over that and, in time, the practice helped me. And to this day, I count myself lucky that I got out of that hole without medication. Praise Jesus! Hallelujah, mi Dios! Many need antidepressants, and there's no shame in that. None. You do what you've gotta do. But in my case, the sessions with Lorraine and my return to the arts pulled me back from the brink. I also cut back on the benders;

I had become quite a lush. And there's another piece of good fortune I'm grateful for—I didn't have to check myself into rehab in order to lower the bottle. I still partied from time to time, but at least I finally knew what I wanted to do with my life.

My classmates became my new circle of friends. In addition to my courses, I signed up for private lessons with Peter. From time to time, he'd take me and his other students to this church space he'd rented. He'd then pair us for scene work. That's how I met Dave and Kat; they were actors on similar journeys. "I'm telling you, Diane, you could really get out there and do this," Dave would often tell me. "The cream always rises to the top." I loved that saying by my sweet friend Dave. I'd be like, "Me? Really? What are you talking about?" I mean, I secretly hoped he was right, but either way, his sweetness boosted me. And Kat was always keeping an eye out for me around the industry. She's the one who'd gotten me the gig in *The Zookeeper*. By the summer of 2010, the three of us had become inseparable.

My confidence gradually improved, and Peter recommended that I have better head shots taken; Boston Casting was hosting a photo clinic, and I signed right up. The pictures were decent, good enough for me to begin submitting them around town. In Boston, there aren't dozens of agents and agencies like there are in New York. There's the main agency, Boston Casting, as well as Carolyn Pickman Casting, also known as CP Casting, and Maggie Inc., a modeling agency. I uploaded my head shot and CV on every site that I could. For weeks, I received not even a nibble. But in the fall of 2010, I got my first official audition—meaning one I hadn't scrounged up for myself on Craigslist. In other words, it was legit. It was a part in a Kmart commercial.

"Oh my God, I can't believe it!" I shrieked when I told Brian the news. You would've thought I'd just won the million bucks on *Who Wants to Be a Millionaire?*, and as far as I was concerned, this was the much bigger prize. "I'm so excited! This means they looked at my head shots and liked them!" You get pretty mindfucked in this industry. Sometimes, a bite of anything brings your hopes to an all-time high, only to have them drop the next day. Making it as an actor is easier said than done, but you have to keep perspective and stay levelheaded—optimistic, but not overly excited.

"Ahh, you'll figure it out!" is what I'd often tell myself. "Just do the work and you'll be fine."

On the morning of the tryout, my enthusiasm gave way to terror. What should I wear? What should I say? Will they like me? I had no clue how any of it was supposed to go, and it scared the hell out of me. I'd been given three lines, and I'd memorized them so thoroughly that I could've repeated them in my sleep. One was something cheesy like, "These cotton T-shirts are incredible!" I'd prepared as if I was making my debut appearance in the year's hottest biopic. Believe me, I took this all quite seriously.

I made my way into the studio. The waiting room overflowed with all sorts of folks, some brown-haired and lanky, others thick, short, and burly. I didn't know who was there for what, and yet I still did what many actors do: I sized up the competition. There were definitely some pretty girls, but I was one of only a couple of Latinas. Who knew? Maybe that'd be the look they went for.

One at a time, the actors were called in. The casting director, a goth woman with straight-edge bangs and a clipboard, at last said my name.

"Diane?" she called.

"Yes," I said, sitting up and straightening the simple T-shirt and jeans I'd so carefully chosen.

"Come right on in," she said.

I followed her into the room. There, a group of casting directors sat in a semicircle. No one cracked a smile.

The goth lady explained the concept for the commercial and handed me my prop, a pink tee to be featured in the ad. "Do you want to give us your first line?" she asked.

"Um, sure," I said. I cleared my throat and stood up tall. "These cotton T-shirts are incredible!" I said with as much zest as I could while holding up the T-shirt. I had the most stupid grin plastered on my face.

The group sat silent. "Okay, great," the goth woman finally said. "Let's hear your other two lines."

I delivered both flawlessly, and again, the directors stared blankly at me. "That'll be all," the main woman told me. "Thank you for coming in." She then followed me into the lobby and called in her next victim.

Three days later, my big break became my heartbreak. I didn't get the part. I tried not to let it sour my mood, but it did sting. The fact that I'd invested so much effort made it feel like even more of a letdown. "You never know what they were looking for," Peter told me. "It could've been something as random as they didn't think you were the right height, or they decided to use a man instead. You just have to keep going out on as many calls as you can." It took me a month to recover from the disappointment, but once I did, I followed Peter's advice and got back up.

Through Dave, I connected with Rebecca Rojer, who was then an undergraduate film student at Harvard. She was auditioning a bunch of people for the principal role in a short called *Ashley/Amber*.

"You should try out," Dave urged.

"I don't think I'm ready for that," I told him. I'd checked out some of Rebecca's other work online and let myself get intimidated. Her stuff was good.

"Diane, you're *totally* ready," Dave goaded. "Just do it."

Another reason for my apprehension: The script contained this scene in which the main character has sex with her boyfriend, and the dude dies. I was like, "I don't want to do an indie film making love with someone who croaks! Or making love on film at all, for that matter." But Dave was like, "Dude, you can sort that out later! Go in and see what happens."

On the day of the tryout, it snowed. The audition was on Harvard's campus. That fact alone was nerve-racking. Dave came along. "This is awful," I told him as we cut across an icy Harvard Yard. "It's a mess out here. I wish I'd never signed up for this. I don't even know what I'm doing here." As we walked, my mind flashed back to all those Sundays when Papi drove us through Wellesley; the look of the Cambridge campus, with all its ivy-covered buildings and gold steeples, reminded me of that community. It was a secret, elite world I never thought I'd get to be part of, and yet here I was—and it freaked me out. "Calm down," Dave told me. "Remember, the cream always rises to the top."

Rebecca called me in almost right away. "How are you, Diane?" she asked, extending her hand. She seemed as nice as they come. *Phew.* "I'm great," I said. Dave shot me a thumbs-up as we went off into a small studio. Literally ten minutes later, it was over. Just as I was preparing to rejoin Dave in the waiting area and delight him with another round of "poor me," Rebecca surprised me.

"I appreciate you coming in today," she said, "and it'd be great if you could come back."

What? Did I hear her correctly? Is this a callback even before I've left the building? "Um, all right," I said shyly.

"How about next Wednesday?" she asked.

"Yes, sure," I answered. OMG.

When I returned for the callback, I took one look around the waiting room and nearly crapped my pants. To my right sat an (insanely) gorgeous blond girl with plump lips and perfect teeth; on my left was a brunette who was almost as much of a knockout. *I'm so not getting this.* We all looked so different that I started wondering how we could all be up for the same role. *Maybe she's auditioning for multiple parts*, I thought. Fingers crossed, 'cause I'd have no shot in hell against Angelina Jolie.

When Rebecca brought me in a few minutes later, I went in there and did my thing—and I held nothing back. "Wait here," she told me afterward. She disappeared from the room and returned wearing a big smile. "I'd love to have you do the part," she said. The room stood still. "Really?" I squealed. "You would?"

"Yes, I would," she said. "I think you would be a perfect fit."

I was stunned. Literally. "I'm so glad Dave connected us," she continued as I stood there looking befuddled. "I'd already auditioned a hundred girls for the part and couldn't find the right person."

I left that room and called Dave on his cell. "She wants me!" I screamed. "Thank you so much for pushing me to do this!" It blew me away that I'd been picked out of so many girls. To say I was amazed is the understatement of the millennium. At last, after so many setbacks and failures in the previous few years, I was getting something right.

Working on the film is still on my top ten list of most fun experiences. First of all, this film had a budget. No, I didn't get paid, but all my meals were provided. And stop the presses: I was the main character! Not to mention that I was getting twenty-three minutes of meeee! I could also get a reel out of this. In the film, which is a dark comedy, Ashley and Amber are the same person, hence the slash. During filming, everyone in the cast had to pitch in (that's the way it goes with low budget). And the "set"? For the set, we shot at Rebecca's co-op, at a café, and sometimes even inside my apartment. We also did a lot of outside shots, in the snow. The whole thing was very crunchy-granola, um, I mean artsy.

I got such a rush whenever I was on camera. Most of the time, I didn't know what I was doing, but I took the fake-it-till-you-make-it approach. I was *soooo* serious, probably because I was fresh and nervous. I wanted everything to be perfect—by the book. I didn't do a lot of what actors call "playing," where you try different things and really make the material your own. When you're feeling free, when you have a handle on who you are, you're more able to go in there and try new things. I hadn't yet grown to that place. The fear of failure stopped me from letting down my hair, and when I look back at the film now, I can see that my performance reflected that. But Rebecca was happy. "You gave me what I wanted from you," she'd tell me, and I guess she was onto something. The film was later chosen to be screened at the Berlin International Film Festival, and I got to travel to Germany with the cast to see the big premiere. And yes: The flashback sex scene ended up in the film. #awkward.

My life was shifting for the good, yet I still wasn't calling my family all that regularly. When I did reach Papi, he seemed proud of me. "I've always known you were meant for this," he'd tell me. "Remember how you used to sing all the time at the dinner table?" I won't lie: It was still difficult for me to even be on the phone with Papi. But I was making progress, and the more we did talk, the better we both felt. Funny how confronting your fears will do that for you. Go figure. As for Mami, I really didn't connect with her at all during this time, or know how things were going in Spain.

Although I had a couple of credits to my name, I remained tight-lipped about my acting. For instance, I never invited the other girls at the bar to watch any of the films I was in. I did test the waters once by mentioning to a coworker that I was experimenting with acting. "So what are you going to do," she said, "be in porn?" That hurt. And it reaffirmed my choice to shut up about everything.

In 2011, my cover was blown. Early that year, an amazing opportunity arose, one that was pretty rare in Boston. I got an audition for the ABC series *Body of Proof.* For the audition, I had to simulate driving and falling asleep at the wheel; when the character awakens, she realizes she's run over someone and is later arrested. By this time, I wasn't a complete neurotic freak during auditions; I was becoming more comfortable. The same day I did the audition, the unimaginable happened: I got the part! Do you know how that felt for me? It was like I'd been told I was a series regular.

A couple of weeks later, we traveled to Rhode Island to shoot the scene, the same one I'd auditioned with. *I've arrived—my first union credit.* I wasn't just an actor; I was a *traveling* actor. I had a trailer and everything, complete with a hair and makeup team. I felt like I'd arrived. Weeks later, without my knowing it, the episode aired—and my scene was the show's opener. You know how on *Law & Order* they always have that first scene before the show really comes on? That's how it was on *Body of Proof,* so I was front and center. I started getting these e-mails from people in Colombia. I also got tons of messages on Facebook. "I just saw you on TV!" Dana wrote. I couldn't believe it. I recorded it on DVR and watched it a kazillion times. It felt wonderful. All I could think was, *That's me! That's really me!*

In retrospect, I'm still amazed at everything that happened during that short period. I did a 360. Many times in our sessions, Lorraine would ask me, "How does it feel to be in front of the camera?"

"I feel free," I told her, "like I can do anything."

Not that performing isn't the scariest thing ever, but the fear is part of the exhilaration. And when you're in it, feeling that rush, it's just bliss. I'd had that rush in high school, when I'd performed at Springfest, and then again during my senior recital. The difference between me back then and me at this point is that I'd grown up. I had material to draw from. The journey I'd taken, even the most heart-wrenching parts, began to shape me as an artist and as a person. And as I let go of some of the judgments I had about my past, I also became less critical of my own work. When you put something out there it's not about deciding whether it's good or bad. It's about creating it, and then letting it go with the hope that others take some light or inspiration from it.

After the big high of the TV appearance, I began considering my next move. Brian's and my relationship was stable, but by this point we both

Me and the shiny Big Apple.

knew it had run its course. We'd become more like roommates than romantic partners, and whether or not I stayed in Boston, it was time for us to part. Life was clearly moving me toward a career on the stage, and, in order to explore that, I needed to be willing to step out. The place to do that was in the mecca of the acting world—New York City. As they say, if you can make it in the Big Apple, you can make it anywhere. I wanted to prove to myself and the world that I had what it took to do this thing.

"There are years that ask questions and years that answer," Zora Neale Hurston once wrote. The year 2009 was the one that asked me why I was here. The years 2010 and 2011 gave their answer.

CHAPTER 15

New York City

It is not true that people stop pursuing dreams because they grow old. They grow old because they stop pursuing dreams.

—Gabriel "Gabito" García Márquez, Colombian novelist and recipient of the 1982 Nobel Prize in Literature

"**H**ow's everyone feeling?" Marishka, a coach at the Susan Batson Studio near Manhattan's Times Square, scanned the row of faces. Eight others and I had gathered for our biweekly therapy session, um, acting course—one called Ex Er Actor. The course included several components, includ ing awareness and emotional flexibility. Marishka, this whip-smart, fiery, and soulful woman, nodded toward the first person in our semicircle. That was Ethan, a Brooklyn guy with wild, wiry black curls springing from his head.

"Ethan, what are you aware of today?"

" I'm aware that I missed my train on my way here and almost didn't make it," he said, sighing. "So to be honest, I'm aware that I'm feeling fucking out of breath right now." A few of us snickered. Marishka smiled approvingly and shifted her gaze to the next person in line—me.

"Diane, what are you aware of?" she asked.

I glanced around at my classmates before I rested my gaze on Marishka. "Um, I guess I'm aware that I'm jittery today," I said, twirling the bottom lock of my hair. "My mom left me this insanely long voice mail this morning, and, well—to be honest, I feel like a terrible daughter." Some people laughed but I wasn't being funny. Maybe I'd been very Kramer in my delivery.

Marishka made her way around to the others. One girl had just lost her beloved cat and was overcome with grief. An older dude, a retired dentist, was aware of his exhilaration after hearing he'd gotten a part in a commercial; he was also aware that he had to be kinder to himself. And a redheaded woman, a mother from Queens, said she was aware that she was feeling neutral, and didn't really feel like sharing. After everyone had gotten a turn, we moved on to part two of our class—the musical interlude, aka emotional flexibility. Marishka walked over to the stereo and put on Stevie Wonder's "Superstition." It was so loud, it practically shook the walls.

"Up on your feet, guys," she shouted over the music. We all stood, formed a large full circle around the classroom space, and stretched a little in preparation for what we knew was coming. "Don't judge yourself, this is a safe space," she yelled out. "Ethan, you go first."

Without any sign of hesitation, Ethan strutted into the middle and began flinging his arms and legs all over the place while snapping his fingers to the beat of his heart, or whatever else he might've been hearing in his head. There was no right or wrong way. The exercise was all about allowing us to connect emotionally and intellectually to our bodies so that we wouldn't be freaking robots. It was a way of getting loose for the work ahead.

"Okay, Diane," Marishka called out a moment later. "Now you."

Reluctantly, I slid out into the middle of everyone and moved lamely along to the music. At first, I was nervous and completely judging myself, but after a few seconds, I got into it and let the music's rhythm carry me as best I could. Each of us took a turn, with Marishka shouting out directives from the side of the room. "Be present to your bodily sensations," she told us. "Give in to yourself. Let go of your shit, Diane. Don't resist. Drop your judgments about what it looks like. Let yourselves be free."

Freedom of emotional expression—our coursework revolved around that principle. Why? Because great acting, as Marishka often reminded us, involves more than simply learning techniques. It's also about getting so comfortable with your own feelings that you can empathize with those of the characters you portray. In class, for instance, we did a lot of what's called "sense memory" work, which is letting sensory conditions, along with the needs of a character, affect the physical and emotional life of that character. "Think about the time in your childhood when you were most vulnerable," Marishka once told us. *Oh my Lord*, I sat there thinking. "Close your eyes and imagine that you're back in that very moment. Notice how your body feels. What can you see? Can you smell anything?" By the end of it, some were in tears. Others, like me, twisted in their seats. A few sat stunned. It was intense. The point was for you to find your truth, as well as the truth in every character you played. The founder of the studio, the Susan Batson who'd coached greats like Nicole Kidman, wrote a book on the topic. It's called *Truth*, and it was required reading in our course. Like I said—therapy.

Susan Batson was my first stop in New York in August 2011. Elizabeth, a friend of mine from Boston who'd already moved to the city to break into the biz, told me to check it out. At the time, Elizabeth was working for a well-known talent manager, this old Italian lady. She also suggested I go in and meet with the manager of the studio to do a short audition. I did—and it was a complete disaster.

"Diane . . . is that Gwo-WHERE-way?" she asked, squinting her forehead as she peered down, over the top edge of her reading glasses, at the sign-in sheet. "How do you pronounce your last name?" she asked in one of the thickest Brooklyn accents I've ever heard. I'm talking deep Benson-hurst thick.

"It's Guerrero," I said, trying to keep up my fake smile.

"Well, whatever," she said, setting aside the sheet and picking up another. "Here's some dialogue for you to read for me. Have a quick look and then shoot." I looked up and down the paper, which contained a few short lines at the top. I stood up straight, lifted the sheet to my face, and delivered the lines as smoothly as I could. *Please, brain—don't do that thing where you jumble up all the letters and I sound like I'm from another country*, I thought. She stared at me without batting an eyelash.

"Hmmm, okay," she said. "The thing is, honey, I don't know if you're pretty enough for this business." I could feel the steam coming out of my ears. "But yeah, I guess we'll give you a try, only because you're Elizabeth's friend."

"Uh, all right," I said. *Thanks for the vote of confidence, you witch.* "That sounds good."

"Do you have any head shots?" she asked. I reached down into my bag, pulled out a folder filled with photos, and handed it to her. She flipped through the packet, barely pausing to look at each pose.

"It looks like you'll need some new pictures," she told me. I guess mine were too Boston for her. "But you're in luck. I know a guy who can do them for you. He's a bit pricey, but he's good. I also suggest you sign yourself up at Susan Batson. Elizabeth probably already told you that."

I nodded. "How much are the photos?"

"You'll have to call him to get an exact price," she told me, "but I think they're around twelve hundred."

I nearly pissed my underwear. "Twelve hundred *dollars*?" I asked.

"Yep," she told me, handing the photos back to me. "But trust me, he's worth every dime. He can make anyone look like a million bucks." Right then, I wished I knew a guy who knew a guy, if you know what I mean.

I'd walked in that morning with the hope of landing a teammate and cheerleader. I left with a snarky Brooklynite on board. And a mandate to round up some serious cash, pronto. And a brand-new set of heart palpitations. At this point, I didn't even yet have a permanent home in New York. The only way I'd been able to afford the courses was to keep my steady bar job in Boston. That's right: Twice a week, I was schlepping from there to the city via Greyhound, four hours in each direction. Once in the area, I stayed with my aunt Milly in Passaic, New Jersey, in a corner of my cousin's bedroom. The commute was a total nightmare. It had also turned me into a bag lady: Most of the time, I walked around with this enormous duffel strapped across my body. Not a good look.

Whenever I came to the city, I took classe and occasionally auditioned. When you're just starting out, you're lucky to get in the room. It's true that as a girl, I'd imagined one day getting into musical theater. But by this point, acting had become my sole focus. And when I look back on those years when I bopped around our house, belting out Selena hits, I didn't do so with the thought that I'd become a famous pop singer. For me, the fantasy was more about just being onstage. Connecting with an audience. Telling a story. Basking in the spotlight.

The first time I stepped off the Greyhound in Manhattan, I felt born to be here. The place pulsates with this insane energy. It's unpredictable. It's gritty. It's real. It's dangerous. The folks who gravitate to New York, people with dreams bigger than the sky, are my kind of peeps. There's a certain electricity in the air here, one created in part by the fierce competition. The stakes are high, the skyscrapers even higher. And you've gotta be a badass to even stay on the ball field. That's true not only in my biz but in every industry. Even a bum here has to be on the double hustle. First of all, it can get cold as hell in this town. Second of all, there's always someone ready to elbow you out of the way. Not to mention that everything happens in a big fat hurry, so no one has time to stop and hear your sob story. The pace and the pressure can be tough, yet that's exactly what keeps you working your tail off. In the city that never sleeps, I quickly learned that I'd better not either.

The audition process was three times more brutal than it had been in Boston. I thought I'd seen my share of gorgeous girls; here, they literally filled the tryout waiting rooms, standing around with their perfect tits and teeth and booties and money and connections. Talent and good looks are as prevalent here as nepotism is. To make it, you've gotta be damn good at what you do, or know someone who can help you to the front of the line—in many cases, you need both. I'd turn up at these auditions and absolutely give it my all. I'd then wait by the phone for days and hear nothing.

No callbacks. No nothing. Which is how I realized that, if I was really going to do this thing, I needed to relocate to the city. Full-time.

So after three months of schlepping, I at last traded in my Boston bar job for another in midtown Manhattan. I also cut ties with Brian. We were sad about it but knew it was for the best. "Can I please have the room in the basement?" I asked my aunt Milly. She'd long since noticed how the commute was wearing me out, and she graciously agreed. It was a tight space, with only enough room for a twin bed, a TV, and a dresser, but it was a place to stay, and I was grateful she wasn't charging me rent. Being there also meant I could hang with my family. When I dragged home late in the evenings, my aunt would often be up waiting to offer me my favorite dish—rice, beans, and plantains with a side of lime or lemon to squirt all over it. So sweet.

Young aspiring actors have often asked me whether I ever wanted to quit. Yes. Sometimes daily. But like it or not, and I do like it, I rolled up in this world as an artist. It's who I am. The alternative to continuing in my struggle was returning to the way I felt after I left high school. In my heart of hearts, I knew I'd veered off the career path I was meant to take, and that's in part why I almost ended my life. So as hard as it was to show up to an endless succession of rejections, I stuck with it. When you want something badly, like to the point of near obsession, the work doesn't feel as strenuous. Don't get me wrong: It's exhausting and often heartbreaking. But while you may be physically tired and your spirit is tested, it cannot be drained. If you love it, you will find the juice. The effort actually gives you energy rather than depleting you of it. This business is so challenging that you're constantly trying to beat your existing score. And when you do—oh, how sweet it is. You've got the wind at your back and that force propels you forward.

Until it doesn't—because that same wind can also knock you flat on your ass, which is what seemed to be happening to me after six months in the city. I was down to my last hundred dollars and still living with my aunt. With an average of maybe two tryouts a week, I hadn't landed a role in anything. And I'd spent what savings I did have on those stupid photos the manager recommended. "Those types of head shots are totally going out of style," a seasoned actor at the studio told me. "That might be one reason you're not getting more callbacks." Which of course wasn't true, but what did I know? Fuck. I'd trusted this woman, and there I was with nothing to show for my investment. And as much passion as I'd brought with me to the city, it had become increasingly difficult to keep my head up. I was at least saving the little cheese I made at the bar to pay for my acting classes, but after months of saving, it wasn't enough for me to afford my own place. Not by a long shot. That's when I needed to take my effort to the next level and round up some cash, gangsta style. Let me explain.

I was so broke that I went on Craigslist; it had kept me busy before. So while poring over the site one evening, I scanned the ads from people seeking to purchase certain items—which included everything from Rolex watches to washing machines. About halfway down the first page, my eyes landed on this headline: "Wanted: Women's Used Shoes." *Secondhand shoes? Who'd want someone else's smelly footwear?* Well, some guy in New Jersey did, and according to his CL entry, he was willing to pay up to $30 a pair for them. "The more stinky and worn out, the higher the price," he wrote. I hadn't brought much with me from Boston, but I've always been a shoe fanatic and still owned plenty of pairs. So I wrote to this dude and arranged to meet him at a bar for the exchange.

The guy was in his early twenties. He had an artist-hipster-type beard. He was wearing a beanie and jeans. I'd imagined he'd be a super-creepy dude with an old-school Kiss T-shirt, a guy who hadn't bothered to brush his teeth or hair for days. But instead, I found someone completely different. He looked clean and cool. This doesn't mean I wasn't careful. I was still nervous and cautious, because after all, I was meeting a random man from Craigslist and selling him my old stinky shoes. The point is that I was desperate. After a quick and nervous hello, I handed him my bag of old shoes, and one at a time, he took them out and inspected them. The heels were run down on one pair; my moccasins had a huge hole in the toe area. I'd gathered five pairs in all.

"Is this all you've got?" he asked.

"Well, yeah, for now," I said with a shrug.

"I can give you a hundred and ten dollars for all of them."

"I thought you said thirty dollars a pair?"

"Yeah, but some of these aren't very worn out," he said. "I'll pay twenty dollars for the ones in better condition, thirty dollars for the moccasins. Do you want the money or not?" It was so sketchy that it felt like a drug transaction.

I paused for a second, but only for a brief one. "I'll take it," I said. I needed the money no matter how weird the situation.

"I might be able to bring you more next week," I said. "We'll see."

"Good," he told me. And off we went in opposite directions.

I met up with the dude at least three more times, and by the last meeting, I realized he was more of a cool guy than a creep; he even gave me some of his artwork, which was pretty good. Apparently, he was selling the shoes to guys all over New Zealand and Australia who had women's foot fetishes. Hey—whatever floats your boat, dude. You take socks? Anyway, all I knew is that I had some cold hard cash in my pocket. In fact, by the end of it, I collected more than five hundred dollars from the guy. Never mind that I'd left myself with two pairs of shoes: black boots for work and a pair of bobos. I laughed/cried at the thought that I could've been murdered and chopped up into little pieces by a Craigslist killer. That move was dangerous, but as I mentioned, I had to go gangsta. I consoled myself with the fantasy of one day telling this story on *The Tonight Show with Jimmy Fallon*. I could have been totally murdered and never seen or heard from again. Haha! Then we'd play Wheel of Musical Impressions. Oh, what a hoot it would be.

By spring 2012, I'd at last saved enough cash to look for my own place. Manhattan was out of the question—rents were too high. "Why don't you move to Hoboken?" my friend Katie suggested. She was already living there with her boyfriend (and now husband, Henry) and loved it. "It's an easy commute to the city, it's a cute area, and you can find a cheap place close to me." A month of pavement pounding later, I signed a lease on a studio for $750 month. It was so small that I hit my butt on the radiator whenever I got out of bed. But hey, it was all mine—and it was affordable.

* * *

Seven. Whole. Years. That's how long it had been since I'd seen my family. Almost weekly, Mami rang me from Madrid. "Honey, I miss you," she'd say on my voice mail. "Please come visit. It's not the same here. It's nothing like Colombia. It'll be just the two of us, no distractions. Ring me back." I rarely did, but that didn't stop my mother from calling again. And again. And again. Someone should give her the award for Most Persistent Parent, because I don't know any mom who has reached out to her child more frequently than my mom—even after she'd been terribly shunned.

In Hoboken, I felt like a real grown-up for the first time. I could come and go as I pleased. I could hang out as late as I wanted, without a boyfriend blowing up my phone with texts. I could sit in peace and think, and the sort of work I did in class had me thinking a whole lot. "What is blocking you?" Marishka would ask, prodding us during our exercises. "What walls do you still have up?" Every wall I'd erected had something to do with the subject I'd chronically avoided—my family's breakup. And yet week after week, class after class, it became increasingly clear to me that I was blocked. Majorly. When I'd try a scene, I'd have a hard time being open to certain feelings. I had trouble with intimacy. The closer I came to any emotion that made me feel powerless, the more I shut down.

In late 2012, I found myself at a crossroads. I knew that in order to get on with this next chapter in my life—to continue growing as an actor and as a woman—I needed to go connect with the woman who gave me life. I had this huge aspiration to be a successful actor, and many times I'd find myself wishing I had my mother there with me, just to share things with her. I missed Papi too, of course, but I've always had a more complicated relationship with my mother. In my mind, Papi had been the one who'd sacrificed so much to keep my life as steady as possible. He'd been the savior. The nurturer. The anchor. They'd both been snatched from my life, but Mami was the one I resented. The one who'd been in and out of my world during that critical passage when my body was changing more quickly than the circumstances in our home. I needed her, and she wasn't there for me. Through her choices, she'd made herself a big target for deportation—and in so doing, she'd missed out on some of the most important experiences of my childhood. Buying my first bra. Dealing with my period. Boys. Growing from a girl into a young woman. Yes, I pretended, at the time, that her absence didn't matter to me. That I was perfectly fine. That Papi's presence was enough. I shrugged it all off as no big deal and refused to talk to anyone about it. But deep down, I judged her, and I held her most responsible for the mess our lives had turned out to be. In my mind, my father was the hero of our family's story line—and I'd cast Mami as the villain.

Mami had relocated to Spain six years earlier out of desperation. In Colombia, she and my dad weren't talking. I'd gradually slipped away from her. And she was struggling financially. So what was the point in staying? None. Her brother, who'd become a Spanish citizen (and who'd since retired from his work as a bullfighter), had taken her in until she could afford a place of her own. She'd eventually gotten a job as a housecleaner, saved up her money, and moved into her own small place. In some ways, she and I were on parallel paths. We were both reinventing ourselves. Starting over. Rewriting our narratives.

"Mami, I'm coming to see you," I called to tell her early one Friday morning. The line went silent, probably because she was twice stunned: first, that I was calling, and second, that I was planning a two-week trip to visit her. "That's wonderful, Diane," she said, her voice shaking around the edges. "It'll be so great to see you again."

In October 2012, I boarded a flight from JFK to Madrid. Most of the way there, I stared dreamily from the window, wondering how my mom would be different. How her life had shifted since that Christmas I'd traveled to Colombia. How she was faring in a new country. So many years had passed since our last meeting that I felt like I was going to see a stranger. Mami had agreed to meet me in baggage claim. The woman who showed up there that evening was not the mom I remembered.

I wheeled my suitcase through the sliding doors leading to the waiting area. "Diane!" I heard. "Over here!" Mami and her girlfriend, another Colombian woman, were both waving and rushing toward me. *Is that her?* I thought. Before I could get a great look, she darted forward and threw her arms around me. "Oh, princess!" she said, squeezing me long and hard. "It's been so long!" I backed up, blinked back the tears, and gazed at her. *Oh my Lord.* My mother's nose was different. Completely.

Back when our family was still together, Mami had often mentioned wanting a nose job. "You don't need one," I'd told her. "I like your nose the way it is." I'd always thought it was pretty and distinguished, large and with an arched bridge. As a small child, I remember reaching up to touch it, and I thought it had a certain elegance to it. For as long as I can remember, she'd called it her "witch nose." At some point during all those years while I was busy ignoring her calls, she'd gotten the surgery. I stood there and gawked at her. Her nose wasn't like Michael Jackson–style different; it had just lost its big arch. She was also fit, tanned, and toned, like she'd been hitting the gym daily. She was wearing a pair of dark-wash Levi's and a cute blouse. Her hair was a little more gray than I'd remembered, and yet it was long and still shiny. Her complexion glowed as if she was seven years younger, not older. She looked happy, happier than I'd ever seen her in Colombia.

Fresh tears welled up in my eyes. "You got your nose done," I said. "Wow."

"Yes, I did," she said proudly. "A few years ago."

Seeing how much my mother had changed made me painfully aware of just how many years I'd locked her out. How much of each other's lives we'd missed. How weak I'd allowed our mother-daughter bond to become. She'd made this big decision to change her nose, and I'd had no part in it, nor any awareness of it. Her life had moved on without me in it. It hit me that we had no real relationship anymore, only the shadow of a former one. That realization made me feel so lonely—not just on my behalf but also on hers.

Mami reached up to hug me again and held me even more tightly than before. "It's okay, baby girl," she said. "I'm here now."

From that first moment in the airport, it was clear to me that I wasn't there to reconnect with the mom who'd raised me; I was there to get acquainted with the person she'd grown into since. Nothing about her life in Madrid resembled the one she had had in Colombia. For starters, she owned a car, one of those budget European models that looks like a toy. After we loaded my suitcase into the tiny trunk, I climbed into the front seat next to Mami and went back to staring. Her side profile made her look even more different than she did face-on.

"Let's get outta here," she said, revving up the engine, turning on the radio, and speeding from the lot. She seemed so independent. So in charge of herself. So spirited and sassy as she zipped through the streets. The last time I'd seen my mother drive, I was a kid; in Colombia, she had gotten around by bike. So it was the weirdest thing, all these years later, to see my mother behind the wheel. She changed lanes with confidence, glancing back and forth between the road and me.

"So how have you been, my love?" she asked.

"Good, I guess," I told her.

"Should we stop by the grocery store and pick up anything special for you to eat this evening?" she asked. "I've already made your favorite, *frijoles y arrocito*."

"That should be plenty," I said. "Thanks."

As Mom curved from one road to the next, I peered out at the city. The place reminded me a bit of New York. Cosmopolitan. Sidewalks overflowing with people. Little cafés with outdoor dining. The architecture, however, made it uniquely Madrid. Gothic churches and basilicas all over the place. Beautifully maintained plazas and squares. Mami lived on the outskirts of the city, and about half an hour into our drive (and after we'd dropped off her friend for an appointment in the city), we at last pulled into my mother's parking lot. "Here we are," she said, yanking up the emergency brake. "It's not much, but it's home." Inside, the one-bedroom was bare-bones—a couch, a table with two chairs, and her queen bed and dresser in the bedroom—yet by comparison to Mami's previous homes in Colombia, it was quiet and it was all hers. The walls were mostly bare, but she had a school photo of me, at age seven, hanging at the center of one of them. I had this wide grin with three front teeth missing. I cringed when I noticed it. I no longer knew that little girl.

Mami still had to work long hours while I was in town, but we spent as much time together as we could. She took me to dinner one night. To a museum one day. And later in the trip, to a flamenco show. I spent a lot of the trip in awe that she had built a life for herself here. I think about it now, and that was probably because any recent memories I had of my mother were of her nervous, scared, and in hiding. There was no need to hide here, and no one was giving her any charity.

A couple of years earlier, she'd gotten a job at a farm, taking care of animals. It didn't pay much, but it was far more than she could earn back in her country, and it was enough to cover her rent. It had also given her back this spirit of independence, this spark I was noticing in her. She wasn't just surviving in Madrid; she seemed to be thriving. At long last, she'd regained control of her life. How Mami got her groove back—I liked it.

I hadn't expected the trip to be a Hallmark reunion, but it was more difficult than I thought it would be. Just as my mother had changed, so had I. And that meant we clashed quite a bit. When you haven't seen someone in years, you have to literally relearn the person, figure out what makes him or her angry, scared, ticked off. And as we made those adjustments, silly tensions arose. "Diane, your food is getting cold." Mami would direct. "Can you not tell me what to do?" I'd shoot back. "I'm not a kid anymore."

Then as the days went on, she frequently wanted to reminisce about my childhood, about the old days. "You remember how you used to play out in the backyard with Dana and Gabriela while I was cooking?" she asked.

"Of course I do," I snapped, "but that was a long time ago, Mami." In her mind's eye, those experiences were as vivid as if they'd happened the day before; and as I'd drifted further from her, she'd held those memories all the closer and more tightly. But for me, the recollections were like old faded photos, ones I'd long since replaced with all the moments that came after. Mami knew little of that life—and her mention of the previous one we'd shared brought up so much anguish for me.

Some of our moments together might've been tough, but many others were sweet. "My muzzy," I'd call my mother. She loved that. During our time together, I'd make her laugh by taking on a Spanish accent and imitating people around us. We took selfies all around the city. It was just me and Mama. I would make up little sketches on the street where I would pretend to be a Spanish reporter interviewing her about whatever monument or church we were in front of. Slowly, my memory of all the great times we'd shared began to come back. Even when I was little, my mother would indulge all my kooky shenanigans and let me play with her for hours. I remembered. Mama, I loved you and you loved me. I was your little girl and you were my favorite.

We filled our evenings with conversation, but seldom on any subject too painful for me to confront. She had figured out that I was not ready to discuss everything; it was still too raw for me. That changed four nights before the end of my trip. Over a bottle of Pinot Grigio, the two of us sat near each other on her couch—and it was the first time I had ever shared a drink with my mother. Mami, a little tipsy, started talking about the deportation.

"That whole time was so horrible for me," she said. "The prison was dirty. I couldn't communicate with your father. I couldn't eat or sleep . . ."

As she spoke, my blood pressure rose. I sat up and cut her off.

"You know what, Mami?" I shouted. "I don't want to hear another thing about how hard things were for you!"

Mami, caught off guard by my anger, stood. "What are you talking about, Diane?"

"You don't even know how hard things were for me!" I shouted. "It's always about you, isn't it? You, you, you!"

Tears came pouring out. "You abandoned me!" I howled, standing to point my forefinger right in her face. The words, ones I'd never uttered aloud, came from some unknown place inside of me, with a fire and a fury that surprised me. "You destroyed our family!" I screamed. "I hate you!"

Mami widened her eyes, and then all at once, she too began to cry. She tried to pull me into her arms, and I resisted. But I was weeping so hard I couldn't keep my body stiff. I finally gave in to her pull and buried my face in her bosom.

"Diane, I never wanted to leave you!" Mami wailed. "I did everything I could to stay with you! Everything! I never meant to hurt you!"

Mami embraced me for the longest time, rubbing my back and swaying me from side to side as if I was again her baby. "I'm so sorry," she whispered. "Please forgive me."

I'd spent nearly a decade making my mother wrong. I blamed her for deserting me. For taking the kinds of chances that put her at greater risk for deportation. For vanishing from my life at the very moment when I most craved her love, her care, her attention. And on that afternoon when I'd watched her wave good-bye through the back bars of a paddy wagon, I'd made a choice, one I wasn't conscious of. In the quietness of my heart, I'd decided that no apology Mami could later offer would be sufficient. No explanation would be enough for me to let go of the deep bitterness toward her that I carried in my belly. I'd built a barrier from that rage, a partition

so thick and so high that no one could peer around it. My mother might've left that detention center in 2001, but for years after, I'd held her a prisoner, the person most responsible for my heartache. I'd rendered her unforgivable, and in so doing, I'd also locked away myself. A part of my soul. And any hope that she and I would ever live at peace. That night, in the dim light of my mother's living room, I made the choice to free us both.

On my last day in Madrid, Mami drove me with her to the farm. When she turned on the radio, a familiar ballad by Cristian Castro called "Por Amarte Así" came on, and after we sang it together for a half minute, I stopped.

"What's the matter?" Mami asked me.

"Nothing," I said.

"What is it?" she pressed.

"This song takes me back," I told her. Before she was deported for the last time, Mami would often spruce up my bedroom, just to make things nice for me. I'd come home from school to find yummy burning candles flickering, and sometimes she'd even have a little present waiting. One afternoon, I spotted Castro's CD, *Mi Vida Sin Tu Amor*, propped up on my pillow. I fell in love with that album and listened to it so often that I almost broke it. Until we heard Castro's song on the radio, I'd nearly forgotten Mami's gift all those years earlier. I'd carefully buried away the memory along with countless others.

"I've missed you so much, Mami," I told her.

"I've missed you too, darling," she said.

I cried the whole flight home. The sweet old woman seated next to me kept handing me tissues. "It's okay, dear," she repeated. "Everything will be fine." These weren't tears of sadness; they were tears of release. Of freedom. Of healing. Of recognition. My mother had been dealt a whole hand of wild cards in life. She'd played them as well as she could, and, in so doing, she'd managed something far braver than I ever might've attempted at her age. I had not yet learned to fully accept my reality, as she had been forced to. Even still, my mother has never been a bitter person. I'm amazed at her great spirit and her ability to soldier on in any challenge life presents her with.

With a heart still burdened from a level of loss and grief I'd wish

upon no one, Mami mustered the courage, with Eric on her hip, to set out for a foreign land. A nation where she didn't speak the language. A country that provided a haven from the poverty and violence and despair she was desperate to flee. Along the way, she fell down, got up, and then toppled to her knees again. But in the end, she always got up. She crawled back to her feet. She stood. And she deserved not my contempt but my deepest admiration.

* * *

It was time for me to get a new manager. My breakthrough with Mami had freed up this huge space inside me, and with my spirit so much lighter, I was eager to move ahead with my work. The Susan Batson Studio hosted showcases, and there, managers and agents could show up and evaluate our work. As soon as I returned from Madrid, I signed myself up for one and began searching for a monologue to present. I settled on one about a girl who had a troubled childhood, married young, and later became a meth addict. When I read the piece for Susan (yes, the real Susan Batson!), she told me, "This is a nice choice for you. It has a lot of dimension to it." She gave me a couple of pointers, and later that week, I gave a powerful enough performance, if I do say so myself. Josh Taylor, an agent from VAMNation Entertainment, was there that day.

"That was amazing," Josh said to me afterward. "Can we talk?"

"Sure," I said, blushing, as he handed me his card. A week later, I was in his office discussing the possibility of him representing me; I showed up wearing a cropped top, ripped stockings, and platform boots. I looked like a homeless person, but thankfully, Josh didn't seem to notice. "I think you're very talented," he told me. "I think I can find you work." Frankly, I didn't know if he was boosting my ego or being serious, but either way, the encouragement felt good after months of being told I wasn't pretty enough. Talented enough. Experienced. So within days of our meeting, I started working with him.

At his word, Josh began sending me out on auditions immediately; and in between auditions, he often checked up on me. "How you holding up?" he'd call and ask. Many weeks, there'd be no auditions. The thing is, when casting directors don't know your work, they rarely want to even see you.

And no matter how much your manager tells them "She's fantastic," they roll their eyes and keep it moving. So during my downtime, I also kept tracking down my own opportunities on websites like Backstage, and of course, on CC: Creeper Craigslist. When none of those roles worked out, I began wondering if I should change my direction. *Maybe I should go back to school for theater*, I thought. *Maybe I need some serious training.* In the meantime, I auditioned myself silly.

You name it, I tried out for it—from series like *Glee*, to procedural dramas such as *Law & Order*. I'd go into these auditions, wait by the phone for days, hear nothing—and later discover I'd been up against a real celeb. I once got beat out for a part by none other than Nina Dobrev from *The Vampire Diaries*. Excuse me, but how did it make any sense that I was even up for that role? No clue. Casting will assure you they want a "fresh face," only for you to later see that the name got it instead. So I'd go into these auditions thinking, *Whatever—I'm sure I have no shot*, and in a way, that eased the pressure. In retrospect, I now realize this whole process was part of what it means to become an actor. You've gotta put the time in. You've gotta get out there and show casting directors who you are, and even if they don't hire you initially, they might circle back and ask to see you down the line. I know that now. You couldn't have convinced me of that then.

I was cast in an episode of *Are We There Yet?*—the TV series (based on the 2005 movie) created by Ice Cube. That was over-the-moon exciting. I then got a central role (!) in an indie film called *Emoticon ;)*. The movie wasn't huge, but they paid me around a hundred dollars a day to film. That's real money. Plus, I got to travel to Mexico for some of the shooting. I also did this small part in a movie called *My Man Is a Loser* with John Stamos. So a little at a time, I was building up my SAG credits and making a (small) name for myself. At least I was working and putting in the hours. "It's only a matter of time before people are really going to get on the Diane Guerrero wagon," Josh always told me. "Just hang in there. Bigger opportunities will come along. You have to build toward that."

One week after I'd been turned down by a fresh slew of casting directors, Josh sent me a text. "There's this part I want you to try out for," he wrote. "It's a prison series, so don't wear any makeup for the audition, and have your hair messy. Keep it as real and natural as possible." He mentioned that it was an Internet thing, and since my big dream was to be on TV and in the movies, I wasn't exactly impressed. But who had time or money to be picky? Ha, not me! Remember, I wasn't above CC: Creeper Craigslist.

Josh e-mailed me the sides that evening so I could begin to work on it. The character was a girl named Maritza, a spunky, tough ghetto girl whose bad choices have landed her behind bars. In the scene, Maritza is running for prison government, and she gets into a scuffle with her best friend, Flaca. At the end of it, she pops off with a smart-ass couple of lines: "Vote for Maritza if you want more pizza! Vote for Flaca, she's full of caca!" *How silly*, I thought. *It's a Web series? Do people watch those?*

The day of the audition, I called my papi with the secret intention of getting a pep talk. "I'm getting really discouraged by everything," I told him. "It's so hard to keep going out on all these stupid tryouts."

"You can't give up so easily, *chibola*," he told me. "You're doing your best, right? And that's all you can do. Something is going to work out. Trust me."

Later that morning at ten, I showed up precisely as Josh had instructed: bare-faced and wearing sweats, a T-shirt, and my combat boots. The look wasn't difficult to pull off, given that I was more down in the dumps than I'd been in weeks. I'd gone through the motions of memorizing my part the night before, but I didn't truly want to be there. I kept thinking. *I'll never get cast in anything, not even a Web series.* I delivered my lines for the casting director, Ms. Jennifer Euston, and unlike so many others she was approachable and happy. She put me at ease.

"That was good," she told me, "but I want you to do it again for me. And this time, I want you to make the character a lot tougher and with a lot more attitude. Let's get it on camera one more time." *Oh good. She's giving me another chance. She must think I'm decent if she wants me to do this over*, I thought. *Let me try and get into this.* I stood up straight, focused myself, and launched into my first line. That's when something unexpected happened.

The moment I began reading, I was transported. Back to Boston. Back to my early middle-school years. Back to all those times when the girls in my hood got in my face and talked trash about me "acting white." My childhood was filled with dozens of Maritzas, and if I hadn't chosen a different path, I'd now be one of them. In those three minutes in front of the casting crew, I brought all those experiences to my character. Then at the end of the piece, just to add some drama, I got close to the camera and yelled out an ad-lib: "Yo, fuckin' *hit* me!" The team looked stunned. Sweetly, Jen said, "Great! That was it. Thanks for coming in, Diane." I left feeling so lifted, like I had lived a little bit of truth in that moment.

Day one went by. No callback. Two days turned into a week, which turned into three. Still nothing. "Forget it," I told Josh. "I'm sure they've gotten J. Lo to take the part by now," I joked.

One day about a month after the audition, my father rang to check on me. I'd just gotten into bed to sulk.

"So how'd that audition go?" he asked.

"I think I did okay," I told him. "But I haven't heard anything. So you never know. I don't even care anymore."

"Well, did you give it your all?" he asked.

"I gave it my all, and then some," I told him.

"Then you've already won," he said.

No, Papi, I thought. *I haven't won if I don't actually get the part.* I didn't say that to my father, of course. I just thanked him, hung up, and scooted down under my comforter.

You don't sell your old shoes to a random dude because you want a metaphorical victory. You don't move your entire life to New York City so you can earn the "Great Effort" trophy. You don't tuck a blue journal of dreams beneath your pillow at age twelve because you want to end up in second place, as the also-ran. You take big risks so you can score big victories. You step out because, dammit, you want to be chosen. You want something to show for your effort. You want to be the girl who got the part. Almost as much as I wanted life itself, that is what I wished for.

Some of the *Orange Is the New Black* crew and Maritza Ramos.

CHAPTER 16

Orange

One press account said I was an
overnight success. I thought that
was the longest night I've ever spent.

—SANDRA CISNEROS, novelist

It's not every day a girl gets to wear a red beak. At a makeup school in downtown Manhattan, I was having my first one ever attached, courtesy of my friend Kourt. I met this beautiful creature at the *Emoticon ;)* shoot a year before. She was the makeup artist on set, and I was immediately taken by her kind spirit and genuine personality. So any way,

Kourt was taking classes at Makeup Forever Academy, and for her final class project, she needed a model she could temporarily turn into a phoenix using prosthetics and cosmetics. Enter me—the (near) starving artist desperate for rent money. "Makeup Forever can pay you a hundred and fifty dollars for your time," Kourt told me. Boom—sold.

The prosthetic was huge and clunky. Kourt was doing her best to fit the latex prosthetic over my nose with spirit gum, a glue that can be used on skin.

"Can you hold still so I can get this on here right?" she said.

I could hardly speak—or, for that matter, breathe—because the nose piece covered so much of my face. "Hmmm hmmm," I managed to get out.

"This is going to be fly," she said. *So to speak.*

Just as she was gluing down the edges, my cell rang. Trying to keep my face as steady as possible for Kourt, I pulled the phone from my pocket and answered it.

"Hello?" I managed to mutter. I sounded muffled, like I'd just stuffed a ball of cotton candy in my mouth.

"Hey, Diane, this is Josh," I heard—and for whatever reason, he sounded out of breath.

"What's up?" I asked.

"I have some news for you," he said. "Do you remember your audition for a show called *Orange Is the New Black*?"

I froze. "Orange who?" I said. Kourt, who was throwing me the stink eye, motioned for me to get off the phone.

Josh laughed. "You know," he told me, "it's that Internet prison show you went out for. And you got it! You landed a recurring role for the character Maritza Ramos."

I dropped the phone. "Oh my God!" I yelled, jumping up and down. The beak's right edge slid off and dangled over my mouth. A couple of the other makeup artists and models stared over at me like I was possessed. Kourt looked at me and smiled like a proud mama.

"I got the part!" I shrieked. "I got the part!" I picked up the cell phone and pressed it to my ear again.

"Josh, are you still there?" I asked.

"Yup, I'm here," he said, chuckling.

"Are you kidding me?" I asked.

"I'm not kidding at all," he told me. "In fact, they want you to start filming in about four weeks."

My head spun. "So, like, how many episodes would I get?" I asked excitedly.

"We don't know that yet," he told me. "Could be two. Could be five. Could be eight. But you're in!"

After a scream-fest with Kourt, I stuck around long enough for her to reattach my beak (role or no role, I needed that hundred fifty bucks by week's end). But once I left the school, I cannot tell you how I even got home, because the whole way there, I was in the zombie zone. *Is this actually happening?* I kept thinking. *Am I going to be on a show for longer than five seconds?* The last time I'd been so worked up was over that Kmart commercial. That was nothing compared to the thrill and shock of *this*. Me? For real? Some actors go years without ever landing a recurring role. I mean look, they weren't committing to me the way they would a series regular, but I didn't care. In my eyes, we had a little time to date and get to know each other before they fell in love with me.

By the next morning, my euphoria had turned into trepidation. What had I gotten myself into? Who was in this? What was this whole Web series thing about anyway? The crazy thing is, I'd done zero research in preparation for the audition. That's how I am: I like to show up and just roll with things. Sometimes that strategy works for me, because I'm open to whatever unfolds; other times, that has bitten me in the ass. Josh had mentioned something about Netflix, but at the time, that didn't mean what it does now. I thought of Netflix as a place to order movies, and although some folks were turning to Web content as their main source of entertainment, that wasn't yet widely known. And then when I heard "Web series," I figured that could involve anything from a few friends making a movie in a backyard to a smallish production. That's basically why I'd dismissed it. Until I didn't get a callback—at which point it felt like the biggest letdown of my acting career.

Over the next couple of days, I went through the same stages that a lot of us actors go through: First, there's the zombie stage. Then there's the super-excited stage. Then there's the scared-as-hell "What if I can't deliver" stage. Followed by the super-diva "Um, excuse me, do you know who I am? Guards, take him away!" stage. In short, I was a mess. But at least I was a mess with a job!

Josh gave me the scoop on the series. It had been created by Jenji Kohan, the badass director who also created *Weeds* on Showtime. The show, which is based on Piper Kerman's bestselling memoir by the same name, is set at a fictional minimum-security women's penitentiary in Litchfield, an actual town in upstate New York (although the real-life town has no prison). The show revolves around the main character, Piper Chapman—an upper-middle-class New Yorker whose past comes back to haunt her and lands her at Litchfield alongside an, um, colorful crew of other inmates. "Some of the scenes will be filmed upstate, in an abandoned children's mental ward," Josh told me. Most others—including Episode Two, which would be my first appearance—would be shot in the city. I still had no idea who any of the other cast members would be, but this was starting to sound like the big time. This was a series with a full budget and its very own set.

One month and many sleepless nights later, I turned up at the iconic Kaufman Astoria Studios in Queens at 9:00 a.m. sharp. The building itself is enormous. As I roamed around looking for the *Orange* set, I passed through a long hallway filled with signed photos of some of the greats who'd worked there. Frank Sinatra. George Burns. Lena Horne. Paul Robeson. Productions such as *Goodfellas* and *Hair* had been filmed in the studio. In one corner of the building, I noticed the set of *Sesame Street*, complete with Oscar the Grouch's trash can and the big Sesame Street sign. *So cool.* Just across from it was the set of *Nurse Jackie*. I finally spotted the double doors marked *Orange*.

Pure insanity—that's what I found inside. In this huge waiting area, throngs of actors, producers, and background artists milled around. I signed in with an associate director (or AD), and then I stood there and drooled like a dumbfounded schoolgirl. Real actors, those with films and TV shows I recognized and admired, were all over the place. Jason Biggs (*American Pie*). Natasha Lyonne (*Slums of Beverly Hills*). Laura Prepon (*That '70s Show*). Taryn Manning (*Crossroads*). I was like, *What is this thing?* These were actors, and I was about to work on the same show with them. Eeek! Good thing I didn't know in advance who'd been hired. If I had, I may not have shown up. That's how much of a nervous wreck I instantly became.

On the set, women—all shapes, sizes, and colors—were all over the place. Some of the bigger stars were chatting with each other and hanging out with the producers, but most of the rest of us, the extras and the newbies, were standing around like geeks, checking each other out. I'm sure I wasn't the only one thinking, *How will I ever measure up in this crowd?* No one said much to me, nor did I speak. Whenever I'm in a new situation, I get shy. Especially when the stakes are high. And especially when almost everyone in the room has been in some of my favorite TV shows and movies.

After a few minutes of gawking, I found my way to a row of side chairs and took a seat. *What's the protocol? And should I be mingling?* From the looks of it, a few of the seasoned actors had already formed cliques, probably when they'd shot the pilot months before. *This must be how it goes in showbiz*, I thought. I had no idea what to say or do, which is why I'll always be grateful to the actor who broke the ice.

"My name is Uzo," said this vibrant black woman with kind eyes. She had such a commanding presence. So regal. She smiled and extended her hand, which I shook. "What's your name?" she asked.

"I'm Diane," I said, fidgeting in the chair. "Diane Guerrero."

She sat in the seat across from me. "Where you from, Diane?" she asked.

"Boston, originally," I told her.

Her face lit up. "Really?" she said. "I'm from there too."

I liked Uzo Aduba from that first conversation. She seemed so sure of herself but also quite warm, which brought my blood pressure back down to normal. We traded stories about Boston, and after I gave her the digestible version of my story, she told me a little about her family; her parents had come to the United States from Nigeria.

"My mom is so amazing," she said. "She's like my biggest fan. She was always like, 'Zo Zo, you can do it. You have to keep going!' And here

I am." On *Orange*, Uzo had been tapped to play Suzanne Warren. As in "Crazy Eyes." As in the portrayal that would eventually earn her two Emmys and a SAG Award.

"What's your character?" she asked me.

"Maritza Ramos," I told her.

"Cool," she said—and just then, the AD interrupted us to pull me aside.

"We're sending you into hair and makeup now," she told me. "Just go back to the right, and down the hall." I nodded, looked over my shoulder to smile at Uzo, and stepped off.

My hair had never been longer—like down past the small of my back. The hairstylist brushed it silky and then pulled it to the side while the makeup artist started working her magic. Maritza and her Latina crew are supposed to have this ghetto glam look. Mission accomplished: By the time the team got done with me, I could've fit right in on the streets of East LA. Very *chola*-y. My liner was thick; dark brown lipstick, almost burgundy, was smeared all over my lips.

Next stop: wardrobe. A seamstress handed me a fresh set of those khaki-colored two-piece scrubs. "Put these on," she told me. Can I tell you a secret? I love my outfit on *Orange* more than any other costume I've ever had to wear. It's simple. It's comfortable. It's basic. And no worrying about how my boobs or butt will look in a tight dress. It's also almost exactly what everyone else is wearing. (Though we all have a different signature way we wear the scrubs; we are stylish women, after all.) The fact that we had to wear the same clothing made me feel like I was part of something. A community. From day one for me, it wasn't about coming in and trying to be the cute girl. I wanted to be a serious actor doing serious work, not the one only concerned about looks.

When I emerged from the changing area, another AD met me. "We're running behind today," she told me, "but we'll come get you when your scene comes up." I nodded. "Make yourself comfortable," she told me. "It could be a while." She dropped me off in another waiting area, one filled with a crop of actors I hadn't seen earlier.

The other faces were new and fresh, just like mine. Danielle Brooks.

Samira Wiley. Emma Myles. Those three were sitting in a circle across the room, cracking up and eating lunch together—and clearly already bonded. I saw an empty chair in a far corner and shuffled toward it. A few minutes later, Danielle got my attention.

"Hey, girl," she shouted across the room, "what's your name?" She wandered toward me.

"I'm Diane," I said shyly when she got close.

"So why are you sittin' over there all quiet?" she said with a grin.

"I dunno," I said. "It's my first day. I don't even know if they're going to use me. Do you think they'll cut me? Do you usually have to sit around for a while?"

She laughed. "Wait, wait, wait—slow down, girl," she said. "They'll get to you. Don't worry. Just chill. Come hang with us until they do."

I followed her back across the room, where she introduced me to her crew. "Hey, guys, this is Diane," she announced, "and she's nervous she's going to be cut. But she's not going anywhere. Can we please show her some love?" The girls snickered and applauded. A couple of them gave me high fives. *Maybe this isn't so bad.*

"So who are you playing?" Emma asked me. I told her all about Maritza, but as I spoke, I couldn't help but notice her horrible teeth. Yellow. Like they were rotting. Gross. I was like, *Damn, they're really using real people for this.*

"Oh, I'm sorry," she cut in. "I meant to tell you—these aren't my real teeth." I let out a chuckle, the kind that told her I'd indeed been judging her dental situation. "I play a meth head on the show," she said. "They just smear crap on my teeth. I'm usually much better looking than this." Hilarious.

One by one over the next three hours, the actors were called in to shoot their scenes. A couple went off at two p.m. Someone else around four. A few others at six and nine. By midnight, only five others and I were still in the waiting room. Finally, at two a.m., my number came up. "Come with me," said the AD. The others and I followed her to video village, that area on the set where all the directors and producers congregate. When I rounded the corner, several senior producers looked me up and down, and then they got into a huddle and started whispering. *Oh Lord*, I thought. *They're definitely sending me home*. After a minute, which felt more like thirty, one of them came up to me.

"You look too pretty," she said.

I raised my brows. "Huh?" I said.

"You're too made-up for this role," she explained. "This isn't going to work. We need Maritza to be way less glamorous. We're sending you back to hair and makeup."

Off I went—and I returned without lipstick. The producers seemed to approve of the new look and escorted me to the set, one of the most basic I've ever seen. A cafeteria. A rec room. A kitchen. A cafeteria and commissary. And a cell with bunks inside, which is where my first star turn took place. All the actors in my scene were already there, waiting for me to return from my cosmetic strip-down. Hardly before I could gather my thoughts, the director called out, "Action!"

Long story short? I blew the first scene. In it, I get into this little dustup with a couple of the Latina girls. Three of the actors in my scene, Elizabeth Rodriguez (Aleida), Dascha Polanco (Dayanara), and Selenis Leyva (Gloria), had worked together in Episode One. They had a rhythm; I, however, had my tongue in my throat. I'd been given three lines to memorize, and I flubbed every. Single. One. "Cut!" the director kept yelling. *How embarrassing.* We tried it again. And again. And again. I still don't know if the director called it a night because he was satisfied—or because, at 3:15 a.m., he was too exhausted to continue. Then again, not everything is about you, Diane. Jeez.

Given how awful that first scene went, I had to pry myself out of bed for the following day's filming. Each episode requires about nine days of shooting; not until day three did I turn a corner and really start to relax. That had a lot to do with meeting Jackie Cruz, who plays Flaca, Maritza's best friend. We instantly hit it off. She's so spunky, so fun, so approachable. "Hey, do you want to have lunch?" she asked me that first week. "Sure," I said. That was the beginning of not just a work camaraderie but a real friendship. I'll tell you more about that in a sec.

The cast was huge, and up to this point, I was meeting a new character every half hour. And as shy as I was, meeting Taylor Schilling (who plays Piper) was very cool. She seemed so dedicated. She was tall with a big smile and an infectious laugh that reminded me of my college roomie, Adrienne. She mentioned she was from Boston, and that filled me with pride. Hell yes—three girls from the Bean on a show together in New York! Eat that, whatever town or city hates on Boston.

My sole focus is playing the hell out of Maritza. "Who is she, really?" I get asked a lot by fans and interviewers. "What's her story?" Here's the thing: On a show like *Orange*, the characters unfold for us actors nearly as slowly as they do for our viewers; the writers only give us the script for the following episode, not for the full season. So I'm still getting to know Maritza myself, and this is what I can tell you about her: She's a spitfire. She's got a silly side. She always tries to make the most of her situation. And she's desperately seeking a family, some security. Sound familiar? And while she's smart, I don't think she cares about trying too hard. She's a girl who's had to use whatever is available to her, like many others in her situation (I can think of a few girls like that). I think you'll find that Maritza is a lot more than she seems.

In Season Four and hopefully beyond, you will see more of who Maritza is, as well as her baggage. I have fun all the time with the different possibilities for her life. In one scenario I've played with, Maritza comes from a wealthy white suburban family who adopted her at birth; she has grown up grappling with identity issues. When her mom shows up at Litchfield to see her, she's like, "Maritza, why are you talking like you're from the streets dear? What would the gals in the country club say if they heard you speaking that way, after all we've done for you?" That storyline, among others, makes me laugh. We'll see how that jibes with what the writers create. The truth is that this show is so freaking good that there is no doubt that we'll continue to amaze and grab your attention with all the wonderful stories we bring to life. Real stories about real women. As Lea DeLaria aka Big Boo would say, "Fuck yeah!"

When I think about the show entering its fourth season, things seem so different than they were in the beginning. My worries have changed. My heart is in a different place. I cannot believe how much I've grown throughout this whole experience. I feel like I belong to a family, like I'm part of something bigger. Since the first season, we as a show have broken so many barriers and brought light to so many important issues in need of attention. How many shows can you say have done that? Not only have we changed the way people watch television, we've bred a whole crew of activists. How wonderful to be part of such social and political awareness. Dope. We are fighting for women's rights, LGBT rights, social equality, prison reform—and now I hope my brothers and sisters join me in my fight for immigration reform.

Maritza's most memorable line (so far!) is the one I auditioned with. And it's not just because I'm in the episode—okay yes, it's because I'm in it, duh!—that it became one of my favorites of the first season. In all seriousness, it was after that episode that I first began noticing that people were recognizing me. I started seeing Internet memes of myself with "Vote for Maritza if you want pizza!" as a caption underneath. I swear, people still randomly come up to me on the streets and yell out that line. I felt ridiculous when I said it (I even cringed when I later watched it), which is why it's funny and ironic that it turned out to be one of Maritza's best moments.

A lot of my scenes are with Jackie, who's about eighty inches taller than I am (seriously, she stands five feet nine to my five feet two). The directors hadn't initially planned for our characters to be such close friends. But when they noticed how cool Jackie and I had become in real life, they went with that and altered our story lines. (Or at least, this is the story Jackie and I have planned to tell our grandchildren, so whether I'm fuzzy on the details of how our characters became so close is of no importance.) In Episode Six of Season Two, our on-camera connection suddenly got hotter. When I read that week's script, it involved a Valentine's party, some hooch (aka prison moonshine), and a smooch between two besties. It was wicked awkward. I immediately started hyperventilating when I realized Jackie and I would have to kiss. I'd never even done a kissing scene, much less a girl-on-girl one. And since Jackie and I are such great buds off camera, it made it all the weirder.

For the entire week, I practiced my kissing technique in the mirror; I put my lips right up to the glass, closed my eyes, and then peeked to see how it appeared. In a word? Disturbing. I looked cross-eyed with lips all poked out. I didn't even want to consider how it would look to other people.

When you're kissing someone in real life, you don't pay attention to how you look; you're not supposed to. You're in the moment. Your face gets ugly. You might even slobber. Jackie and I didn't talk to each other about any of this in advance; she probably felt just as strange about it as I did. So when we showed up on set that day, we were both nervous.

"You ready for this?" she asked.

"Ready as I'll ever be," I said, giggling.

It's one thing to simply peck someone on the lips; it's an entirely different matter to perform a make-out session. In the case of the latter, you get self-conscious. People are watching you. Repositioning you. And talking you through it. "Try to angle yourself to the left, Diane!" the director instructed. By the end of it, I didn't care whether I was kissing my girlfriend or a hippopotamus. I just wanted the ordeal to be over with.

And soon enough it was. Flaca (and yes, it helped to keep reminding myself that it was Flaca kissing Maritza, not Jackie kissing Diane) leaned in and planted one on me. Things got heavy, and then we both stopped and went, "Naaaah!" Afterward over lunch, Jackie and I had a laugh about the whole thing and got right back to being what we are to this day—platonic pals.

Although now and again, she gets a little grabby and I have to splash cold water on her face to get her little paws off me. "You totally want me," she'll joke. "OMG Jack, get over yourself—I do not!" I'll tell her. "Then why are you blushing?" "Uh, because you're making me blush." We crack up at the fact that I'm so uncomfortable with people touching me and giving me long hugs. Leave it to your friends to point out your weird hang-ups and quirks. "You're not touchy-feely are you?" she'll tease. *What, me?* Right then, a slew of moments when I've gotten stiff in various social encounters will flash through my head. I'll be your rock and a shoulder for you to cry on, but don't get too close to my body or I'll turn stiff as a board. Unless I'm drunk or actively trying to seduce you. Yup, very primal over here. I'm still working on that. My mom says its because I have trust issues, because of my trauma as a kid, blah blah blah.

Even if we weren't on a hit show together, I'd hang with Jackie. I can be my goofy self around her. No judgments. In fact, she's just as silly. We do a lot together off set. We've gone to the ballet. We like to try different restaurants. And above all else, we're black-belt shoppers. After a day of filming, for instance, we always hit up the stores of Soho. From there, we might go get our nails done but not without a few hundred selfies courtesy of selfie queen Cruz. I protest, but I have to say that without her I probably wouldn't have any accounts of my outings.

With so much estrogen on the set of *Orange*, some might think there'd be constant bickering. In fact, it's empowering and full of free expression—an environment mostly run by women, for women. This is one reason I appreciate Jenji Kohan and the *Orange* producers so much. Not only has Jenji changed my life, she has inspired me through her leadership. Working on a production like this one has taught me that there's no limit to what I can do. I can be strong and be a woman at the same time. I know this sounds dated and that the women's liberation movement already happened, but we still deal with societal pressures that tell us we're not as strong or as competent as men. Jenji is a constant reminder that that's not the case. She is a fighter for women and has chosen Piper Kerman's story—along with the story of millions of women in the prison system—to show how powerful we really are. She's shining a light on the injustices that we face. We need more women like you Jenji, and I hope to be one of them—someone who's contributing for a better and more just world in which women are equal to men.

I'd say the ladies on the cast of *Orange* are some of the best I've ever met in my life. It's not uncommon to walk by a dressing room and hear laughter or singing or even crying. We're real people, and we bring our true selves with us to the set. We're there for each other, and not just the cast, but the whole doggone crew. I've never seen a better-run production. We're hardworking and happy. I feel respected and valued. Being there reminds me of my time at Boston Arts Academy. There's no filter on what you can say—and I know that my feelings are safe there.

Even with all the love and warmth on the show, there have still been some tough days for me. For one thing, no one in the cast, including Jackie, knew what had happened in my family. I kept that to myself because I was ashamed of it—and because I didn't want to think about or discuss it. But how can you refuse to acknowledge something when your whole environment is one big screaming reminder? With just about every script, in almost every corner of the set, I was faced with the truth: *This was my parents' life.* My mother had sat in handcuffs; my father had once worn an orange jumpsuit like the dozens that sat folded in our wardrobe department. For the other actors and me on our show, this was all fantasy, the re-creation of a world we knew little about; for Mami and Papi, it could not have been more real or painful.

I tried to use the experience—to access my raw feelings and channel them into my portrayal—the way I'd been taught to do at Susan Batson. Some days, that worked beautifully; other days, I'd end up upset or numb. I've had so many scenes in which Flaca and I are doing the dirty work, like cleaning the kitchen or mopping the floors, which is when I think of my parents most. Long before they ended up in prison, they'd spent years handling the nastiest jobs, the ones often avoided by others. Manual labor. Low pay. No respect. They must've felt so trapped. It must've been so hard for them to maintain their dignity when others looked down on them or, worse, didn't see them at all.

As we wrapped up shooting Season One, the show's material suddenly hit even closer to home. My brother called me with some news about his daughter—my niece, Erica. The two of us had long since fallen out of touch, and I'd always deeply regretted that. So when Eric told me that she'd gotten caught up with the wrong crowd in high school and had ended up in jail, it broke my heart. A few years earlier, Gloria had apparently realized Erica was headed toward trouble, and she'd done all she could to steer her back on track. But with my brother away in Colombia, and with the struggles that go along with raising a child on one income in a tough neighborhood, Gloria's efforts weren't enough to save her beloved daughter from a difficult situation.

I experienced many emotions when I heard about Erica. Guilt that I hadn't somehow managed to stay connected with her. Anger that she'd been forced to grow up without the nurturing presence of my parents and the guidance of her father. And sadness that she'd stumbled into a hole she couldn't pull herself out of. Here I was, experiencing the happiest moment in my career, portraying a woman's life in a fictitious penitentiary, and my only niece, my own flesh and blood, was living through her lowest point while in an actual prison. That, along with all my parents had survived, made my work on *Orange* bittersweet. Life can indeed imitate art—and at times, it does so agonizingly well.

* * *

During my second season of filming for *Orange*, I got a call from Josh. "There's another show we want you to go in for," he told me. I went into the audition, and two weeks later I got a callback and flew to Los Angeles to test for a role. The series? *Jane the Virgin*, a comedy-drama to air on the CW. The story is about Jane, a virgin who is mistakenly artificially inseminated and becomes pregnant.

That trip was my first time in California—and everything was so vast and big. This was a huge deal for me. I couldn't imagine starting over again in a new place, and I'd always told myself that if I ever went to LA, it would be if I were called there for work. LA was a different animal, and I wanted to be introduced to it formally.

When I arrived, everything about the city made it different from New York. But I liked the change of pace. And it was beautiful: the nature, the sunsets, the green juice. *I could totally do the whole bicoastal thing just fine*, I thought. *Now I all I have to do is book the job.*

On the day of the audition, I was bright eyed and full of wonder and amazement. I was LA chillin' *fo sho*, brah. My theme song even changed from *Gypsy*'s "Some People" to 311's "Amber." The same thing had happened when I first set foot on the CBS lot—my theme song music turned into the one from *Jaws* . . . ominous and grand. That was my first time in a Hollywood studio lot, and oh how scary it seemed. I'd never seen anything like it. I felt like a little mouse. This was Hollywood, baby! And why not me? On the afternoon of the audition, I tested and waited patiently to hear if I was going to leave LA with a job or just a great experience, or both! By the time I landed in New York, I had bitten off all of my nails. As soon as I got into the car, my phone rang. It was Jennie Urman, the show's creator. "We'd like to offer you the role of Lina, Jane's best friend."

"What?" I said.

"We think you'd be wonderful for that part," she explained.

"Really?" I squealed.

"Yes, really," she said.

And just like that, in the space of ten seconds, I'd doubled my number of recurring roles. No, it wasn't a principal character, but not too shabby for my first time in LA. I got a job and that was huge! More than ever, I was determined to keep working hard and allowing myself to dream big. (Press PLAY for *E.T.* theme music). Never in my wildest dreams did I think that I, this little mouse, would have a shot in this space. I was humbled and hungry. It's the only way I've learned to tread water in this business.

We shot the pilot, and what a fantastic experience that was. It was great to be able to play a character so different from Maritza. I had all this great set experience from *Orange*, and I used that knowledge to keep myself from being awkward on set. I still frequently have to pinch myself that I am on two awesome shows! I love portraying Lina. She's so cute and feisty. I also love it when young girls come up to me and comment on how they love Jane and Lina's friendship, #bestfriendgoals. Lina loves Jane and would do anything to protect her. She's a loyal friend and always down to do whatever! Not to mention that she's always trying to get Jane to lose her virginity. I mean, that is the ideal girlfriend, right? "C'mon, Jane, just do it already!"

Another great perk of the sweet new job was getting to know my dear friend Gina Rodriguez. Most of my scenes are with Gina, and she's not just wonderful as an actor but as a person. She's a ball of energy. She's smart and funny. And she really cares about the cast and knows how to bring us together. On many filming days, she'll gather up all the background actors, stand up on a little podium, and thank them for the work they do. "We couldn't have done this scene without you," she has often said. "I mean, we would look pretty stupid at a club with no people in it! Thank you for being here." Wow, what a gal! We can all learn a thing or two from her, you know. It's hard not to like and feel connected to someone who's so generous and open.

And, of course, it's good when you get along with the folks at work— and the rest of the cast makes that easy. They are just as beautiful and generous as Gina is. I couldn't have asked for better. Another thing that makes this show so special is that it's telling, for the most part, the story of a Latino family. Jane and her family are from Venezuela. The series reflects a lot of what is beautiful about my culture and what it's like to grow up in America. It shows a family that is connected to its roots, but also grounded and connected to American values and way of life. It shines a light on a generation of families that is rarely portrayed on television. This is huge! And the fact that the show has done so well just proves how high the demand is for this kind of content, as well as shows how large and important our community really is in the United States. Our stories are interwoven in the fabric of this country, and it's about time we accept it as part of our norm. I can't think of a better way to celebrate who I am and where I come from. Thanks, Jennie.

After *Jane* got fully under way, I took off a weekend to hang with my girls in Atlantic City and celebrate our friend's birthday. We stayed at the Golden Nugget Hotel and Casino, and at around ten p.m., we headed down to the hotel's dance nightclub, Haven. I had no expectations of any sort, other than to get white-girl wasted with my bests! I was on the dance floor doing my hottest shoulder moves when out of nowhere, this guy comes up to me. Handsome. Clean-cut, beautiful chiseled face, and impeccably dressed. It was as if God had drawn his face using one of His finest pencils. And he smelled like heaven. My goodness, what a delicious scent. *Who are you?* I thought.

When it comes to two people meeting, the following events will sound clichéd—like a scene right out of your favorite romantic comedy. It was like he and I were the only ones there. No distractions, no noise, just sparkle and glitter. "Hi there, I noticed you from across the room, and I wanted to introduce myself. My name is Hov, OH, H-to-the-O-V." Just kidding. What he actually said was, "My name is J, and I think you're very beautiful."

"Hello," I said, pretending I didn't have any time for smooth talk. *This night is for my girls, not for you. As pretty as you are and, oh God (sigh) as good as you smell, go on your way and impress some girl looking for love tonight, because I am not the one.*

"Can I get you a drink?" he continued.

"No, that's all right, I have a drink already. But thank you for asking." And like that, I shut down the possibility of us getting to know each other.

"Okay, if you change your mind, my table is over there," he said. His ego didn't seem hurt in the slightest. *Huh*, I thought. *He was cuuuute!* Then I shook it off and kept it moving.

Minutes later and still sort of fuzzy from the encounter I'd just had, I rejoined my friends. And for some reason, I couldn't stop smiling. Could it be possible that this guy had charmed the hell out of me? No! I make the calls around here! It was probably just the three whiskey neats I'd taken to the face, I was sure. I tried my best not to be affected by the situation, but alas, I made my way over to his table. "I'll take a Jameson neat," I told him—and I never looked back. And he also had no idea what he was in store for.

I loved being around J. He was so debonair, but with an edge. His accent was so authentic New York. Think *Goodfellas*. He was the real deal with a kind of swagger some people would kill for. This was all his. He was and is an original.

Since that evening, I've come to appreciate far more than J's accent. I've never felt more supported, more seen, and more heard by one person. We are partners. He's responsible and hardworking. He's curious about the world and things that are important to me. He does his best to connect with me and gain insight into who I am. He's what I call "fancy," meaning that he usually knows the better bottle of wine to purchase or the best places to go. There's no snobbery in his game, and I like that about him. He's my little white baby.

The truth is, if I'd connected with J only a few years earlier, I probably wouldn't have been anywhere close to being ready for him. In those days, I was the girl who longed for someone, anyone, to fix my life, to do for me what I could only do for myself. But by the time I met J, a space had been cleared in my heart. I'd found Lorraine. I'd at last confronted the ugly, gut-wrenching experiences in my rearview mirror. I'd flown all the way to Madrid to rekindle one of the most important relationships I'll ever have. The day you finally start dealing with your past is the day you stop dragging it into the present. I'm still dealing. I'm still facing the hard stuff. I'm still getting better and growing up. In J, I've found a man who's willing to take that long road with me.

* * *

I am blown away by *Orange*'s success. I mean, c'mon: It's Netflix's most-watched series. Critical acclaim has poured in from every corner of the planet. Viewers send the cast hundreds of letters every month. In its first season alone, the show received twelve Emmy nominations and, hello, we won that 2015 SAG Award for Outstanding Performance by an Ensemble in a Comedy Series. What more could a girl ask for?

A mani-pedi, for starters. Because let me assure you that when the award show rolled around, I took great pleasure in getting dolled up. The prep process is the ultimate good time, particularly for a girly-girl like me. First, you've gotta choose a dress (I picked out this stunningly bright red Jill Stuart number). Then you've gotta get your accessories together (I chose these beautiful delicate diamond earrings with blue detail, as well as thin diamond bangles). Then you've gotta pick out your shoes. I always try to be as comfortable as possible but I can't help that the shoes I'm most attracted to are the most painful ones. It's okay—beauty is pain, right? Oh, and the red carpet. My goodness. The affair itself is as glamorous as it appears on television, and I should know, since I've tuned in to just about every SAG, Emmy, Golden Globe, and Oscar show that has ever aired.

Sashaying down the crimson carpet at the SAG Awards is both exhilarating and overwhelming. Reporters are sticking microphones in your face. Bright lights and cameras are flashing all over the place. Major celebs are all strutting and posing. Just ahead of me on the walkway were Emma Stone and Meryl Streep. Some of my cast mates later met Meryl personally at an after-party. I said hello to Keira Knightley, but other than that, I kept my lips zipped. I'm notoriously nervous about going up to other actors to introduce myself, because I'm worried that, after the initial hello, I'll have nothing more to say. I did muster the courage to walk up to a certain big actor I won't name, and, well . . . let's just say she wasn't very receptive. She gave me this look like, *Who are you and why should I care?* Ha ha—those encounters always make me laugh and remind me to never be like that.

The highlight of the evening is, of course, the show itself. I don't care how many actors claim it's "just a thrill to be nominated"—everyone wants to win. If we didn't, we wouldn't spend dozens of hours and way too much money trying to look as if we've just stepped effortlessly from the pages of *Vogue*. And when you take your seat at one of the tables, it's not like you're thinking, *Gee, I know I'm up for this big award, but I hope someone else gets it this year.* Nope. I, for one, sat there holding my breath when that magic sentence was uttered: "And the SAG goes to . . ." It's hard to adequately describe that moment when *Orange* was announced as the winner. *Surreal* is the word that comes to mind. I had this mini-flashback to that moment when, as a senior at Boston Arts, the crowd applauded at the end of my final recital. There's this incredible energy in the air, this tingling in your body, this feeling that makes you want to stand up and shout, "Yes!"

Both of my parents have been lapping up every minute of this wild ride. A day after the SAGs, Mami called me (we'd been talking more since my visit) and yelled, "I'm so happy for you!" She'd seen the broadcast. Papi and my other family in Colombia sent me texts and WhatsApp messages, congratulating me on the win and mentioning every magazine they'd seen me in. Mami and Papi were paying close attention to every detail and seldom missed an episode of *Orange*. Did the show's, um, spicy content turn their faces red? Maybe a little, but my parents are pretty open when it comes to artistic expression. If anyone is blushing, it's me. I know it's hard to fathom, given that I used to work as a cocktail waitress rocking a bustier, but these days I can be a little on the conservative side. I think that just goes back to my idea of what represents a good and proper lifestyle—in my mind's eye, that has always involved a wealthy woman wearing a high-collar shirt, a double strand of pearls, and big stylish sunglasses as she makes her way to summer in Nantucket or the Hamptons. It's like, "Oh, no—let's not talk about sex in public. It's not polite." That's also why I've sometimes been like, "Mami, stop being so loud! White people aren't loud." The hilarious thing is, I had no idea what white people did or didn't do—or, for that matter, how anyone lived behind closed doors. And Lord knows, loud folks come in all colors. But in the world I was raised in, amid the countless media images I took in as a girl, I got this crazy notion that being white and well-heeled and educated made one inherently superior. Sadly, I thought that being brown and broke, as well as hiding out from authorities for most of my childhood, somehow made me less valuable in the eyes of others and, at moments, in my own eyes. I was dead wrong.

I feel fortunate to be part of a series like *Orange*. It's entertaining, yes, but I'd like to believe that its value goes beyond that. The stories are so real. Many viewers write to me and say, "My sister is in jail," or they've spent time in a penitentiary themselves. The United States has the largest prison population of any developed country, with more than two million behind bars by some estimates. There are more jails in this country than there are colleges. It's a privilege to be able to shine a light on a world that many people in our country seldom even think about.

It's also important for Latino viewers to see actors who look like them. I'm proud of the fact that both *Jane the Virgin* and *Orange* have casts that include brown girls. Not long ago, Jackie Cruz and I were wrapping up a day on set, and a Honduran woman approached us outside our set; her daughter, a fifteen-year-old shy girl with a mouth full of braces, stood at her side.

"Would you mind if my daughter took a photo with you?" she asked.

"No prob," Jackie told her.

After we'd posed with the girl between us, she cupped her hands over her face and started to cry. "What's wrong?" I asked.

"I'm sorry," her mother cut in, "she's just nervous. You're such an inspiration to her. We are so proud of you girls."

Jackie and I looked at each other like, *Us? An inspiration?* It was another reminder that, as an actor, I have a powerful platform; whether or not I realize it, I'm influencing people I've never even met. And that means I can't just do or say whatever I want. I have a responsibility to use my stage well.

I hope *Orange* and *Jane the Virgin* are only the beginning for me. I plan to keep pushing myself. I want to take roles that stretch me. I want to climb all the way to the top of this business, and I have no shame in making that public. Some people shy away from boldly claiming what they most wish for. Maybe they fear it'll make them look pushy. Or greedy. Or ungrateful for what they have. But when you keep your dreams hidden away, when you hide them under a sofa cushion, they never get the light they need to grow. I'm all about that growth, which is what keeps me swinging every day. I literally cannot wait to see what's around the corner. Imagine all I would've missed if, on a rooftop in Boston on a snowy December night, I'd thrown everything away.

With my boyfriend by the sea.

CHAPTER 17

Into Daylight

The United States is the kind of place
where you can choose your own path.
We should never forget that.

—HENRY CEJUDO, US Olympic gold
medal–winning wrestler who was
born to Mexican immigrants

Three things will always be enough to make me flip. First, receiving flowers or even a phone call from my sweetheart, J. Second, shoes—enough said. And third? Receiving an invitation, as I did in 2014, to meet the president of the United States. I'm just going to go ahead and say it; President

Obama is my boo. Oh, stop! You all think he's your boo, too. And shouldn't we feel that way about our presidents?

All joking aside, let me back up and tell you how I got the chance to meet the first black president of the United States, Barack Obama (or Barry, as J and I call him). In September of that year, I attended an awards ceremony sponsored by *Cosmopolitan for Latinas*. The mag was honoring all these great women who've done amazing community work. I was really inspired by one woman in particular, Grisel Ruiz. She's an attorney for the Immigrant Legal Resource Center (ILRC), a nonprofit offering resources to those facing deportation. As I listened to her speak so passionately about her work, I was like, *Wow—I want to be like her.* I'd been itching to get involved, to do something to help immigrant families with nowhere to turn. I loved the fact that Grisel and the ILRC were educating people about their legal options.

A few days after the awards ceremony, I reached out to Grisel and told her I wanted to somehow use my voice. "Why don't you write an op-ed piece?" she suggested. The ILRC had been pushing for the president to provide temporary legal protection for undocumented workers. "Sharing your experience will keep the country focused on the issue," she told me. So for the first time—and a little apprehensive about what I might've just gotten myself into—I wrote about the day my parents were deported. The story ran on November 15, 2014, in the *Los Angeles Times*, five days before the president's big announcement. I had no clue what response the article would get or what might happen afterward. As I write these words, I'm still astonished by what happened.

Within twenty-four hours of its publication, the op-ed went viral. Thousands were suddenly talking, tweeting, texting, and Facebooking about my story. In the press office of the ILRC, the phone rang off the hook with media requests following a press release. NBC. ABC. *The Huffington Post*. NPR. Every major press outlet was requesting a comment from me. Me! Rather reluctantly (this all happened so dang fast . . .), I agreed to a short interview with *New Day* host Michaela Pereira on CNN. On the morning I went on her show, nervous as all hell, it was the first time I'd spoken publicly about my family's ordeal except for a brief mention to a Fusion reporter a few months earlier. Even some people I've known for years, like former high school and college classmates, didn't know about the deportation.

"That seems to be every child's worst nightmare, that your family is taken from you," Michaela said to me with compassion in her voice. I nodded, and then told her I'd gotten to visit them in Colombia. "How is that?" she asked. That's when I broke down.

"It's tough," I said, the tears toppling out before I could squelch them. "We've been separated for so long I feel like sometimes we don't know each other. . . . There are things about them that are new, that I don't recognize. It just . . . It hurts." And to this day, it still does.

After that interview, the story seemed to get even bigger. Strangers were coming up to me on the street saying, "Aren't you that girl from *Orange* whose parents were deported?" I cringed every time I heard that, because my family's entire struggle had been reduced to one humiliating sound bite. With as much fervor as I'd written the op-ed, I wished I could un-write it. *I've revealed too much*, I thought. *This has been a big mistake.* I'd opened the floodgates for people to judge me. To say crude things about my parents. To think they knew all about me because they'd seen one article or video clip.

And let me tell you, the hatefulness abounded. People wrote nasty letters to me, declaring that my parents should've been shipped back to Colombia years before they were. "In fact," someone wrote, "they should've deported you along with them." Some used racial slurs I won't give airtime to by repeating. If I'd been criticized about, say, my work on camera, I would've been like, "Whatever, dude." I'd learned how to buffer myself when my performance was critiqued or when I was rejected for a role. But this was different. I wasn't used to others going after my family. I didn't yet have the thick skin for it. And aside from that, I was also pretty sure my career was over. *No one's ever going to mess with me again*, I thought. *Maybe I'm being too political. Maybe I need to stick to the arts or talk about saving the whales.* The topic of immigration is so polarizing.

The shift came for me as I read through all the other letters I received. As crippling and toxic as negativity can be, there will always be greater power in the positive. For each of the haters, three others wrote to me with stories of recognition; in hearing me speak about what happened in my family, their private fears had been given a voice. A face. An affirmation. At last, someone understood them.

The most heartrending notes I received were from children. "I'm so afraid this is going to happen to me," a nine-year-old told me. "What if I lose my mommy and daddy? What will I do?" One sixteen-year-old girl stopped me in downtown Los Angeles and said, "My mother and father were deported last year. I've been on my own ever since." And one woman, although she hadn't been personally impacted by immigration, connected to the feelings of grief and abandonment I'd described. "I lost my parents when I was twelve," she told me as she held back tears. "I know what you're going through. It's so hard."

The more I heard and read, the clearer it became that this was about something much bigger than just my family's tragedy. Millions were living under the radar, ashamed, as I have been, to say a word about their situation. For their benefit, I needed to tell my story—and not just some of it, but the whole ugly truth of it. As I made the choice to step out rather than retreat, I got some support from so many people I respect. My cast mates, the crew, my friends. "We had no idea you'd gone through this. We think you're brave to open up." That really touched me. It reminded me that while it's tough to put myself out there, I shouldn't shy away from it. Any cause worth taking up requires courage. And you can't wait until you're feeling bold to act; if we did, most of us would never do anything. You have to step out in spite of the fact that you feel scared. And I often do.

Shortly after my op-ed piece ran, the White House rang. Gebe Martinez, a longtime reporter and now a publicist for Mi Familia Vota (and these days my right hand gal) relayed the message to the team at the ILRC: "President Obama would like to invite you to attend his speech on immigration reform," they told me. "He'd be honored to have you attend." I almost choked when I heard it—that's how stunned I was. What a huge deal. At that point, I was like, forget the hateration—I'm going to hear my idol speak! The historic address, which was to be televised during prime time, would take place at Del Sol High School in Las Vegas, Nevada. I flew in with no expectations that I would meet him personally—but between you and me, I prayed I would.

The speech was as riveting as it was important to the future of our country. The president had taken executive action to extend deportation relief to millions and lay the groundwork for the undocumented to work here legally, rather than separating families. I stood there in the audience, tears threatening to spill down onto my white dress, and I thought about my mami and papi. I thought about how the president's new order might've meant the difference between their presence here with me and their immediate deportation. I thought about all the years of uncertainty they'd endured, the thousands of dollars they'd handed over to that lawyer, and the effort they'd expended just trying to do the right thing.

After the address, a White House aide approached me. "The president would like to greet you," she told me. OMG. About twenty of us were led to a private reception area at the back of the arena. Among the guests: Wilmer Valderrama, the talented actor who has been an outspoken advocate for immigration reform. I've looked up to him and been inspired by his example, so it was a thrill to stand in line with him as we waited to meet the president. "Is this your first time meeting Mr. Obama?" he asked. I told him yes. "Don't worry," he told me. "It'll be great. Obama's cool."

Even before I said word one to the president, I was a hot mess! Just as my turn came up, he looked directly at me and said, "I know you." I began to weep. "Oh no," he said, taking a step toward me. "Don't cry." I was in shock that the president of the United States, the leader of the free world, was talking to *me*! Unbelievable. I pulled myself together well enough to shake his hand. "I've heard your story and I know why you're here," he told me. "And I want you to know that you're important. You matter." (Or at least that's how I remember it.) That brought more tears from me. Big time. I almost passed out.

From there, the conversation went left: The president mentioned *Orange*. "Michelle and I can't wait for the new season," he told me. *For real? The president and the first lady actually watch the show?* "You're feisty in those kitchen scenes," he said with a laugh. "Don't try anything funny in here—I've got security." Hilarious. He asked a couple of questions about the upcoming season, and I was like, "No, Mr. President—I'm not giving you any spoilers."

A moment later, a photographer snapped an official photo of us, which was later signed and sent to me. "Diane, it was wonderful to see you," it reads. "Thank you for getting involved. Barack Obama." *Be still, my heart.* The president made his way around the room, hugging people; somehow, *wink-wink*, I ended up back near him.

"Ah!" I go. "I'm here again! Sorry, I don't know what I'm doing here."

"No," he told me, "you belong here." And that's when he reached down to hug me. Afterward, I called Mami and screamed into the receiver, "I just met the president!" Disclaimer: I rarely get excited about seeing famous people, but when I admire someone, I act like some rookie at a 1999 NSYNC concert.

The picture of me and the president ended up on the front page of *El Tiempo* in Colombia, a very reputable newspaper. My parents couldn't believe it. The CNN clip had also gone viral, and they'd watched it multiple times. To tell you the truth, I had been concerned that I'd embarrassed my parents. I brought that up to my mother. "This is your story," she told me. "Tell it the way you want to, and don't be afraid. Use what we've been through to help others." Papi was encouraging as well, but true to his nature, he seemed a little apprehensive. The same thing that stung me bit him—seeing our all-time worst experience summarized in a five-word headline. For others, that was so-called news. For us, it was an agonizing reminder of the trauma and separation. "Always remember that you're in charge of your own story," Papi told me. "You get to decide what you want to share. Don't let others push you into talking about anything you're uncomfortable with."

That advice served me well. In the weeks following the op-ed, anyone with a notepad or a mic seemed to think it was fine to play Diane Sawyer and ask me the most personal, probing questions—questions I'm sure would've made them squirm if they were in my position. Much of the time, I didn't know what to say, which is why I'd come off as curt and a little bothered. But after having that conversation with Papi, I drew my line in the sand. This is my story. I own it. So if I don't feel like talking about it during a particular interview, I make that known beforehand. I want to open up about my life, but on my terms. In my time. And with the complete context of all we survived. That's one reason I chose to write this book.

Putting my ordeal on paper has been gut-wrenching. I've felt vulnerable through every step of it. I've had to look back at moments I'd rather forget and stare into dark places. I've had to examine my choices, my motivations, and my missteps, as well as those of my loved ones. The process has been like therapy to the tenth power, and although, yes, I've ultimately found some healing and relief in opening up, the path to that point has been personally taxing. In fact, I nearly called my publisher and said, "Let's just forget this. I'm not ready." What kept me going? The gripping e-mails I still receive by the dozens. The husbands and wives who, at this very moment, are being forced to live apart from each other. The realization that, tomorrow and the next day and the one after that, a child will come home to find a home with no one in it. I've written the book I wish I could've read when I was that girl—and my hope is that, in these pages, others will find the solace I once ached for.

* * *

My mother is back in Colombia—at least for now—so she could be closer to my brother. I don't know what the future will bring—Mami wants to return to America and live here with me—but she does have the option of going back to Europe. When she left Madrid, I gave her my word on something. "I will not forget about you," I told her.

I'm grateful that my brother has rebounded. He at last reached out to a counselor, and he's not only feeling much better, he's working full-time as a teacher. I'm proud of Eric. In our culture, it's not easy to even talk about mental health, much less bravely step out and ask for help. I wish we lived in a world where more people did that—and I wish more of us would support rather than judge those who do seek help.

During Christmas 2014, I traveled to see my parents. J came with me. I was a little anxious about taking him; I've never introduced my parents to anyone I was dating. But this felt right. I soon realized I had zero reason to be apprehensive, because my parents absolutely adored J. Mami was charmed by his sweet face and eyes, his cool demeanor, and how gentle he was with me. Papi appreciated his work ethic. "He's a serious young man," he told me. "He's disciplined." He'd noticed that J was usually early to bed, early to rise; he'd get up and handle his business in the mornings so he could chill with me and the family in the afternoons and evenings. My parents were so fond of J that, a couple of times, when I got hissy with him, they scolded me. "You should watch your tone with him," Mami told me. I've been away from my parents for more than a decade, but one thing hasn't changed: They're quick to tell me when I'm being an ass.

J and I took a side trip to Armenia—the area of Colombia where one of its finest exports, coffee, is grown. Papi came with us. J, who has become increasingly involved in building his family's business, was particularly interested in visiting the region. We fell in love with Armenia. The area is nestled in gorgeous countryside, with coffee fields stretching as far as the eye can see and breathtaking hills and mountains in the backdrop. And of course, there's a beautiful coffee culture there. In that city and in the surrounding towns, locals frequent the outdoor cafés and enjoy the country's best brews.

The visit gave me a chance to bond with my father. Dad and Diane together again! We were like peas and carrots. Although I'd visited Mami in Madrid not long before, I hadn't seen my father since that Christmas during college when I'd flown to Colombia. We didn't do anything big, but just spending time with him felt special. It made me recall those times, years earlier, when my father would take me to the beach or carnival. And it was cool to watch him and J get to know each other. For many years, my father had been down because of the way things turned out; but as he and J sat over coffee, talking and trading stories, he seemed more like his old self—the open, funny, and warm father I remembered from our days in Boston. And although he'll probably always be on the shy side, he was actually a bit talkative with J. Good sign.

One afternoon when Papi and I, just the two of us, meandered through the fields, I struck up a conversation.

"Papi," I asked, "if you were able to come back to America, what would you do?" In the previous year, my father had been bugging me like never before to look into his return to the States. I was curious what life he envisioned for himself there.

He stopped for a moment, swept his palm over his forehead, and gazed out over the rows of lush greenery. "I'd do anything," he said. "Any job would be okay."

"Anything?" I pressed.

"Yes," he said. "Maybe I could find another factory job. Doesn't really matter."

"What do you mean, it doesn't matter?"

He turned, looked directly at me, and didn't flinch. "I just don't want to miss any more of your life," he said. "I only want to go to be near you. We've been away from each other for too long already." I reached over and hugged Papi, and as I did, he leaned down and pecked me on the forehead. "I love you, *chibola*," he told me. "Always will."

I'll be honest: Up to then, I'd been annoyed about my father's insistence on his return to the United States. He seemed obsessed. He brought it up just about every time we talked. "When are you going to start looking into the paperwork?" he'd urge. I wanted to tell him, "Look, you've got to make the best of your life in Colombia." But during that moment in the field, I got it. I understood him. My dad wasn't looking for some grandiose life. He simply wanted to be close to his only child. And even in his early sixties, a time when many are settling into retirement, he was willing to take a lowly job just so he could be around me. That afternoon, I made a quiet choice. I would do everything in my power to bring my papi back to the United States.

I'll do the same for Mami. These days, she and I talk at least a couple of times a week. What a pivot after seven years of silence. My mother's so cute: Every morning, she sends me my Cancer horoscope on WhatsApp. Or she passes along a photo, an inspirational quote, or any articles in which I've been featured. If a few days go by and she doesn't hear back from me, I sense the panic in her. "Diane, where are you?" she'll write. "Can you please answer me?" When I sense her desperation, it hurts. It makes me aware again of all the ways I shut her out. Look how many years we lost. I daydream about reclaiming some of those moments by sharing the simplest things with her. What would it be like for us to go to HomeGoods and pick out a mirror or a little chair? How would it feel to be able to say, "Hey, Mami—how would this look in the living room?" Those are the little things I miss. And when you think about it, they aren't little things at all. They're the experiences that, one moment at a time, make up a life.

More than fourteen years have passed since Mami and Papi were taken, and in a way, I need them more now than I did then. Every day, I have new questions about which direction I should take, both in my career and in my personal life. I long for their guidance. I get some of that over the phone, but it's not the same as having them in the room. Because they're in a country where day-to-day existence is so arduous, they're often distracted by the basics of survival.

It's clear that my parents will never rekindle their relationship. That's a sorrow I'll have to live with. And yet I do keep one fantasy alive. I imagine the day when I can bring Mami and Papi back to America, buy them a little duplex near me, and have one live upstairs, the other down. They wouldn't even have to see each other much, and yet they'd both be within a couple of miles of my place. They could pop over for dinner, or I could linger at Mami's table and enjoy her homemade stew. Each would have a copy of my spare house key, so I could call up and say, "Hey, I forgot the plumber was coming by today. Can you stop over and let him in?" Years from now, if I am blessed to have my own children, I envision my parents cradling their grandbabies in their laps, rocking and swaying and singing them to sleep the way they once did me.

I wish I could tell you my story has a perfect ending; such a finale exists only in the make-believe worlds of my childhood. Even in the best of times, life is a mixed bag of disappointments and triumphs, heartaches and highs. Life hands out all of the above, and we don't get to pick how many of each we'll get, or in what order they'll show up. But we do get to choose how we'll walk through our days. Whether we'll cower under our covers every morning, or rise up to take on the challenges. Lord knows I've done both. And now that I'm on this side of things, I'd recommend the latter.

I have a lot of gratitude for what I've been given. I'm still breathing, still kicking up dust, and I count it as a miracle that I want to be in this world. I now have J in my life. I've got this incredible career, one that continues to surprise me with all its twists and turns. Nearly every day, I have an experience, be it tiny or enormous, that reminds me that something bigger is at work—that God hasn't turned His back on me. And though I don't have my parents in the States, I do still have them in this world and in my heart. It'd be so easy for me to dwell on their absence, and for years, I did. I have my days, even now. But a little at a time, I'm learning to cherish whatever moments I do have with my family, even if that's across an ocean. I dream of the day when we can reunite in this country, and I believe we will. Until that happens, I'll hold on to that hope.

Diane — It was wonderful to see you! Thanks for getting involved.

Me and POTUS.

Call to Action

A life not lived for others is not a life.

—MOTHER TERESA,
Roman Catholic missionary

The afternoon I crawled under my parents' bed, terrified and shivering, I'd been completely overlooked by our government. I still find it surprising that, from that place in the shadows, my life has carried me all the way to the set of a critically acclaimed Netflix series. Down the red carpet at the SAG Awards. And into a meeting with the US president.

Along that road, I spent a lot of time trying to make sense of why I'd gone through what I have and what I was put here to do. I realized, years into my search, that one answer had been staring me in the face. I am the girl whose parents were stolen. I am also the girl who is here to make sure no other family is put through that hell.

Our immigration system is especially hurtful to children. The Department of Homeland Security reports that in 2013 alone, more than seventy thousand parents of US-born children were deported. Kids who have at least one undocumented immigrant as a parent make up about 7 percent of K–12 students, and the vast majority of those are citizens by birthright, according to Pew Research. On any given day and without warning, these boys and girls may come home to discover they've been suddenly orphaned. I was fourteen when it happened to me. Can you imagine how overwhelming it would feel for a five- or eight-year-old? I can. Wherever we may stand on the issues surrounding immigration, there is no excuse for our government to abandon its children. None.

Those whose parents are snatched away frequently end up in foster care, bounced from family to family as they deal with post-traumatic stress disorder and severe clinical depression; without the consent of their birth parents, they can be adopted by people who may further mistreat them. Those who remain in the care of a second parent or relative are often forced onto public assistance, particularly when the person deported had been the family's main breadwinner. And what happens to the ones who, like me, aren't contacted at all by ICE or Child Protective Services? Some slip into homelessness, or they have to beg friends to take them in, as I did. All are susceptible to sex traffickers, drug dealers, and gang leaders. The lack of due diligence by our government repeatedly leaves our youngest citizens hanging without a safety net. When immigration officers sweep in and arrest a housekeeper or factory worker without checking to see if a child will be deserted, families and communities become unstable. Both directly and indirectly and in dozens of ways, that instability affects you. Me. And every other person who lives in the United States.

When I first shared publicly that I'd been left behind, many sympathized—but others suggested I book a one-way flight to Colombia if

I wanted to be with my parents; they, of course, had wanted to stay with me here. Yet in my own family and in the families of scores of others, the solution is far more complicated than deciding who exits the country and who stays. For one thing, my status as an American citizen—and my ability to earn a living wage, which Mami and Papi cannot do—allows me to cover their basic expenses. And second, this country, one founded by those who sought the same refuge my parents came here seeking, is my home. It is the only nation I have ever lived in or known. For thousands of parents, taking the children back to their homelands would mean putting them in dire, life-threatening situations; that's usually why these mothers and fathers have escaped to here in the first place. In Honduras, which the UN says has the world's highest homicide rate (followed by Venezuela, Belize, El Salvador, and Guatemala), violence has become so widespread that locals live in terror that their little ones will be kidnapped or murdered. And they have good reason to be afraid, reported the *Los Angeles Times* in 2014. Hours after a teen boy stepped off his deportation flight in San Pedro Sula, Honduras, he was savagely shot and killed by gang members.

Children who stay in the United States have no choice but to find their own way. After my parents were detained, I knew of no hotline to call. I had no idea what my rights as a citizen were. And aside from that, I'd spent my childhood underground, discouraged from ever mentioning my parents' legal status. Although resources existed, I wasn't aware of them—and even if I had been, taking hold of a helping hand would've meant overcoming enormous fear. I'd been taught to trust no one.

That fear is still alive and well for countless children. It's what initially led me to partner with the Immigrant Legal Resource Center (ilrc .org). Back when my parents were trying to become citizens, they were never told that, despite their immigration status, they still had basic rights (in prisons, agents who conduct interviews with detainees don't have to identify themselves as ICE officials; and many of those imprisoned, like my parents, have no idea that they have the right to remain silent). Mami's and Papi's actions were largely based on fear and hearsay. Connecting with an advocacy group would have made a world of difference for my parents. In fact, if they had been properly guided, I might still have them here with me today.

***

Undocumented workers add millions to America's piggy bank. Our country's economy depends heavily on their labor. "Immigrants take jobs from Americans," it has been said. "They're a financial burden." The exact opposite is true. Undocumented workers contribute well beyond what they can ever recoup. How so? For starters, they regularly buy goods and services, and in so doing, they fork over sales tax. They also pay into Social Security and Medicare (via invalid Social Security numbers and taxpayer identification numbers, the latter of which can be obtained regardless of one's legal status). The money these workers cannot recover is passed on to citizens. Stephen Goss, chief actuary of the Social Security Administration (SSA), has reported that undocumented workers are investing nearly $15 billion a year into Social Security. Without these deposits, estimates Goss, we'd be 10 percent deeper in our funding hole for this program. It's in our best financial interest to give immigrants a path to citizenship. Without their labor, our economic train would screech to a halt.

People who flee to America customarily accept the most backbreaking work as janitors, housepainters, and, of course, farmers. Our nation doesn't just gain from the cheap labor of agricultural workers; it would absolutely suffer without it. "If we deported a substantial number of undocumented farm workers," labor economist James S. Holt once told Congress, "there would be a tremendous labor shortage." That's because more than half of America's 2.5 million farmhands are undocumented, some picking grapes and blueberries and apples for as little as four dollars an hour; their paltry earnings are what keep your food prices low. They are literally doing America's dirty work while living well below the poverty line. That's why many have to string together two or three jobs in order to make ends meet. That's what my parents had to do.

Exploitation of these workers is rampant. In my father's factory job, the conditions were deplorable, his supervisors abusive. His boss at times humiliated and threatened him. On the weeks when he was paid on time, he considered himself lucky, and on a few occasions his earnings were altogether withheld. Many business owners, particularly those who employ low-skilled workers, know they won't be held accountable for their abuses. They have the unchecked power to dole out cruelties on the powerless—those who often don't speak English and who are terrified of deportation. In the worst cases, the exploitation is coldhearted and downright shameful.

The mistreatment has been widely documented in the press. As part of a 2015 series entitled Unvarnished, the *New York Times* shone a light on the abuse of manicurists, many of whom are undocumented immigrants. In interviewing 150 nail salon workers and owners, the paper's reporters found that an overwhelming number of employees were paid below minimum wage; many weren't paid at all. The indignities were constant: Manicurists' tips were docked for the slightest errors. They were berated and cursed at. Owners secretly monitored their every move.

In one salon on Manhattan's tony Upper West Side, the *Times* learned, workers were paid just $10 a day, all while massaging the hands of the city's wealthiest. At a salon in East Northport, New York, manicurists filed a lawsuit claiming they'd been paid $1.50 an hour for a sixty-six-hour workweek. In a chain of Long Island salons, workers said they were kicked when they made mistakes. And don't get me started on the health hazards: Some of the chemicals and fumes found in nail products (and inhaled daily by these workers) have been connected to cancer, birth defects, and miscarriages. This issue is much larger than an occasional eye roll by a grumpy boss. It is barbaric and prevalent mistreatment that puts people's lives in danger. And it should not be tolerated by anyone with a conscience.

The *Los Angeles Times* brought attention to the plight of Josue Melquisedec Diaz, an unauthorized contract worker hired following Hurricane Gustav. Diaz and eleven other workers were brought in to clean up a community ravaged by floodwaters, reported the paper in 2011; while nearby American workers were provided with gloves, masks, and boots to protect against infection, Diaz's group was not. "We were made to work with bare hands, picking up dead animals," he said to the *LA Times*. "We were working in contaminated water." Later, Diaz told Congress that he and the others had asked for safety equipment. In response, the supervisor cut their pay in half, at which point they went on strike. Police and immigration officers then showed up to throw Diaz and his counterparts in jail, and they were later transferred to federal immigration detention.

Do our country's laws protect construction workers like Diaz? Yes, but those laws are meaningless because employees know they can ignore them. It's pretty unlikely that an undocumented worker will fight back as Diaz did. Employers know they can get away with putting their employees' lives and health at risk—and so they do.

The abuse of detainees is equally inhumane. When my parents were arrested and carted off to detention centers, neither had a chance at a fair hearing with a good lawyer, since, of course, they didn't have enough money to hire one. Every day, at least thirty-four thousand immigrants—that's the minimum quota of detainees who must be kept in detention at all times, as mandated by Congress—are forced to dispute their cases while isolated and imprisoned. Due process protections for these inmates? Forget it. In the criminal justice system, people are provided a pro bono attorney if they cannot afford one, but that same right does not exist in deportation proceedings. According to the ILRC, 84 percent of those detained go totally unrepresented, as my mother and father did. Thousands may qualify to stay here legally but are sent away because they can't get legal representation. A disproportionate number of those arrested and detained are brown or black, and that's not a coincidence. Our immigration system, just like the criminal justice system, routinely targets people of color through over-policing, racial profiling, and incarceration.

Deportation can be a double punishment. Someone who has previously been convicted of a crime and who has already paid his or her debt to society can still be transferred to ICE and deported. If, for instance, an undocumented worker is pulled over by police for a traffic violation, that driver would be required to pay the fines involved, and then he or she would be turned over for deportation and permanent banishment from the United States; oftentimes, such a person is sent back to a violent country where his or her life is immediately in jeopardy. And even if someone is arrested and detained for missteps that occurred decades earlier—and they've since become totally rehabilitated—that does not matter in immigration courts.

My work on *Orange* has taught me this: Human beings are not categorically bad because of their mistakes. They can learn from their errors and get back on track. No one should be forever written off because of one part of his or her history. Nor should anyone be held in our prisons in the name of making a buck. Legal permanent residents with long-standing family ties, torture survivors, and victims of human trafficking are among those detained for months or even years, worsening any mental health problems associated with their past traumas. The prison industry is a multibillion-dollar operation in which corporations literally earn money on the backs of society's most broken. And this is flat-out wrong.

My mother and father tried as hard as they could to work here legally. They did so using the only immigration system available to them, which is our broken and outdated one. Very few options exist for people to come to the United States lawfully, and many have no path to legal status. That's right—none. They're often directed to "get in the back of the line." Let's get clear on one thing: There is no back of the line. In fact, there is no line, period. We're long past the years when newcomers queued up at Ellis Island to be screened for eligibility and possible entry. And even if such a line existed, it would stretch from coast to coast and back again; anyone in that line could wait for decades to get to the front.

If, for instance, a US citizen files the paperwork to sponsor his or her sibling from Mexico, the wait to have that application processed would likely be twenty years or longer. And those here with a citizen child or spouse who can sponsor them are out of luck. A series of restrictions forces most already in the States to wait for ten years *outside of the country* before a green card application can be filed and considered. That's about as unreasonable and nonsensical as someone suggesting that we round up all undocumented workers and send them back to their respective countries. Logistically, how do you track down, detain, and deport eleven million people, and who on earth would foot the bill?

The American Forum, a right-of-center policy institute, did the math on the potential cost of mass deportation. Their research shows that we'd spend between $400 billion and $600 billion—and with that blow to our workforce, the nation's real GDP would plummet by more than $1.5 trillion. That is obscenely expensive, not to mention impractical and time-consuming.

(The American Forum estimates that the deportation process, if it can even be implemented, could take as long as two decades.) When we're trying to come up with solutions, we should keep it real. And we should do what's most intelligent—like putting reforms in place that will make our economy boom rather than falter.

Another idea that's thrown around a lot: building a wall or fence along America's borders. I'm here to tell you that it won't work. Nearly half of the people who settle in this country arrive on planes and overstay their visas. My mother and father had no wall to climb over, no fence to navigate. A 1,954-mile physical barrier between the United States and Mexico would've done nothing to keep my Colombian mother and father out. And the obstacles to finishing the existing border fencing and walls and replacing them with something even bigger and stronger, as some conservatives have proposed, are numerous: Ranchers who live along the border will continue fighting to keep their land; the wall would have to cut through Native American reservations; and the terrain in, for instance, the Arizona desert and New Mexico mountains, not to mention the lakes and rivers along the border, would make constructing a wall a major challenge, if not an impossibility.

Even if a wall was constructed, it's not a cure-all. When any human being is facing starvation and unimaginable violence, he or she will do nearly anything to survive—including scaling a wall or crossing an ocean, as we've witnessed among the throngs of Syrian refugees escaping to Europe. If a wall is the only thing that stands between near-certain death and the possibility of life, you and I would risk everything to climb over it, because the risk of staying put is far greater than the fear of being caught. "Show me a fifty-foot wall," former secretary of Homeland Security Janet Napolitano once said, "and I'll show you a fifty-one-foot ladder." The Berlin Wall should serve as proof to all of humanity that walls do not work. Building bridges that foster communication between countries does.

"People who enter America without their papers are breaking the laws," some argue. "It's not fair." It also wasn't "fair" for our ancestors to roll up and take land from the Native Americans, but I don't hear too many folks complaining about the benefits we enjoy because they did. Neither was it fair for our forefathers to import slaves to toil in their cotton fields;

plantation owners built this nation's wealth by degrading blacks, a group once declared only three-fifths human by Congress. So-called fairness has seldom been this country's primary compass in determining the best action to take. So instead of arguing about whether immigrants should be here, let's focus on creating a plan that actually moves us forward: immigration reform.

The Senate passed a commonsense immigration bill, but the House—led by anti-immigrants—blocked immigration reform. Congress's abdication of its duty led President Obama to use his executive authority in November 2014, the week that I met him for the first time. The president extended a lifeline by creating DAPA (Deferred Action for Parents of Americans and Lawful Permanent Residents) and expanding DACA (Deferred Action for Childhood Arrivals). For anyone who got lost in that alphabet soup of acronyms, here's the least you should know: The president's executive action provided relief for as many as five million undocumented community members. (At the time of this writing, those benefits are on hold, pending review by the US Supreme Court.) It was a step in the right direction. Our future depends on electing leaders who'll keep this issue on the front burner, because make no mistake: You don't have to be the relative, the friend, or the employer of an undocumented worker to be financially impacted. Every single one of us is affected, simply because we live here.

If you're in favor of a commonsense immigration system that gives people an opportunity to work here legally, you've got company. Gallup reports that 87 percent of us would like to offer a citizenship path to undocumented immigrants, a lot of whom have been paying taxes here for years. And, according to a Gallup poll, Americans' general support for immigration is on the rise, with 75 percent of US citizens viewing others' relocation to our nation as positive. Facebook founder and CEO Mark Zuckerberg agrees. He has called immigration reform "the biggest civil rights issue of our time" and is speaking up on behalf of the powerless.

We need your voice too. There's one simple, yet powerful, action every American can take: We can vote. Many once sacrificed their lives to give us that privilege, and we should use it to its fullest extent. If you're as horrified as I am by some of the 2016 presidential candidates' proposals ideas such as amending the Constitution to end birthright citizenship—you can do more than sit around and debate about it. You can take action by registering to vote, if you're not signed up already. Voter information is available at MiFamiliaVota.org. Then, vote on November 8, 2016, and urge your friends and family to turn up and cast their votes as well. I stand with actress America Ferrera, who penned an open letter to Donald Trump that ran in the *Huffington Post*: "Thank you for reminding us to not sit complacently at home on election day, but to run to the polls and proclaim that there is no place for your brand of racial politicking in our government," she wrote. "Thank you for sending out the rallying cry." Amen. In the 2016 presidential election and in all those to follow, let's make sure our opinions get counted.

Voting is the first step—but it's not the only one you can take. We can keep the pressure on Congress to do what's right and pass a comprehensive immigration reform bill; until that's completed, our efforts must continue. You don't have to be a policy bigwig to get involved. You can call and write to your elected officials. And yes, your input matters. "Never doubt that a group of thoughtful, committed citizens can change the world," cultural anthropologist Margaret Mead once said. "In fact, it is the only thing that ever has." I'm fighting for the most expansive relief possible, which would grant millions the right to reside here lawfully, continue contributing to our country's financial well-being, and keep their families intact. Not another mother or father should be torn away from their loved ones—nor should a child be left trembling beneath a bed.

* * *

My story represents all that should be celebrated about America. Only here could the daughter of immigrants grow up to succeed in the competitive and exciting world of acting. And only here could a girl like me be invited to have a conversation with the president. I will always cherish those opportunities.

And yet my experience in this country also reflects a reality that's still tough for me to face. In a nation that values keeping families together and safeguarding children, I was invisible. Either the immigration officials didn't see me or they chose to turn their heads. I'll never know which. But I do know that as Americans, we can do better than that. We can extend greater compassion. And we can push our leaders to protect the most vulnerable among us. It's one way we can help people who desperately need it.

Service to others—I believe that's the purpose every person on the planet shares. "The best way to find yourself is to lose yourself in the service of others," Mahatma Gandhi once said. Dr. Martin Luther King Jr. put it another way: "Everyone has the power for greatness, not for fame, but for greatness, because greatness is determined by service . . . You don't have to have a college degree to serve. You don't have to make your subject and verb agree to serve. You only need a heart full of grace." We may be divided over how to bring about reform, but let's unite in our desire to leave our planet better than we found it.

My desire to be of service to others is not limited to immigration reform. I have come to realize the power of my vote, and that each one of us has that power. I want to remind all voters—and especially young new voters—that we have the power to change policies. Through our votes, we also can ensure the rights of women to earn wages that are equal to those of men; we can speak out about our reproductive rights; we can ensure that our public health policies include better gun safety laws; and yes, we can work toward leaving our planet more environmentally safe than we found it. So don't be surprised if you hear me advocating on behalf of a broader range of rights. Dignity for immigrants is just the beginning.

I still don't comprehend all the reasons my life has turned out the way it has, but that's no longer the central question for me. What matters more is how I can turn the trauma of my experience into some kind of meaningful change for myself and others. There's no point in going through anything difficult if, on the other side of it, very little shifts. That's as true for me personally as it is for us collectively. Does pain have a purpose? I'm not sure. But it can if we give it one—and I've chosen to view my ordeal as an opportunity to be a voice for millions. For the sake of all those who come to our shores, I hope you'll join me in that cause.

Want to learn more about the immigration reform debate and get involved? A few resources:

- Immigrant Legal Resource Center (www.ilrc.org)
- Mi Familia Vota (www.mifamiliavota.org)
- Community Initiatives for Visiting Immigrants in Confinement (CIVIC) (www.endisolation.org)
- Detention Watch Network (www.detentionwatchnetwork.org)

Acknowledgments

Words aren't enough to convey the overwhelming love and gratitude I have for all those who've trekked through the muddiest of waters with me. But since words are all I have, here goes. Thank you, because without your presence in my life, I would not be the person I am today. I'd need another book to list all those who've been part of my journey, and I want each of you to know how grateful I am for giving me a chance, offering me a shoulder to cry on in difficult moments, and cheering me on when I didn't think I could keep going. Here are just a few of the people I'd like to mention by name:

Mami: Thank you for being fearless and never giving up on our family, even when the odds against you were stacked higher than Mount Everest. Thank you for teaching me the true meaning of love.

Papi: Thank you for being the kindhearted gentleman you are. I can call myself a feminist because you taught me to believe in myself and to feel equal to men. You taught me how to respect others and be respected.

To both of my parents: Mami y Papi, thank you for being the caring mother and father you are and for supporting me through every moment of my life, whether we lived near or far. I will never stop fighting for us. Never.

My brother: Thank you for being my big brother and for always being kindhearted. You will never know how much I truly love you.

Tia Milena: Thank you for always being yourself no matter what. Thank you for teaching me the importance of selflessness and kindness to all people. Thank you for always respecting me and guiding me with the utmost positivity and truth. Also, thanks for all my cousins. ☺

Tio Jose Guerrero: Thank you for naming me in 1986, when my mother was about to make a big mistake by naming me Maria Emilia. You stopped the presses and gallantly walked into the hospital and said, "No, her name will be Diane." Thank you for being there for me always. I love you.

All my *tios*: Edgar Guerrero and Cachi, Pacho, Moiso Becerra—thank you for your love and support always.

All my *tias*: Maye, Omir, Tenda, and Luceni Guerrero and Maria Eugenia thank you for being the best *tias* I could ever dream of having, and thank you for passing on your wisdom and care to me. Thank you for making me feel loved and for making me see that I do have a family.

My cuzzos: Alejandro Cobo, Gisella, Jackie, Dayron, Jasmine Alvarez, Harris Davino Garcia, and Jasmine Alvarez—thank you for loving me always, no matter how corny I was or still manage to be.

My *primos*: Andres Sanclemente, Lina Maria Urbano, Omar, Sara, Aura Maria y Fabian Guerrero, Felipe, Juan Sebastian Becerra—thank you for being sweet and loving, no matter how much time passes without us seeing each other. I can feel your hearts and smiling faces miles away. Also, *no me llamen Ñañan por la mañana.*

Andres Sanclemente: My partner in crime. From pranking each other as kids, to our endless witty repartee, I cherish our bond. Thank you for always having my back and being a source of knowledge and calm for me. Also thank you for having the guts to be the only doctor in our family. I love you, buddy.

Orfilia, Diana, and Anthony: Thank you for always being there for my family and me. Your love and support has been undeniably significant to my life. Thank you for teaching me the importance of cleaning up after myself and not being a little brat.

Lucy: My family and I are very grateful for your love and support.

Ana: Thank you for welcoming me in when I thought my life was over. You were there to hold and protect me during the worst of tornadoes. Your strength as a woman is unwavering. You taught me how to buck up and go for the World Series. Also, thanks for giving me and all of us Grisell. ☺

Grisell: My homie for life. Hardly a moment goes by without my thinking of our time together, from the blizzard of '96 to the time we got to be sisters for real. I thank you for always being a woman of your word and for teaching me to always question and fight the power.

Stacy: Thank you for being an amazing friend through and through. I'm not sure I would have survived high school without you. You hot ticket, you.

Diana: Thank you for making my childhood one filled with laughter. I still think of our days in class together, making up songs and coming up with ways to torment Mrs. Clifford. Jack! Ha!

Emma y Don Fernando: Thank you for showing me what family looked like. Thank you for your warmth and for making me feel wanted, understood, and special. You stood in for my parents and never missed a beat. Also, thanks for Nani. ☺

Stephanie aka Nani: My sister from another mister, thank you for sharing a slice of your life with me. It was love at first sight at the Halloween contest, where we competed wearing the same costume. I knew we'd be best friends for life, and that has proven to be true. Thank you for your love and trust, my dear friend.

Boston Arts Academy: Thank you for saving me. Thank you for providing a space and curriculum that allowed me to develop as an artist and explore my potential.

Kelly: Thank you for being the greatest white friend a little brown girl could ask for. You have shown me true friendship through and through, and without you, I wouldn't have made it in NYC. You're my angel.

Kyle: Thank you for being the best Asian friend a little brown girl could ever ask for. Thank you for always listening to me and being a voice of maturity and reason. Had you not been in my life, I would've fallen down a few wells by now. Your beauty and kindness always resonate, and I'm lucky to have you.

Vamnation Entertainment: Thank you guys for having my back no matter what—I wouldn't be here without you!

Josh Taylor: Thank you for being the most amazing manager I could ever ask for. Thank you for seeing something in me and giving me a chance to show my stuff. You are an integral part of my success and my sanity. You're more than a manager; you are my friend. Thank you.

Abrams Artists Agency: Man are you guys classy! Thank you for being such a great team and supporting me always.

Danielle DeLawder: You are a phenomenal agent, and I seriously do not know what I'd do without you. Thank you for believing in me and keeping me on track and punctual, even when I'm a pain in the ass.

Steve Ross: Thank you for being the best literary agent on the planet. Thank you for believing in my story and for encouraging me to take on this project. This book is out in the world because of your passion and your powerful advocacy. I appreciate you. Really.

Jenji Kohan from *Orange Is the New Black*: Thank you for taking a chance on me, and for giving the world the opportunity to get to know me. Without you, none of this would be possible.

***Orange* cast:** It has been an honor to work alongside such talented and interesting people. I'm so grateful to be part of this family.

Grisel Ruiz of the ILRC: Thank you for inspiring me to do more. Seeing you give so much and dedicating yourself to this work has activated something in me I never thought possible. You taught me that my voice has more power than hate and intolerance could ever have. Thanks for helping me discover my purpose.

Gebe of Mi Familia Vota: You are incredibly important to my work. Thank you for your guidance and generous spirit. I couldn't imagine doing any of this without you by my side. You are not only my mentor, but my friend. PS: Meeting POTUS together wasn't too shabby either. ☺

Regis girls: Thank you Abby Kuzia, Jaime Girard, Jen Glass, Sam Lynn, and Paulette Benetti for being my college homies and staying connected to this day. I love you girls.

Jackie: Our friendship began exactly like the scene in *Forrest Gump* where all the seats are taken, but then Jenny tells Forrest, "You can sit here if you want." Thanks for letting me sit with you on the first day of school. Thank you for being my girl throughout this amazing journey.

My buds: Thank you to all these beautiful souls in my life—Nathan Anthony, B.B., Lesley Coehlo, Amaris Delgado, Dascha Polanco, Selenis Leyva, Uzo Aduba, Lea DeLaria, Emma Myles, Danielle Brooks, Adrienne Moore, Esther Caporale, Erica Lavelanet, Ahn Mai, Dan Libman, Peter Berkrot, Alex Metz, Gina Rodriguez, Shane Patrick Kearns, Michael Harney, Doreen Maya, Susan Batson Studios.

Toni: Mama, thank you for always being such a positive force in my life, and for showing me true kindness and selflessness. No one could ever compare to you, but I do hope that the values with which you lived your life will somehow manifest in mine. I will work hard and be worthy of your beautiful family and make you proud. You are a true light in my life, and there is not a single day that I don't think of you. I love you.

J: My love, thank you for being my partner and my best friend. Thank you for the trust and support you have given me since the very first day I met you. Thank you for being patient with me and my very colorful personality, and thank you for not shying away from potentially one of the greatest loves in history. You are one of a kind, and I'm a very lucky girl. The rest of our lives awaits.

Gianna: Oh, Bethany, thank you for being the best sisi ever. Thank you for being so darling and caring. I love spending time with you and can't wait for our relationship to grow into a beautiful Christmas tree. I will always be here for you as your big sisi because ya bad.

Jim: Thank you for being so generous and welcoming. You are a wonderful father, and I thank you for sharing your beautiful family with me. I look forward to what the future brings for our families. Also, thank you for J. ☺

My coauthor, Michelle Burford: *Girrrrrl.* Thank you for all your hard work. This book is literally a reality only because of you. Thank you for your patience with me, and for your intelligence all around. I appreciate how well you've understood my vision, and how you've helped me to bring that to life in the form of this memoir. And above all, thank you for handling my story with so much care and sensitivity.

It truly does take a village to put together a memoir, and my team at Holt has been absolutely incredible. Thanks to Gillian Blake and Serena Jones, who believed in my story from our very first meeting and have supported me across the finish line. Serena, thank you, too, for being a top-rate editor. Special thanks to Patricia Eisemann and Leslie Brandon in publicity. Much appreciation also goes to David Shoemaker, Meryl Levavi, Molly Bloom, the extraordinary sales force at Macmillan, and every person, those publicly named as well as those behind the scenes, who had a hand in this project. I am as grateful for your competence as I am for your enthusiasm for the book.

About the Authors

DIANE GUERRERO is an actress on the hit shows *Orange Is the New Black* and *Jane the Virgin*. She volunteers with the nonprofit Immigrant Legal Resource Center, as well as with Mi Familia Vota, an organization that promotes civic involvement. She has been named an ambassador for citizenship and naturalization by the White House. She lives in New York City.

MICHELLE BURFORD is a founding editor of *O, The Oprah Magazine* and the writer of many bestselling books including memoirs by Olympic gymnast Gabby Douglas, singer Toni Braxton, and Cleveland kidnapping survivor Michelle Knight.